The Kuyper Center Review

New Essays in Reformed Theology and Public Life

The Kuyper Center Review publishes substantial essays of a historical or critical kind that relate the tradition of Reformed theology to issues of public life. Although it will take a special interest in the writings of Abraham Kuyper (1837-1920) and in the neo-Calvinist style of thought that he initiated, the aim is also to provide a vehicle for the widest-ranging exploration of the history and contemporary relevance of Reformed theology to important topics in politics, economics, and culture. Contributions from a variety of disciplines — history, philosophy, the humanities, and social sciences, as well as theology — are warmly welcomed.

The Kuyper Center Review

VOLUME 3 *Calvinism and Culture*

Edited by

Gordon Graham

WILLIAM B. EERDMANS PUBLISHING COMPANY
GRAND RAPIDS, MICHIGAN / CAMBRIDGE, U.K.

© 2013 Gordon Graham
All rights reserved

Published 2013 by
Wm. B. Eerdmans Publishing Co.
2140 Oak Industrial Drive N.E., Grand Rapids, Michigan 49505 /
P.O. Box 163, Cambridge CB3 9PU U.K.
www.eerdmans.com

Printed in the United States of America

19 18 17 16 15 14 13   7 6 5 4 3 2 1

Library of Congress Cataloging-in-Publication Data

Calvinism and culture / edited by Gordon Graham.
    pages   cm. — (The Kuyper Center review; volume 3)
    Includes bibliographical references.
    ISBN 978-0-8028-6876-3 (pbk.: alk. paper)
    1. Calvinism. 2. Kuyper, Abraham, 1837-1920. 3. Christianity and culture.   I. Graham, Gordon, 1949 July 15 — editor of compilation.

BX9422.3.C335   2013
261 — dc23

2013003543

Poetry of Emily Dickinson reprinted by permission of the publishers and Trustees of Amherst College from THE POEMS OF EMILY DICKINSON: READING EDITION, edited by Ralph W. Franklin, Cambridge, Mass.: The Belknap Press of Harvard University Press, Copyright © 1998, 1999 by the President and Fellows of Harvard College. Copyright © 1951, 1955, 1979, 1983 by the President and Fellows of Harvard College.

Contents

Editorial: Calvinism, Art, and Culture — vii

Contributors — xii

Culture Regained? On the Impossibility and Meaninglessness of Culture in (Some) Calvinist Thought — 1
 Neal DeRoo

Reply to Neal DeRoo — 23
 Albert M. Wolters

The Pilgrimage to Kuyper? Adolf Schlatter and Abraham Kuyper on Theology, Culture, and Art — 32
 Michael Bräutigam

Theology and Architecture: Calvinist Principles for the Faithful Construction of Urban Space — 51
 Matthew Kaemingk

Calvinism, Necessity, and the Death of Tragedy — 63
 John De Soto

Contents

The Correlation between Creation and Culture in the
Theology of Abraham Kuyper and Colin E. Gunton   76
   William Baltmanis Whitney

The Calvinian Eucharistic Poetics of Emily Dickinson   94
   Jennifer Wang

Beautiful Harmony: Kuyper, Dooyeweerd, and the
American Musical Avant-Garde   102
   Janet Danielson

From Neo-Calvinism to *Broadway Boogie Woogie*:
Abraham Kuyper as the Jilted Stepfather of Piet Mondrian   117
   James D. Bratt

The Music God Likes and the Calvinist Tradition   130
   John Barber

The Vampire Squid: Abraham Kuyper on Public Entertainment   149
   Clifford B. Anderson

To Transcend and to Transform: The Neo-Calvinist Relationship
of Church and Cultural Transformation   163
   James Eglinton

Editorial: Calvinism, Art, and Culture

There are many differences between the Reformed tradition and other varieties of Christianity, but one of the most noticeable is what James Bratt, in his paper for this volume, calls "the litany of Calvinism's aesthetic underperformance; no monumental architecture, little in the way of sculpture, a music long on Psalm-singing and short on everything else, an aversion to nudity in painting, and a virtual prohibition on the theater." This impoverished state of affairs provides the background for Abraham Kuyper's concern, in his Princeton lectures and elsewhere, to uncover and give articulation to Calvinism's enduring relationship with the arts. It is the same concern that animates this third volume of the Kuyper Center Review. Many of the papers (though not all) derive from the 2011 conference of the Abraham Kuyper Center for Theology and Public Life at Princeton Theological Seminary, the theme of which was "Calvinism and Culture."

The peculiarity of Calvinism's aesthetic austerity can be overstated. Protestant churches whose origins lie in Anabaptism are not any more noted for their contributions to Christian painting, sculpture, or architecture, for example. Nevertheless, it would be difficult to dispute the contention that with respect to artistic expression there is indeed a striking difference between Calvinism and most other manifestations of the Christian religion. The contrast is sharpest, no doubt, in comparison with Roman Catholicism and Eastern Orthodoxy, but Lutheranism and Anglicanism have taken a dif-

---

I am grateful to James Bratt for helpful comments on this editorial.

ferent tack also. Bach's St. Matthew Passion, for example, has an aesthetic richness no less marked than the altar paintings of Caravaggio, while Thomas Cranmer's Book of Common Prayer was able to inspire and shape the Oxford Movement's renewal of ritual.

Abraham Kuyper is the towering figure in the revival and renewal of Calvinist thought generally known as neo-Calvinism, and H. R. Rookmaaker's classic *Modern Art and the Death of a Culture*[1] stimulated special interest in the question of neo-Calvinism's relation to visual art. In *Voicing Creation's Praise*,[2] Jeremy Begbie extended the investigation to music. The papers in this present volume constitute a further and more wide-ranging exploration of neo-Calvinism's relationship to the arts, both at a general level and in connection with specific art forms. Their investigations are part historical, part theological, and part practical. Overall they suggest that the neo-Calvinism espoused by Kuyper can and should make more of the arts than the traditional view of Reformed Christianity might be thought to allow. There is, however, this underlying question: Why does it matter? Why should there be any concern about Calvinism's aesthetic austerity?

Kuyper himself raises this issue. In the lecture on "Calvinism and Art" he writes, "Do the writings of John, Peter and Paul, the three pillars of the Christian Church, in a single word betray any special appreciation of artistic life? Yes, be it asked reverently, is there any instance in the Gospels of Christ ever pleading for art as such, or seeking its enjoyment?"[3] For anyone who takes the doctrine of *sola scriptura* seriously, these are compelling questions. Yet even though they must be answered in the negative, Kuyper continues, this generates no "right to deny the fact that Christianity as such has been of an almost invaluable significance to the development of art." He then goes on to argue that "the want of an art-style of its own, far from being an objection to Calvinism, on the contrary indicates the higher stage of its development."[4] This is chiefly because it has released art from its previous thralldom to religion, and thus freed it to claim its true status as an independent sphere of common grace, one that has a special power all its own by which the glory of God and of creation can be revealed.

This response to the accusation that Calvinism is essentially anti-art, I feel inclined to say, is ingenious but too easy. To begin with, the art that is

1. H. R. Rookmaaker, *Modern Art and the Death of a Culture* (InterVarsity Press, 1970).
2. Jeremy S Begbie, *Voicing Creation's Praise: Towards a Theology of the Arts* (T. & T. Clark, 1991).
3. Abraham Kuyper, *Lectures on Calvinism* (Eerdmans, 1931), 144.
4. Kuyper, *Lectures on Calvinism*, 157.

"freed" by Reformed theology is art of a rather restricted kind. Kuyper has his "eyes fixed upon the Beautiful and the Sublime in its eternal significance," and this turns out to be compatible with rejecting the art world of his times because of its "vulgarization of art." In fact, by accusing "the present aesthetical movement" of "an almost fanatical worship of art," Kuyper thereby reveals his sensitivity to a notable feature of European culture in the late nineteenth century; partly in response to the apparent conflict between Christian theology and empirical science, art had generally ceased to be religion's spiritual ally, and had become its spiritual rival instead.[5] In short, Kuyper could view the art world benignly, and accord it the freedom of common grace, only insofar as it did not go its own way.

It is possible, of course, to insist that the art world of which Kuyper speaks is a degenerate one, and to appeal to a conception of "real" art that the sensuous aestheticism of the late nineteenth century had largely abandoned. Indeed, by focusing on the beautiful and the sublime as the essential categories of aesthetic experience, Kuyper appears to adopt some such line. He objected to much actual high-art production from the Impressionists, for example, for not aiming at the beautiful and the sublime anymore. Yet paradoxically, by making this criticism he is endorsing precisely the same conception of art as its "fanatical" worshippers. Over the course of the eighteenth century the "fine" arts had been ever more sharply distinguished from the "mechanical arts," to the point where the qualification "fine" could be dropped. "Art" properly so called was now to be contrasted with (mere) craft. Its proper home was the gallery, the museum, or the concert hall — cultural oases set apart from the institutions of ordinary life, such as home, workplace, school, or college — or the church. It was the business of the craftsman, not the artist, to supply the functional needs of ordinary life. This divorce between form and function could never be complete, of course. Everyday life continued (and continues) to have its self-consciously aesthetic dimensions. But these were now supplied by fashion and furnishings, alongside the theater, the lending library, and the music hall.

Kuyper expressly embraces, and seeks to justify, Calvinism's traditional objection to theater and dance. Combined with his elevation of beauty and the sublime, he thereby relegates the aesthetics of everyday life to entertainment and diversion. "Art is no fringe that is attached to the garment, and no amusement that is added to life, but a most serious power

---

5. I explore this rivalry at length in Graham, *The Re-enchantment of the World: Art versus Religion* (Oxford University Press, 2007).

in our present existence."⁶ This contention would have won the enthusiastic support of the most ardent aesthete. But what is that power? Here too Kuyper implicitly subscribes to the dominant Kantian aesthetic, and gives art a quasi-epiphanic role. "Standing by the ruins of this once so wonderfully beautiful creation, art points out . . . both the still visible lines of the original plan . . . and the splendid restoration by which the Supreme Artist and Master-Builder will one day renew and enhance even the beauty of His original creation."⁷ His remarks about, and pride in, the Flemish School of painting illustrate his conception of art's special power. The "light of common grace" showed that "non-churchly life was also possessed of high importance and of an all-sided art-motive," but it took a Rembrandt to "open the eye for the small and the insignificant" as manifestations of the divine. Painting such as Rembrandt's, then, invites us to look upon ordinary life. As art, it does not enable us to participate in it.

In *Art in Action*, Nicholas Wolterstorff notes and reflects at length on the radical divorce that has come about between high art and the lives of ordinary people. "Between our producers of high art and the human tribe," he says, "[there] is a vast gulf of mutual indifference, widening ever since the Christian church lost its hold on the mind and heart of Western man."⁸ As the title of his book suggests, Wolterstorff wants to emphasize the aesthetic dimension of action, and break away from the conception that confines art to contemplative experience. He locates art's special role in its ability to secure a certain "fittingness" between what we believe and how we act out those beliefs, and he looks to the exploitation of this ability in a renewal of Christian liturgy. For art to play this role effectively, however, it must leave the museum and the concert hall and reconnect with what Wolterstorff calls "the art of the tribe," which is what I have been referring to as "the aesthetics of everyday life."

Art in Action, it seems to me, gets many important matters right. For Calvinism, and by implication for neo-Calvinism, however, Wolterstorff's program presents special difficulties that relate chiefly to the form and context of its worship. Kuyper did make allowance for the didactic role of everyday art. In his rectorial address "Calvinisme en Kunst," he praises at length the poetry of the seventeenth-century Dutch statesman/writer Jacob Cats, who penned moralistic verse in folk idiom for "emblem books," a purpose

---

6. Kuyper, *Lectures on Calvinism*, 151.
7. Kuyper, *Lectures on Calvinism*, 157.
8. Nicholas Wolterstorff, *Art in Action* (Eerdmans, 1980), 198.

for "folk" art that endured a long time in the parlor literature of sober Dutch Calvinists. The practice of moral teaching, though, is distinct from that of worship, and it is here that the Calvinist's aesthetic lacuna is most evident.

Luther, famously, abandoned the beautiful music characteristic of the pre-Reformation mass in favor of popular tunes familiar to ordinary churchgoers. But starting with Luther himself, a sequence of gifted musicians from Hassler to Bach provided harmonizations that raised these same tunes to new heights of musical excellence. In a similar fashion, Charles Wesley used attractive rhymes and rhythms to make complex theology accessible to large numbers of poorly educated people, while at the same time producing religious poetry of enduring worth and mystical power. Eastern Orthodoxy has provided the world with a seemingly endless supply of devotional images that are iconic in both the literal and the analogical senses of the word. Lutherans and Anglicans never wholly abandoned, and later more extensively recovered, the richly colored vestments that visually enhance the practice of worship, as well as retaining the Christian holy days that were allied to public holidays. American evangelicals, especially in the South, absorbed and transformed country music and theatrical style in their hymn singing and their preaching. As a result, all these are styles of worship that have aesthetically rich traditions upon which to draw for their renewal. Even in a highly secularized world they can hope to reconnect with the aesthetics of everyday life because it was from the aesthetics of everyday life that they arose.

But here Calvinism confronts difficulty. The aesthetic austerity produced by its emphasis on the Word and its suspicion of the sensual served to sever its connections with the aesthetics of everyday life, and hence makes reconnection for the purposes of evangelism problematic. Because Kuyper's own account of "Calvinism and Art" is committed implicitly to a high estimation of Art as a revelation or contemplation of the beautiful and the sublime, and explicitly to a low estimation of "folk" art as entertainment, it has little to offer that could remedy this. That is why the question of Calvinism's relation to the arts matters, and why new avenues of thought about it need to be explored. The essays in this volume, like the conference from which many of them originated, are presented in this spirit — as a fresh, varied, and serious attempt to do just that. It is to be hoped that they will act as a stimulus to more sustained treatments of the subjects they broach.

GORDON GRAHAM
Princeton Theological Seminary

Contributors

CLIFFORD B. ANDERSON is Director of Scholarly Communications in the Jean and Alexander Heard Library at Vanderbilt University in Nashville, Tennessee. He is currently preparing an annotated edition of Abraham Kuyper's *Lectures on Calvinism* for Wm. B. Eerdmans.

JOHN BARBER, Ph.D., is a pastor in the Presbyterian Church in America and an adjunct professor at Bryan College, Dayton, Tennessee. A trained classical musician, he is the author of numerous articles and books on Christianity and culture, including *The Road from Eden*. He is also a founding member of Uzima Reformed College, Nairobi, Kenya, where he teaches several times a year.

MICHAEL BRÄUTIGAM is a doctoral candidate at the University of Edinburgh. His research, under the supervision of Dr. Paul T. Nimmo, focuses on the Swiss theologian Adolf Schlatter. He holds degrees in psychology (University of Trier) and theology (University of Glasgow and Free Church of Scotland College, Edinburgh). Michael Bräutigam was the 2011 visiting Puchinger Scholar at Princeton Theological Seminary.

JAMES D. BRATT is professor of history at Calvin College in Grand Rapids, Michigan. Although first of all a historian of American religion and culture, he has devoted significant time to studying the life and thought of Abraham Kuyper. He edited the annotated anthology of some of Kuyper's key shorter works, *Abraham Kuyper: A Centennial Reader* (Eerdmans, 1998). His biography, *Abraham Kuyper: Modern Calvinist, Christian Democrat,* is appearing in 2013 (Eerdmans).

Contributors

JANET DANIELSON is a composer, music theorist, and lecturer at the School for the Contemporary Arts at Simon Fraser University in Vancouver. Her compositions include an opera, *The Marvelous History of Mariken of Nimmegen*, along with orchestral and chamber works. Danielson was composer-in-residence for the 2010 *Sonic Boom Festival*, which premièred her *Suite Vancouver* for string orchestra and erhu, and is presently working on a collaboration for a 2012 festival/conference, *Music and Mercy: The Performing Arts and Restorative Justice*.

NEAL DEROO is an Assistant Professor in the philosophy department at Dordt College. He is the author of *Futurity in Phenomenology: Promise and Method in Husserl, Levinas and Derrida* (Fordham University Press, 2012), and has co-edited several volumes, including *The Logic of Incarnation: James K. A. Smith's Critique of Postmodern Religion* (Pickwick, 2009) and *Phenomenology and Eschatology: Not Yet in the Now* (Ashgate, 2010).

JOHN DE SOTO graduated from the University of California, Irvine, with degrees in English, Philosophy, and Classics. He is preparing to pursue graduate work in Classics. His research interests include Greek tragedy, Platonic philosophy, and the theology of time.

JAMES EGLINTON, Ph.D., is a postdoctoral research fellow at the Theologische Universiteit Kampen (Netherlands). His current research, under the direction of Prof. George Harinck, concerns the relationship of Scottish and Dutch Calvinisms. His doctorate on Herman Bavinck, supervised by Prof. David Fergusson (University of Edinburgh), has been published as *Trinity and Organism* (T & T Clark, 2012). Eglinton has contributed articles to *Calvin Theological Journal, Scottish Bulletin of Evangelical Theology, Theology in Scotland,* and *La Revue Réformée*.

MATTHEW KAEMINGK is a Ph.D. candidate in Christian ethics at the Center for Advanced Theological Studies at Fuller Theological Seminary. His research interests include theology and culture, Reformed social and political ethics, and the role of faith in the marketplace.

JENNIFER WANG is a graduate student at the New School for Social Research in the philosophy department. Her concentrations are psychoanalysis and phenomenology, and she has a research interest in their intersections with theology as a holistic discipline. Her long-term goal is to continue working toward a Christian ontology that builds upon the insights of theologically oriented phenomenology while taking seriously the psychoanalytic critique of religion.

WILLIAM BALTMANIS WHITNEY holds his Ph.D. in Systematic Theology from Fuller Theological Seminary and his Master of Science in Marriage and Family Therapy from the Fuller Graduate School of Psychology. He currently teaches at Fuller Seminary and Azusa Pacific University while also providing counseling services for individuals, couples, and children at La Vie Center in Pasadena, California.

ALBERT M. WOLTERS is professor emeritus of religion and theology/classical languages at Redeemer University College, and former adjunct professor of biblical studies at the Paideia Centre for Public Theology, both in Ancaster, Ontario. Originally trained in philosophy, he is the author of works on Plotinus, the Song of the Valiant Woman, and the Copper Scroll. He is best known for *Creation Regained: Biblical Basics for a Reformational Worldview* (1985; 2nd ed. with Mike Goheen; Eerdmans, 2005).

Culture Regained? On the Impossibility and Meaninglessness of Culture in (Some) Calvinist Thought

Neal DeRoo

The notion of "transforming," "reforming," or "redeeming" culture — long a staple of neo-Kuyperian reformational thought — is coming increasingly under fire, not just from evangelical or Anabaptist "outsiders," but from within the Reformed tradition itself. Some critics claim that merely transforming or reforming culture is too reactive and is therefore insufficient to our human calling.[1] Others claim that, given that Christ will return and "burn this old world, in fire and flame,"[2] there is no point in trying to reform or redeem culture. The most recent advocates of this latter position in the Reformed tradition advocate a "two-kingdoms" approach: Christians must live in the common kingdom (of everyday life and culture), which will one day be brought to a cataclysmic end, and in the redemptive kingdom (of the church), which will one day be fulfilled in the new heaven and the new earth — but these two kingdoms must be kept distinct, even as the Christian is called, here and now, to participate in both.[3]

---

1. For a recent statement of this position, cf. Andy Crouch, *Culture Making: Recovering Our Creative Calling* (Downers Grove: InterVarsity Press, 2008).

2. Belgic Confession, Article 37.

3. Cf. David VanDrunen, *Living in Two Kingdoms: A Biblical Vision for Christianity and Culture* (Wheaton: Crossway, 2010) and *Natural Law and the Two Kingdoms: A Study in the Development of Reformed Social Thought* (Grand Rapids: Eerdmans, 2010). VanDrunen is at pains in both works to show that the two kingdoms approach is not *merely* a recent phe-

---

I would like to thank several of my colleagues at Dordt College, most notably John Kok and Jay Shim, as well as Albert M. Wolters for comments on earlier drafts of this paper.

At stake in the reformational idea of "transforming" culture is not whether or not we will, or should, participate in culture. Culture is not optional; not being cultural is, for humans, not possible. Rather, at stake is the precise manner in which we engage in culture. Are our cultural pursuits thoroughly infused with Christian meaning and calling, or are the standards of cultural morality and excellence "ordinarily the same for believers and unbelievers"?[4] That is, the question concerns whether there is a specifically Christian way of acting in cultural pursuits or instead if there are merely moral and immoral ways (in which case Christians should probably opt for the moral ways). Is there a Christian task or calling to develop, rather than merely participate in, culture?

Reformational[5] thought clearly asserts that there is a uniquely Christian calling to develop culture, and has produced a philosophical vocabulary to explain and explore this calling and its relation to the biblical narrative. In brief, reformational thought ties this task of transforming culture to the mandate given to Adam and Eve to "fill the earth and subdue it" (Genesis 1:28). This, in turn, is related to an understanding of: creation as ordered by divine laws; sin as the violation of those laws; and redemption, ultimately, as the restoration of creation by bringing it again in line with those divine laws.

Yet, as a person working, writing, and living within the Reformed tradition, I have become aware of the myriad ways in which this vocabulary is used and understood that run counter to its own reformational intentions. This misuse of the vocabulary of reformational philosophy is not, I think, malicious, but the result of a misunderstanding and misapplication of the complex notion of creation order at work in that tradition. Without properly navigating this complexity, it is easy to inadvertently slip from advocating a transformation or redemption of culture to advocating something like a two-kingdoms approach, in which culture is either mindlessly and univer-

---

nomenon, but in fact has roots older than the Reformed tradition itself (cf. *Natural Law and the Two Kingdoms,* chapter 2).

4. VanDrunen, *Living in Two Kingdoms,* 31.

5. Perhaps a word is necessary here on the distinction I have introduced between Reformed thought and reformational philosophy. The latter term applies to the branch of philosophical thinking that arose first in the neo-Kuyperian Calvinism of early twentieth-century Holland, and is typified in the work of Dooyeweerd, Vollenhoven, and their various followers. By Reformed thought, in contrast, I mean to signal the wider adherence to the thought of the Reformers (Luther, Calvin, Zwingli, etc.). In this sense, the Reformed-reformational distinction I am after here mirrors Kuyper's distinction between the denominational and the scientific understandings of Calvinism; cf. Kuyper, "Calvinism a Life-System," *Lectures on Calvinism* (Grand Rapids: Eerdmans, 1961), 9-40, 13-17.

sally affirmed (as long as I do it "for Jesus") or in which culture is suspiciously and universally denied (as worldly and therefore "unimportant"). In this easy slippage, more is at stake than theological or philosophical minutiae. What is at stake is the nature of the Christian life and task itself.

My claim in this paper is simple: that understanding creation order as a system of fixed and unchanging laws renders the notion of cultural development impossible, meaningless, or both. In order to preserve the cultural mandate as an essential Christian calling, then, we must abandon the notion of a fixed and unchanging creation order by re-emphasizing certain elements already found in the reformational tradition. To show this, I will argue first that there is a necessary threefold complexity at the heart of the reformational understanding of creation order that is often overlooked (Section I). This complex, threefold creation order is instead too often subordinated to the structural understanding of creation order, a subordination that manifests itself in an understanding of God's laws as fixed and unchanging structures (Section II). These fixed law-structures lead to the elimination of the distinction between the creational and the redemptive mandates, a distinction that is necessary to the claim that culture is a good that must be transformed (Section III). By removing the conditions that make cultural development and redemption possible (Section IV), these fixed law-structures end up making culture — as an essential Christian task — impossible, meaningless, or both (Section V). The conclusion is that we must abandon this notion of the creation order as fixed and unchanging law-structures if we are to maintain a meaningful place for culture in the Christian calling, and that such an abandonment can be best achieved by recovering other aspects of the reformational understanding of creation (Section VI).

I. An Ambiguous Creation Order

To see why this would be the case, we must begin by understanding the role that creation plays in reformational thought. To do this, let us look at *Creation Regained*,[6] a work that has, as one of its most salient features, an argu-

---

6. All in-text citations are to Albert M. Wolters, *Creation Regained: Biblical Basics for a Reformational Worldview*, second edition (Grand Rapids: Eerdmans, 2005). Given its foundational importance to Reformed thought, this book is important as much for what people *think* it says as for what it intends to communicate. That is, while some of what I am about to say about the book may not be entirely in line with the author's intentions, this does not, unfortunately, mean that it inaccurately portrays what many in the Reformed community

ment for the universal scope of creation: everything that exists is part of God's creational design, and as such every area of creation is the scene of the religious struggle between the kingdom of God and that which opposes that kingdom. This is possible because God's creating activity is one and the same as the laws God establishes that rule creation (15), and according to which creatures are able to be what they are (59). These laws — and God's creating activity — can then be understood as operating upon, or as, the "creation order."

Here we stumble upon a slight ambiguity, but one that becomes ever larger and more damaging the more one looks at it. How are we to understand "creation order" here? There is surely a difference in saying God's laws act "upon" the created order, and saying that they *are* the creation order. And even within this latter possibility, there remains an ambiguity: if God's laws are the creation order, is that order temporal and changing, or is it transcendent[7] and fixed?[8] All of these various understandings of creation order are at work at various points in *Creation Regained* — and in reformational philosophy more generally.

There are three distinct senses of creation order at work in reformational philosophy. First, creation order is the speaking of a law or command by a superior, which his subordinates are called to obey (e.g., a sergeant in the army ordering his troops into battle).[9] Second, creation order is the to-

---

believe the book to teach. I offer the following, then, as an exploration of a strand in Reformed thought and not as a critique of Wolters or his book.

7. Several people in the reformational tradition claim that the laws that structure creation themselves transcend that creation, most notably Vollenhoven (cf. *Introduction to Philosophy*, trans. John H. Kok, ed. John H. Kok and Anthony Tol [Sioux Center: Dordt College Press, 2005], 16). This opens up the entire discourse of the nature of the law as the "boundary" between Creator and creation, an issue that would take us too far afield to be pursued here. Let me just note briefly that, since temporality is the mark of creaturely existence (cf., e.g., Kalsbeek, *Contours of a Christian Philosophy* [Toronto: Wedge, 1975], 152), to posit laws as "transcendent" to creation is to raise questions regarding their status as temporal and/or eternal. This question is one of many that tend to operate under the surface in Reformed discourse on creational laws.

8. For a discussion on this question, cf. Jacob Klapwijk, *Purpose in the Living World: Creation and Emergent Evolution* trans. and ed. Harry Cook (Cambridge: Cambridge University Press, 2008); for his critique of Dooyeweerd as an essentialist (i.e., as understanding laws as eternal and fixed), cf. chapter 12 of this work.

9. Cf., for example, Vollenhoven's statement in "The Consequential Problem-Historical Method," in *The Problem-Historical Method and the History of Philosophy*, ed. K. A. Bril (Amstelveen: De Zaak Haes, 2005), 89-135: "Structural law is rooted in the divine command to exist, a command issued in the act of creation" (106). Johan van der Hoeven

tality or collection of individually created things or creatures (the way one would speak of the Jesuit order, for example).[10] Third, creation order is the system of necessary, law-governed, and fixed relations that constitutes our world (in a way analogous to how we talk of the sequential "order" of numbers: 1, 2, 3, etc.). These three understandings of order — let's call them the verbal, the collective, and the structural understandings of creation order, respectively — relate to the previously mentioned accounts of creation order: the verbal sense regards the laws of God as a fundamentally temporal and changing creation order,[11] the collective sense regards the created order as the totality of things subject to God's laws (those things acted upon by God's laws, i.e., those things for which God's law holds), and the structural sense emphasizes the transcendental and fixed nature of the laws of God.[12] The reformational understanding of creation order, then, can best be summarized as *the totality of created things that exist because of a divine law spoken into existence by a sovereign, Creator God.*

The three different senses of creation order are necessary to answer the three "transcendental basic problems" that face every philosophical framework, namely, to give an account of reality's coherence, totality, and origin.[13]

---

also insists that our understanding of creation is "entirely dependent on God speaking"; van der Hoeven, "In Memory of Herman Dooyeweerd: Meaning, Time and Law," *Philosophia Reformata* 43 (1978): 130-44, quote 135. For more on the notion of God as a speaking agent in the reformational tradition, cf. also Nicholas Wolterstorff, *Divine Discourse: Philosophical Reflections on the Claim that God Speaks* (Cambridge: Cambridge University Press, 1995).

10. This is sometimes referred to as the creat*ed* order, or simply as creation.

11. This can be considered temporal and changing because, as verbal, it emphasizes the spoken, rather than the revelatory, aspect of God's commands. In so doing, it emphasizes the relation between God and humanity, thereby opening the door to the temporality and change that such a relation will undergo, due to the temporal nature of (created) humanity. We will return to this in our final section below. For more on the distinction between spoken discourse and revelation, cf. Wolterstorff, *Divine Discourse*.

12. Unlike the verbal sense, here it is the revelatory, rather than spoken, aspect of God that is emphasized. In this sense, it tends toward an emphasis on the transcendent, eternal, and unchanging, in keeping with the transcendent, eternal, and constant nature of the God who is revealed.

13. Cf. Dooyeweerd, *A New Critique of Theoretical Thought*, trans. D. H. Freeman and W. S. Young (Amsterdam: H. J. Paris; and Philadelphia: Presbyterian and Reformed Publishing Co., 1953-58), Volume 1, 41ff.; and Jonathan Chaplin, *Herman Dooyeweerd: Christian Philosopher of State and Civil Society* (Notre Dame: University of Notre Dame Press, 2011), 42-47, and 335 n. 13. On the model I describe above, the structural, collective, and verbal senses of creation order would provide the account of reality's coherence, totality, and origin, respectively.

Difficulties arise, then, when these three distinct — though related — senses of order are not kept in ambiguous tension. But it is difficult for anyone to keep three distinct senses of one word in mind at any one given time, and so this well-rounded sense of creation order has been progressively lost in the reception of *Creation Regained*, most often by preserving the structural sense of order at the expense of the others.[14] This manifests itself, not in an *abandonment of the other senses of "creation order,"* but in *subordinating* them to the structural sense that views order as a system of fixed relations that cannot change without violating its own laws.[15]

II. Creation Order as Fixed Laws

The structural understanding of creation order moves to the fore when we discuss the laws that characterize the created order. These laws are often understood to be given facts, i.e., the way the world "is." On this account, the task of human knowing is to uncover or discover those "facts" so as to understand the way God has designed the world to operate. This understanding of law is then qualified by a distinction in the two types of laws that exist in the world: laws of nature, in which God governs immediately in the areas of "physical things, of plants and of animals"; and norms, through which God governs mediately in the realms of culture, society,

---

14. Thus people tend to equate creation order with the notion of structure understood as a kind of permanent (or constant) essence. For example, when discussing this threefold sense of creation order with some colleagues here at Dordt College, a longtime Dordt professor, one who admittedly does not specialize in reformational philosophy as a discipline but who very much views himself as teaching and thinking within the reformational tradition, said, "That one you call the 'structural' sense — I had always thought that's just what creation order is." Such an equation finds some backing in the reformational tradition (cf., for example, *Creation Regained*, 59: "structure refers to the order of creation, to the constant creational constitution of any thing, what makes it the thing or entity that it is"), though it lacks the fullness of the picture of creation order described above, and therefore misses something significant, as this paper hopes to demonstrate.

15. Indeed, this system of structural, fixed relations is how the philosophy of the "cosmonomic idea" is usually understood, despite the fact that such an interpretation of the cosmonomic idea is not without its critics, including Dooyeweerd himself in some places; cf., for example, the competing visions of Dooyeweerd's understanding of order by Hendrik Hart and Johan van der Hoeven in Walsh et. al., eds., *An Ethos of Compassion and the Integrity of Creation* (Lanham: University Press of America, 1995), as well as Klapwijk's *Purpose in the Living World*, chapter 12.

and "interpersonal relationships" (16). While understanding laws as facts may not seem problematic in regards to the laws of nature,[16] it is applied also, usually implicitly, to norms. In trying to explain the way in which God governs mediately (through humans) in the realm of norms, some people take the claim that God's decrees — and God's alone — are law, combine it with the understanding that these laws have been given once and for all in the original act of creation described in Genesis 1 (cf. *Creation Regained*, 13), and determine, therefore, that our job, as stewards of creation, is merely to interpret those fixed decrees correctly in the current situation. In this regard, our job as knowers of norms is not markedly different from our job as knowers of the laws of nature — to uncover, but not to create or shape, the law. With norms, there is then an added second step in which we determine whether or not some particular action contradicts the uncovered law, but it is apparent that we are not legislators, but merely the police: we enforce a set of laws that existed before us and transcend our ability to affect them. With this understanding of "norms," it seems to me that both laws of nature and norms are understood as facts, that is, as pre-established rules.[17]

This understanding of norms as given laws or facts then impacts the sub-

---

16. Though the notion of pre-established laws is not widely accepted in most contemporary philosophy of science, as Wolters himself seems to recognize when he admits that "sophisticated" people would probably "reject the term *laws* as too metaphysical, and speak of 'models' instead" (17), even in regards to the laws of nature.

17. So, while Wolters critiques "the secularized Western mind" for overemphasizing the distinction between laws of nature and norms through the competing categories of facts and values, respectively (17-18), I am here suggesting that we can also underemphasize the distinction between laws of nature and norms by treating them as if they both indicate the way things are — with norms merely being easier to violate than laws of nature.

Equating norms with "facts," understood as pre-established rules, seems to ontologize these laws into distinct entities, existing in their own right. There is a long line of reformational discourse that seems to move in this direction. Dooyeweerd's understanding of the antithetical *Gegenstand* nature of theoretical thought can seem to trend in this direction, as do the notion of individual or type laws, both as applied to biological and to social or cultural *types*. Several readers of Vollenhoven also seem to believe his talk of law as the boundary between creator and creature ontologizes the law into a third distinct category. I do not wish to argue for or against reading either figure in this way, as doing so would take us too far afield of the current discussion; I merely want to indicate that this line of thinking is not absent from reformational philosophy, and hence it is understandable that people understand norms in this fashion. On Dooyeweerd, cf. Hart and van der Hoeven's contributions to *An Ethos of Compassion*; on Vollenhoven, cf. John Kok, *Vollenhoven: His Early Development* (Sioux Center: Dordt College Press, 1992).

sequent distinction between general and particular norms. General norms are those that hold for all cases (that fit a particular description),[18] and particular norms are more individualized, restricted to a particular time and place. Wolters offers us as examples of general norms "the imperatives to be just, to be faithful, to be stewardly, and so on," while particularized norms include an individual's "calling" or "guidance" (19). But this distinction is between general and particular norms only if we equate generality with vagueness or indeterminacy, and particularity with determinacy. In this case, general norms acquire their generality, and so also their "universal" validity, from a certain indeterminacy — but the particularity of norms (i.e., do this now) comes from their determinacy. Therefore, norms can be universally valid only to the extent that they are empty of content, and once a norm has some content (some specific command or regulation regarding behavior), that very content deprives it of the indeterminacy needed for universal validity. The normative command "be just," for example, can have universal validity only because it has little (if any) particular content — there can be a general norm to be just, but not a general norm to be just by treating your slaves well or to be just by giving all you have to the poor. Particular norms, then, draw their normative weight only from their being a particularized instan-

---

18. The inclusion of the phrase "that fit a particular description" is key to Wolters's understanding of general laws, yet it is itself problematic. Without it, the sphere of general laws would be severely restricted in scope. Indeed, it would seem confined exclusively to laws of nature (or facts), as even the most general norm-related laws (e.g., "Don't kill") seem to not be true for all people in all situations (e.g., self-defense, defense of others, the God-commanded genocide of the Israelite conquest of Canaan, etc.), and Wolters is adamant that the distinction between general and particular laws does *not* map on to the distinction between laws of nature and norms. Yet, with the inclusion of the phrase "that fit a particular description," it becomes difficult to come up with a law that is *not* general. A hair does not fall from my head without a reason, of course, but because of gravity, and my nutritional intake versus the amount of energy I expend, etc. Similarly, sparrows do not fall willy-nilly from the sky, but do so for reasons which any sparrow, in that situation, would also comply with: their wings became coated with ice, or they had a heart-attack, or God struck them with lightning, etc. (note: a hair falling from my head and a sparrow falling from the sky are both examples Wolters gives of particular laws; cf. 19). Wolters tries to get outside this by adding the additional phrase "for as long as the legislation is in effect" to his descriptor of general laws, but I do not see how this helps defeat the problem: is this not just another condition, another "relevant particular," that must factor into the application of the universal law? That is, isn't the law still general, in the sense that it applies to *all* people who find themselves in that particular spatio-temporal position? In this regard, I don't see how Wolters's temporal index removes the universal validity standard, except in a purely arbitrary way.

tiation of a more general normative claim, but they can do so only as long as they are, in fact, a genuine positivization (17)[19] of that more general claim. The norm "Neal, give that thirsty man a cup of water," for example, can only have normative weight — it can only be ethically compelling — if it is a genuine application in the present of the general norm "Be just."[20]

If this is true, then the distinction between general norms and particular norms seems to explain the differing modes of ruling held by God (as immediate sovereign) and humans (as mediate stewards). But then it is equally true that particular norms are the human interpretation of God's (general) norms, and are therefore not norms (i.e., God's law) at all, but merely human rules that try as best they can to positivize God's (general) norms. That is, human "norms" are our attempt to decipher, interpret, and apply the unchanging and fixed (general) norms laid down by God.

III. From Fixed Laws to Sin and Redemption

By arranging things this way, the structural view of creation order entails that human activity cannot distinguish between the creational (or cultural) man-

---

19. "Positivization is a matter of putting into practice a creational norm" (98).

20. Technically, one would still need another level of normativity that could compel us to obey general norms as positivized in particular norms. This higher level is often ascribed to obedience — the most general norm being "Obey God," and other norms carrying normative weight only insofar as they are actual examples of calls or commands of God.

In some strands of reformational philosophy, however, this highest-order norm is thought to be love, rather than obedience, in which case we must obey norms not because they have been commanded by God, but because they are positivizations of the most general, God-given norm to love. This notion makes an appearance already in Vollenhoven's threefold sense of law (structural law, law for love, positive law); cf., for example, Vollenhoven, "The Consequent Problem-Historical Method," 106; Vollenhoven, "Short Survey of the History of Philosophy," in *The Problem-Historical Method and the History of Philosophy*, 21-88, 30; and Wolters, "On Vollenhoven's Problem-Historical Method," in *Hearing and Doing: Philosophical Essays Dedicated to H. Evan Runner*, edited by John Kraay and Anthony Tol (Toronto: Wedge, 1979), 231-62. It should be noted that Vollenhoven's distinction between "structural law" and the "positive law" does not map neatly onto the distinction between laws of nature and norms, nor can the distinction between the "law for love" and "positive law" be explained in the way that general and particular norms have been described here.

In focusing on obedience — which can result from emphasizing the structural (fixed and unchanging) sense of creation order — something is lost between reformational philosophy and its reception in Reformed thought.

date and the redemptive mandate.²¹ In norms, humans are given the "responsibility" of "making tools, doing justice, producing art, and pursuing scholarship" (16). But Wolters's explanation of this responsibility is ambiguous in a way that, upon closer inspection, is very significant for our discussion here. Here, human responsibility is about bringing about some greater good (i.e., instantiating God's norms in concrete situations). However, almost immediately, Wolters will begin to talk about human responsibility in a (theologically) distinct sense: rather than being responsible for bringing about a greater good, we now become responsible, instead, for obeying and following a set of already given commands: "we are held to account for the way we execute God's commandments, and we are liable to punishment if we do no[t] execute them at all" (17). This subtle shift in the understanding of responsibility betrays a much larger issue: we can be creationally responsible in the first sense, but only redemptively responsible in the second sense.²² When these two senses of responsibility are conflated, the cultural and the redemptive mandates are also conflated, a move that we must condemn (and one that Wolters explicitly condemns on p. 15) if we are going to maintain two distinct tendencies in Wolters's account of reformational thought: first, the understanding of the universal scope of creation, fall, and redemption; and second, the fundamental distinction between structure and direction.

Unfortunately, these two desires, which Wolters describes as complementary, may in fact be contradictory instead. The universal scope of creation affords creational goodness to everything, and while the universal scope of the fall affects all of creation, it does not destroy this original goodness, but is rather parasitic on the good "creation order" (46). If we continue to apply the structural sense of creation order that characterizes the understanding of law under discussion so far, we immediately see the need for the distinction between structure and direction: the creational structure (order)

---

21. VanDrunen also claims that Wolters conflates the redemptive and the creational mandates; cf. *Natural Law and the Two Kingdoms*, 381.

22. Hence, the two notions of responsibility are not, in this unique instance, two sides of the same coin, but in fact mark an essential distinction in the human condition: non-sinful vs. sinful humanity. That is, there is a fundamental theological distinction between the two senses of responsibility: we cannot violate God's norms and risk punishment in our pre-lapsarian condition, but only in our post-lapsarian condition. Hence, the first sense of responsibility described above, responsible$_1$, is the only sense in which we can be *creationally* responsible; the second sense of responsibility, responsible$_2$, is a matter of being *redemptively* responsible. There is no role for redemption in creation before the fall, but rather we "can only speak of redemption after misery has made its appearance"; Vollenhoven, "The Unity of Life," trans. John H. Kok, in *A Vollenhoven Reader* (unpublished manuscript), 150.

remains good, while the "direction" or way that structure gets used can be either good (in which case we call it redemptive) or bad (in which case we call it sinful). Here we see the necessity of keeping the creational mandate distinct from the redemptive mandate: the creational mandate dictates the goodness of the created order (understood as structure), while the redemptive mandate dictates that creation is not entirely good, but has been pervasively affected by the fall into sin. While the redemptive mandate is premised on the fact that things can be good or bad, the creational mandate operates in a realm in which things must be good; indeed, the goodness of the creation is precisely what enables Wolters (and others who follow in his footsteps) to claim that cultural products and institutions — as part of the created order/structure — are inherently good, though now affected by sin, and therefore in need of redemption. It is only because of the distinction between the creational and the redemptive "axes" of the world (cf. 57-58) that reformational philosophy can view all of life as religion, and therefore view cultural transformation and redemption as an essential Christian task.[23]

IV. From the Creation Mandate to the Cultural Mandate: Creational Development?

I would argue that the conflation of the creational and the redemptive mandates is necessary once we have agreed to view creation order only through the prism of its structural sense, ignoring — or at least heavily subsuming — the verbal and collective senses of creation order. Such a myopic view renders the creation order static and unchanging, and development ceases to be a meaningful creational word. If the created order is a set of fixed laws or re-

---

23. VanDrunen also claims that reformational thought requires the affirmation of both the creational and the redemptive mandates in its defense of culture as an essentially Christian task. However, VanDrunen then claims that the reformational tradition affirms both of these mandates only by conflating them into one mandate, rather than by maintaining the sharp distinction between the creational kingship of God (exhibited in common grace and the common kingdom) and the redemptive kingship of God (exhibited in special grace and the redemptive kingdom of the church). What I am arguing here, and below, re-emphasizes, contra VanDrunen, the necessity of this distinction for reformational thought, and the rooting of the cultural task specifically in the creational, and not the redemptive, mandate. That there is perhaps redemptive and eschatological power at work in the cultural task is an issue that must be divorced, I think, from the original creational calling to that task, if we are to properly understand the reformational tradition. Cf. *Natural Law and the Two Kingdoms*, chapter 9.

lations, how can it be said to "develop"? What, precisely, is being "developed," and how are we to understand this development, given that the created order is, apparently, unchanging?

I am not claiming that reformational philosophy teaches a static and unchanging creation order. Rather, I want to argue that if one wants to maintain a creational (and not just redemptive) notion of development, and still hold to some kind of structural understanding of creation order, one must recover something of the other senses of creation order at work in reformational philosophy.[24] To do this, one could attempt to recover something of the collective sense of creation order by claiming that, while the laws that structure creation are fixed and unchanging, the creatures subject to those laws remain temporal, and therefore dynamic, creatures.[25] Then we can say that the created order develops in so far as particular creatures (agents, humans) shape other creatures (resources)[26] in previously unknown ways. In this case, the task of creational development would become synonymous with the task of human civilization, of making culture.[27] By having some creatures shaped by other creatures, the created order (understood as the totality or collective of creatures) comes to include things in configurations not previously seen, and hence can be said to develop or grow.[28]

---

24. To quote Vollenhoven again, but now, perhaps, in more prescriptive or corrective manner: "Structural law is rooted in the divine command to exist, a command issued in the act of creation"; "The Consequential Problem-Historical Method," 106.

25. Hendrik Hart has questioned whether there is in fact a genuine dynamism to the theory of temporality put forward by Dooyeweerd, and echoed by many in the reformational tradition; cf. "Reply to my respondents," in *An Ethos of Compassion* (pp. 115-128); see also *Understanding Our World* (Lanham: University Press of America, 1984).

26. Here, indeed, is the root of many of the ecological and stewardship questions that emerge from this structural view of creation order. If other creatures are merely resources for cultural development, then we seem authorized to do what we will not only with natural resources like water, oil, coal, lumber, etc., but also with other animals. Hence, the principle of, e.g., farming is not that of the ethical care of other living creatures, but the (economic) frugal use of limited (animal and other) resources. This divergence in understanding of the nature of the farming enterprise is, I think, at the root of many of the stewardship debates currently going on in Reformed understandings of agriculture.

27. A point emphasized by Wolters: "From now on the development of the created earth will be *societal* and *cultural* in nature. In a single word, the task ahead is *civilization*" (42).

28. However, it seems that these "new" shapes given to resources cannot be unknown to God if the laws God has given that creation order are unchanging and fixed. To maintain this notion of creation order, development as currently discussed must, in fact, be nothing other than the eventual outcome or discovery of the potentials already laden in creation by God's

V. Judging Cultural Development

But recovering the collective sense of creation order alone is not sufficient. If creational development is possible on this account, it is so only in a very loose sense of the term "development." Creation seems to change, at least in appearance — creatures are arranged in previously unseen ways (trees become cabinets, ore becomes cars, etc.) — but is "change" enough for "development"? This latter term tends to take its meaning by reference to an external standard: something develops if it moves closer towards some particular telos. So what is the telos of cultural development in Reformed thought? The answer in *Creation Regained* seems to be: the pre-ordained, transcendent divine norms that are to act as the reference point for judging cultural development. We can then apply Wolters's distinction between general and particular norms to help us make sense of how that would work. God provides us with general, indeterminate guidelines (e.g., "Be just!"), and human culture is our attempt to provide determinacy to these general norms by interpreting how these norms apply in our current cultural context.

We are now finally in a position to see how conflating the creational and the redemptive mandates leaves culture either meaningless, impossible, or both. If cultural developments are to be judged by their conforming or not conforming to God's norms, then those developments must be either sinful (i.e., they violate those norms) or good/redemptive (i.e., they are in accordance with those norms), since violation of God's laws/norms is the definition of sin.[29] Redeeming culture[30] would then be the process of moving cul-

---

divine and eternal decrees. In this regard, anything that is developed must have been known by God from the beginning (at least, known as a potential outcome of creational development). Epistemologically, this seems to return us again to Late Medieval and Early Modern notions of truth as existence in the mind of God. Such a view is still used in certain reformational circles; cf. René van Woudenberg's contributions to the "Truth Matters" conference in Toronto in August of 2010.

29. For Wolters, sin seems to be equated with the "perversion" or "distortion" of creation (58-59). Assuming we can hold "perversion" and "distortion" to be roughly synonymous with "violation" here — and I think we can — then sin as the violation of God's creational laws/norms would be an adequate description of Wolters's account of sin as well.

30. I acknowledge that the issue of "redeeming" culture is problematic to some in the reformational tradition, who would prefer to speak of "reforming" or "transforming" culture, leaving redemption to God alone. I echo the concern of putting humanity in the position of redeemers, and also would wish to avoid this problematic outcome, though I am also not sure that "redemption" and "transformation" or "reformation" are used in a meaningfully different way here, since the "transformation" of culture we are meant to achieve is to

tural activities from a position of being in violation of norms to a position of being in accordance with norms.

This assumes that every cultural development is redeemable. But on what ground can we make such a claim? There seem to be two possible avenues available here. First, norms remain general (i.e., "Be just!"), and the task of redemption is to bring each and every cultural process/product in line with these general norms. This entails that cultural institutions are not rooted in the creation order, but only serve to help us instantiate these general norms: for example, the imperative "praise God" is instantiated by human creative expression in the arts. If this is the case, then the moment they cease to help us instantiate those norms, they can be abandoned. This does not entail that they must be abandoned, for surely some imperfect institutions could be redeemed. But it does suggest the possibility that certain cultural institutions are not developments of creation at all, but are merely misguided attempts to shape creation, and therefore must be abandoned.[31] That is, either not every cultural development is redeemable or not every product of human activity is a development.[32] There is no impulse or force behind development, except the redemptive impulse to bring things in line with God's commands.[33] Development becomes, in this sense, merely an instantiation of the most general norm ("Obey!"), and therefore development itself becomes something that must be brought in line with that norm (redeemed) or abandoned if it is not in line with that norm. Development becomes, in other words, equivalent to redemption. Here, specifically cultural development is a meaningless term, and culture is lost. The question becomes not how to transform or redeem "every square inch" of culture, but rather to determine — somehow — which cultural products or institutions can be used to help humanity comply with God's norms, and to abandon the rest.[34]

---

bring it in line with God's norms, which seems to be how we are to understand redemption as the response to sin.

31. James K. A. Smith makes an argument along these lines in various places in *The Devil Reads Derrida and Other Essays on the University, the Church, Politics and the Arts* (Grand Rapids: Eerdmans, 2009).

32. Because (creational/cultural) development has become conflated with redemption (bringing things in line with God's laws/norms). Here we see the root of the difference between "evangelical" and "neo-Kuyperian" understandings of the Christian task.

33. Here, the reformational notion of the love command could perhaps provide a creational account of development that would be distinguishable from the redemptive impulse of obedience.

34. I take this to be a position consistent with the two-kingdoms approach: that Christians must act in accordance with those cultural laws that are in keeping with God's norms,

The second avenue by which one could consider all of culture redeemable — necessary, since the first avenue did not lead us to this conclusion — is to claim that the purpose of cultural institutions is not merely to help us instantiate general norms, but rather to instantiate norms that apply particularly to them. This line of thinking suggests that norms have become particularized — already by God — so that there are norms that apply particularly to, say, the state or the educational institution (cf. 96-100). In this case, the existence of norms for particular institutions entails that these institutions must themselves have a foundation in the transcendent structure of creation (97).[35] If this is the case, then they must have always been present *in nuce*, because, as unchanging, the creation structures of these institutions must have always existed; and given that the law is "the totality of God's ordaining acts toward the cosmos" (15), there can be no sharp distinction made between the structural sense of creation order and the collective sense of creation order: there are no creational structures that exist without a correlate in created things, in creation.[36] To deny this is to divorce the structural law from creation, instead positing the structural law as some kind of realm of Platonic forms that require a second act (i.e., of creation, or bringing-into-existence) in order to become existent. This entails that, if the State, for example, is a part of the eternal creation structure, then there has always been a State, even if, at times, it was not a very good one (i.e., not in keeping with God's norms regarding statehood).[37] Therefore, the "development" of State-

---

and abandon the rest. This does not conflate cultural laws and God's norms, but precisely keeps them distinct: cultural laws are binding on the Christian only to the extent that they do not openly compel us to sin (i.e., to violate God's norms). In this regard, culture is not a unique Christian calling, but is, rather, merely another avenue in which Christians can display (or not) their compliance with God's redemptive laws in personal and moral ways, but not in the pursuit or construction of culture itself.

35. This seems to be Dooyeweerd's view, and probably Kuyper's also, with the caveat that it is not clear that either of these thinkers took the structure of creation order to be fixed and unchanging. Dooyeweerd seems to lean in this direction at times, but against his own best intentions. J. P. A. Mekkes, one of Dooyeweerd's students, seems to have taken Dooyeweerd's thought in the non-structural direction. There is much work to be done yet, I think, in English-language reformational thought, on Mekkes's understanding of Dooyeweerd and of reformational thought in general. I refer the reader to Chris van Haeften's translation of Mekkes's *Creation, Revelation and Philosophy* (Sioux Center: Dordt College Press, 2010). This is the first of Mekkes's works to be translated into English, a move that should greatly boost Mekkes's place in English-language reformational thought.

36. Hence, the correlation of the law and the subject-sides of creation in Dooyeweerd.

37. This must be true, given that God's laws (including norms) are transcendent and unchanging, on the structural account here under discussion. This also assumes the exis-

hood is not a cultural development at all, but is merely a reworking of what has always already existed from the beginning, because it was created by God's own decree. If culture is the mark of human activity, then these institutions rooted in the creation structure cannot be cultural institutions, for they are the result of God's creating activity, not humanity's. Now every cultural development is redeemable, but only insofar as it ceases to be a specifically cultural development. Culture — as a human activity — is impossible, and culture is, therefore, again lost.

So, if there are particular norms for cultural institutions, then either they are not cultural institutions (but instead divine ones), or they can be considered cultural only to the extent that culture-making is one and the same as the larger process of redemption. Perhaps one would want to counter by claiming that while State-hood itself — the "essence" of State-ness — might be God's activity, our particular manifestation of State-hood is a cultural artifact, as it is our (human-made) attempt to instantiate God's call to State-hood. But this returns us to our previous set of problems: if there is an unchanging, God-given norm for the State, then our manifestations of State-hood are attempts to bring a contemporary state of affairs in line with those norms, and as such are an act on the redemptive axis, rather than the creational/cultural one.

As such, the task of a positive development of culture is lost for Christians. When viewed from the perspective of the divine, unchanging norms, culture is rendered impossible (since God creates the norms, and we do not). When viewed from the perspective of our contemporary state of affairs, culture (and especially cultural development) is meaningless, since it is subsumed under (and must be subservient to) the larger issue of redemption.

VI. Recovering Culture

Viewing the creation order as a transcendent and unchanging structure, then, loses a robust notion of cultural transformation and reformation. Given the pre-existent and unchanging nature of the norms that would guide culture, the question of cultural development becomes conflated with the question of sin and redemption. In this case, we have several options:

---

tence of social "type" laws, laws typical of certain types of (social) things. The notion of type laws, while having a foundation in Dooyeweerd, is highly controversial in reformational circles; cf., e.g., Klapwijk, *Purpose in the Living World,* chapter 12.

(1) all development is good, and must be brought in line with God's norms;[38] (2) all development is movement away from God's divinely ordained structure, in which case culture is not creationally good, and therefore it is not our task to redeem it;[39] or (3) development is the temporal interpretation/application of transcendent and unchanging divine laws/norms, as we have been discussing here. This third view renders culture (a) meaningless by making it the attempt of humans to ally ourselves with God's pre-ordained wishes and, therefore, reduces culture to a question merely of obedient submission to authority (in which case it is not creative or meaning-making, meaning-full, but only, at best, imitative or mimetic), or (b) impossible, by making "cultural" institutions divine, rather than human (and therefore cultural) products. Either way, if creation order is understood only according to its structural sense, culture in any meaningful, positive sense is lost.

So where does that leave us? In order to recover or regain culture, we must abandon the equation of the creation order with its structural aspect and the related notion of the transcendent and unchanging law-structure, and recover not only the collective sense of creation order (since that has already been "recovered" in our discussion — see Section IV), but also the verbal sense of creation order as well. A renewed focus on the verbal dimension of creation order can help provide us an account of changing creational laws only if we can abandon the hypothesis that creation as God's creating activity took place long ago — that is, if we can move beyond the claim that God *spoke* the creation order into existence, and instead affirm that God *speaks* creation order into existence. In order to avoid the Platonic paradigm discussed above (in which creation laws exist separately from the created order and thereby require another act to bring something into existence that is in accord with those pre-existent laws), we would need to affirm that one and the same act[40] — or at least the same power — creates the world and holds it

---

38. This way of thinking is evident in many of my students, who think one can do any cultural activity (including Mixed Martial Arts) as a Christian, as long as you do it "for Jesus."

39. This way of thinking parallels that of the two-kingdom approach, though is not necessarily equivalent with it. Though VanDrunen is adamant that he is not anti-culture (*Living in God's Two Kingdoms*, 25-26), he does admit that our cultural activities have no lasting, eschatological value, and that the functioning of culture is entirely distinct from the Christian task (*Natural Law and Two Kingdoms*).

40. Hence, we can affirm Wolters's claim that "the same Creator God and the same sovereign power that called the cosmos into existence in the beginning has *kept* that cosmos in

in existence. If this is true, providence cannot be an act secondary to, or distinct from, the original act of creation; rather, "God's daily work of preserving and governing the world cannot be separated from his act of calling the world into existence" (14).

The verbal sense of creation order helps us here by suggesting that the creational/providential Word of God was not given once for all, but is still being spoken into the world today. If creation and providence are one and the same, then we can consider that God is still speaking today, that creation is still here because creating is still happening. Such a view — which is consistent, I would maintain, with the reformational tradition[41] — has many implications that must still be laid out. While I cannot do so fully here, let me sketch out briefly what this might entail for the question of culture that is at hand.

I have argued that culture and cultural development are impossible, meaningless, or both when it is assumed that the norms and laws governing culture and cultural development are fixed and unchanging because that assumption leads to a conflation of the creational and the redemptive axes. By treating creation as an ongoing activity, we avoid those problems, and can consider perceived change to be (a possible) part of the divinely ordained creation. As such, the notion of cultural development can be rather easily recovered as a meaningful term.[42]

This does not, however, recover cultural development as possible. Indeed, it seems to make culture even less possible, since it roots all creational change in the ongoing speech of the Creator. Taken in a certain way, this could suggest that all creational change is divine in nature, and as such is not cultural at all (given our earlier equation of culture with specifically human activity). If this is true, cultural development can be meaningful, but not possible.

---

existence from moment to moment to this very day" (13), while perhaps questioning the distinction contained therein between "calling into existence" and "keeping in existence." This seems to be in keeping with the meaning of the Hebrew and Biblical concept of *bara*, which is often translated as "creation," but which also includes the notion of "holding" in existence, of what would traditionally be called providence. I thank my colleague Jay Shim for this reference, as well as for the Bavinck reference given below.

41. For example, with Bavinck's claim that "the Word of God is not only the maker of all things; it remained in the world as the sustainer and ruler of everything"; cf. Herman Bavinck, *Our Reasonable Faith*, trans. Henry Zylstra (Grand Rapids: Eerdmans, 1956), 53.

42. This also enables us to recover the possibility of divine norms for particular social and historical institutions. Whether other elements in reformational thought would mitigate this possibility, I cannot explore further here.

To recover cultural development as both meaningful and possible, we have to acknowledge that God acts in the world in multiple ways. Again, a renewed emphasis on the verbal side of creation order can help us in this regard: by emphasizing the speaking/spoken aspect of creation, we can more easily create an image of multiple modes of divine action working through multiple types of divine speech. This would help further explain the distinction between laws of nature (performative speech acts) and norms (cajoling or requesting speech acts), and so reinforce that divinely ordained norms do not function like pre-given "facts" — that is, as pre-existent and unchanging statements that we must try to decipher and then apply to our lives. This could help us counter the more moralistic (rather than cosmic) understanding of sin at work in much evangelical theology, as well as counter the recent trend in Reformed thought to equate creation order with Natural Law,[43] at least in regard to societal norms.

But the verbal sense of creation order can also help us make deeper sense of the way in which God acts directly (laws of nature) and indirectly (norms) in creation, by helping us think in terms of direct vs. indirect speech. Speaking directly, God uses God's own words to make God's own points. To use the language of speech-act theory: in direct speech, God's locutionary and illocutionary acts are one and the same.[44] In the case of indirect speech, however, we can understand a person saying something "with words which he himself has not uttered or inscribed."[45] That is, God speaks indirectly in the world by adopting someone else's speech as God's own, by speaking through appointed agents that act and speak on God's behalf. These persons, then, can be understood as being "deputized" by God to be unique representatives — or stewards — of God here on earth, as the prophets had been during biblical times, and as ambassadors are for heads of state today.[46] This does not remove authority from God and place it in the deputy, any more than the president ceases to be president when he allows an am-

---

43. While VanDrunen is clear that Dooyeweerd's conception of creational laws constitutes a departure from natural law as it had traditionally been conceived, he contends that this constitutes a move away from the Reformed tradition (including Calvin and Kuyper); cf. VanDrunen, *Natural Law and the Two Kingdoms,* chapter 3 (Calvin), chapter 7 (Kuyper), and chapter 9, esp. 362-68 (Dooyeweerd).

44. Cf. J. L. Austin, *How to do Things with Words,* second edition (Cambridge: Harvard University Press, 1975); see especially Lecture VIII.

45. Wolterstorff, *Divine Discourse,* 38. Wolterstorff refers to this as "double agent discourse" rather than indirect speech.

46. Cf. Wolterstorff, 42-51 for the notion of "deputized discourse."

bassador to carry out negotiations on his behalf. Rather, it entails that God acts in the world through the actions performed by those God has deputized, and God speaks in the world, still today, at least in part through the words uttered or written by those deputies.

There are multiple ways of understanding this deputization, two of which will be of special interest to us here. First, God provides a message that someone else is commissioned to communicate to a third party; second, God authorizes someone else to compose speech and share it with others as if it were God's own.[47] This distinction significantly impacts our understanding of the possibility of changing creational laws and of a Christian calling to culture. Those who maintain that creation as God's creating activity took place long ago contend that God has already spoken the creational laws and norms, and that what is transmitted to us is a completed "message" which we may then have to decode/decipher and share with others. In this regard, we are commissioned to communicate to a third party (the world) a message that we have no hand in shaping. However, if we understand the Christian calling not merely as a commission but as a deputization in the strong sense,[48] then we can mark some cultural developments, and the production of (certain) cultural laws and norms, as acts of (indirect) divine speech in the present.

Such deputized discourse yields "a peculiarly fascinating blend of two personalities."[49] If we lose this blend of personalities, we slide into dangerous territory. If we focus too much on the divine authorization, we tread dangerously close to rendering culture impossible again; on the other side, if we focus too much on the human composition of what is said, we tread dangerously close to the divinizing of humanity. We must emphasize, instead, that while God is still sovereign, and has with that sovereign power authorized certain people to speak, the resultant speech is not merely divine nor

---

47. The key claim here is that when the deputy speaks, God speaks; the differences result from how much say God would have in what is spoken on God's behalf, and in the way in which the deputy is authorized by God to be God's representative. For a more thorough explanation of the ways in which indirect speech can happen than is necessary for our purposes here, cf. chapter 3, "The Many Modes of Discourse," in Wolterstorff's *Divine Discourse*.

48. In which case the Great Commission must be understood as the moment of God's authorization of us as deputies, and not merely as God giving us a message to deliver. Hence, the call to "go and make disciples of all nations," and not the call to "go tell people the following message."

49. Wolterstorff, *Divine Discourse*, 44.

merely human, but rather a matter of of humans who "know the mind" of God[50] speaking their own words, words that help constitute divine speech because God authorizes them to do so (i.e., God uses their locutionary acts to achieve God's illocutionary purpose).

Now, a more thorough account of this particular attempt to re-emphasize the verbal side of creation order would have to give a sustained argument regarding who precisely would be God's deputies, how they would have been authorized to be so,[51] and how we could know who was so authorized.[52] For now let us be content with the assertion that some people could be so authorized, and therefore could become God's deputies or God's stewards here on earth. This notion of stewardship is undoubtedly more familiar to Reformed folks than is my earlier talk of deputies, and seems to function similarly in that a steward is one who administers something (property, finances, etc.) as the agent of another.[53] Assuming that these stewards and/or deputies are in some way related to the church, the question in regards to culture becomes whether these stewards are asked to rule in the name of the king, or merely to disseminate the rulings laid down by the king. I have tried to show in this paper that understanding the church as merely commissioned to deliver a message is not sufficient to yield a reformational account of a call to transform or redeem culture. Rather, the call to culture is best understood if we recover a deeper notion of the stewardship of the church.

Given the presence of the Holy Spirit in the church,[54] and the fallibility and sinfulness of human action, this is far from placing humanity in the role

---

50. This is not to say that they know fully what God thinks, but merely that they have a sense — inspired by careful attention to God's revelation and through the kerygmatic work of the Holy Spirit — of how God would respond in a given situation; cf. Wolterstorff, *Divine Discourse*, 41.

51. The Holy Spirit would have to play some significant role here, as alluded to in the Reformed notion of sanctification. On the relationship between the Spirit's guiding and creational and redemptive law, cf. Vollenhoven, "The Unity of Life."

52. We get the beginning to an answer to such a question already in Deuteronomy 18.

53. For use of the notion of stewards in relation to the notion of ambassadors, which we have been using as equivalent to deputy, cf. James K. A. Smith, "Christian Worship as Public Disturbance," in *The Devil Reads Derrida*, 71-77.

54. Here, reformational philosophy would put the emphasis on the notion of spiritual communities; cf. Dooyeweerd, *Roots of Western Culture: Pagan, Secular and Christian Options*, trans. John Kraay (Toronto: Wedge, 1979); *Transcendental Problems of Philosophic Thought* (Grand Rapids: Eerdmans, 1948) and *The Christian Idea of the State*, trans. John Kraay (Nutley, N.J.: Craig Press, 1968).

of God, either as Creator or Redeemer.[55] Indeed, human sinfulness entails that not all the words of the church are divine speech, but only those that God authorizes as God's own. As the church, then, not only are we called to speak the words that God can authorize as God's own, but we must also, subsequently, live up to the words that are so authorized, and leave behind those that are not. In so doing, we must still employ the creational mandate of loving development alongside the redemptive mandate towards obedience.

As such, recovering a sense of creational laws and norms rooted in the context of divine speech, as Vollenhoven asks us to do, enables us to account for changeable creational laws, and so to maintain two distinct Christian callings: one, to develop creation, in part by developing culture; and two, to act in accordance with God's laws and norms. Though related, these two callings can and must be kept separate. In doing so, we not only recover the complexity of the reformational account of creation order, but we also maintain a meaningful Christian calling to develop culture.

---

55. Though we might function as sub-creators, that is, as agents who can help create cultural laws and norms as we go along rather than merely trying to replicate or mirror divinely ordained structures. I take the word from Jeremy Begbie, *Resounding Truth: Christian Wisdom in the World of Music* (Grand Rapids: Baker Academic, 2007). James K. A. Smith also uses it in *Desiring the Kingdom: Worship, Worldview and Cultural Formation* (Grand Rapids: Baker Academic, 2009). I was first pointed in this direction by Bob deSmith, in reference to J. R. R. Tolkien, "On Fairy Stories," in C. S. Lewis, ed., *Essays Presented to Charles Williams* (Grand Rapids: Eerdmans, 1966).

Reply to Neal DeRoo

Albert M. Wolters

I am pleased to have the opportunity to respond to Prof. DeRoo's stimulating article. He situates himself squarely in the same confessional and philosophical tradition in which I stand myself, and does me the honor of entering into dialogue especially with my book *Creation Regained*. If I understand him correctly, his purpose is to clear up some misunderstandings that have arisen about the notion of creation order as this has been developed in the Kuyperian tradition, especially in the one strand of that tradition associated with the philosophy of the Dutch Calvinist thinkers Herman Dooyeweerd and D. H. T. Vollenhoven and their school, a school of thought often referred to as "reformational" (which I prefer to spell without a capital). It is especially its emphasis on creation order, defined in terms of cosmic law, which distinguishes this strand of the Kuyperian tradition from the more recent philosophical movement which has been developed in that same tradition, namely that of "Reformed epistemology," associated with such names as Nicholas Wolterstorff and Alvin Plantinga. DeRoo is concerned especially with the relation of creation order and culture in "reformational" thought, but not without drawing on the work of Wolterstorff as well.

There is much to like about the fresh and bold way in which DeRoo seeks to come to clarity on the issue of creation order in its relation to culture in the reformational philosophical tradition, and the creative and provocative proposals he makes for renewing this aspect of that tradition. Especially his emphasis on what he calls the "verbal" sense of creation order, and his proposal to conceptualize this in terms of Austin's speech-act theory and Wolterstorff's concept of divine discourse, attests to an imaginative critical reception of the reformational idea of creation order. He is clearly concerned both to appropriate and renew the philosophical tradition he has inherited.

Although I am pleased that he has singled out especially *Creation Regained* as a work representative of this tradition, I believe he exaggerates its influence. It is no false modesty on my part if I protest that my little book is very far from being "of foundational importance to Reformed thought" (as DeRoo claims in note 6) — especially if Reformed thought is defined very broadly (see note 5) as those "wanting to adhere to the thought of the Reformers," including Luther and Zwingli! Moreover, I find it a bit odd that DeRoo should engage my popular booklet as the focus of his discussion. *Creation Regained* does not purport to be a work of philosophy; it was written as a way of laying out the biblical background of the "world and life view" widely shared in the Dutch Kuyperian tradition, and which is the often unspoken presupposition of the philosophical work of Dooyeweerd and Vollenhoven. It thus deals with matters of biblical interpretation and worldview as a preliminary to understanding reformational philosophy, but does not actually expound or defend that philosophy. Furthermore, it takes positions that are self-consciously out of step with standard reformational views (for example on the relationship between theology and philosophy, or on general and particular laws). I would have thought that DeRoo, himself a philosopher, would have been better served to engage directly a more strictly philosophical and representative work of the reformational tradition.

For all that, I am happy to enter into dialogue with him on issues of creation order and culture. In what follows I will endeavor to focus first on the main points of his argument, and subsequently to single out a number of subsidiary points which seem to be worthy of comment. I am aware, however, that there is much in DeRoo's scintillating article that I pass over in silence, partly because of space limitations, and partly because I do not always understand what he means.

As I understand it, the thrust of DeRoo's article is that the reformational tradition has developed a threefold notion of creation order, which he designates as "verbal," "collective," and "structural." Unfortunately, in his view, the structural sense of creation order has tended to be emphasized (especially among readers of *Creation Regained*) at the expense of the two others, with the result that creation order has been popularly conceived in rather static terms, which does not really allow for genuine culture and development. What is needed is a recovery of the "ambiguous tension" (p. 6) that properly obtains among the three senses, and the development of a new appreciation for the verbal sense, perhaps to be understood in the categories of speech-act theory, which will make clear that the creation order is in fact dynamic and changeable, and does allow for real cultural development.

I must confess that I have great difficulty in following DeRoo in his analysis of creation order as understood in the reformational tradition. Let us take a closer look at the three senses of creation order which he discerns in that tradition. The "verbal" is the one in which "creation order is the speaking of a law or command by a superior, which his subordinates are called to obey (e.g., a sergeant in the army ordering his troops into battle)" (p. 5). Presumably what he means is that creation order in this sense is *God* speaking a creative word, in a way analogous to an officer issuing a command. But where in the reformational tradition is creation order spoken of in this way? To substantiate his claim, DeRoo refers in a note to quotes from Vollenhoven and J. van der Hoeven, as well as Wolterstorff's book on divine discourse. But Wolterstorff's book is not about divine discourse in creation, but in human speech, and in any case Wolterstorff would probably be surprised to see himself treated as a representative of "reformational" philosophy in the way DeRoo defines that term (see note 5). As for the quotation from van der Hoeven, when the latter states that our understanding of creation is "entirely dependent on God speaking," he is referring to biblical revelation, not creational ordinances. And when Vollenhoven writes that the structural law "is rooted in the divine command to exist, a command issued in the act of creation," he is clearly not *identifying* the structural law with that primordial command. The idea that the creation order can be understood as a kind of ongoing commanding speech on God's part is certainly intriguing, and potentially quite fruitful, but it has very little precedent, as far as I can see, in earlier reformational philosophy.

In the second sense DeRoo discerns, the "collective" one, creation order is "the totality or collection of individually created things or creatures (the way one would speak of the Jesuit order, for example)." DeRoo here has a footnote saying that this is sometimes referred to not as creation order, but as "created order" or simply "creation." He seems to be referring to what in reformational thought is designated the "subject-side" of creation, the factual phenomena that are subject to God's creational law. However, it is inaccurate to call this a sense of "creation order" without qualification, since the subject-side of creation is not the same as creation itself. Why this "collective" sense of creation order should be compared to a religious society like that of the Jesuits is not entirely clear to me.

Finally, DeRoo distinguishes what he calls the "structural" sense of creation order in reformational thought, according to which it is "the system of necessary, law-governed, and fixed relations that constitutes our world (in a way analogous to how we talk of the sequential 'order' of numbers: 1, 2, 3, etc.)." I am at a loss to know what DeRoo is referring to here. From the way he speaks about "structure" elsewhere in his essay, one might suspect that he means the law-side of creation, but that does not fit here, since he speaks of creation order in this sense as being "law-governed." The reference to "order" in the sense of numerical sequence is also rather opaque. The closest analogue to the idea of such a "system of . . . law-governed . . . relations" in reformational philosophy would again be the subject-side of creation, although neither this nor the law-side would normally be described as "necessary" and "fixed." Although DeRoo does refer to the classical reformational distinction of "law-side" and "subject-side" (see e.g. note 36), it does not seem to play much of a role in his own analysis of how creation order has been understood in this philosophical tradition.

My conclusion is that DeRoo is introducing a new idea of "verbal" creation order, and that he fails to recognize the significance of the distinction between law-side and subject-side of creation. The failure to take this distinction into account also comes through in the overall summary description he gives of the reformational understanding of creation order: "the totality of created things that exist because of a divine law spoken into existence by a sovereign, Creator God." Again, "the totality of created things" would ordinarily refer in reformational parlance only to the subject-side of creation.

In the light of this evaluation of DeRoo's threefold analysis of creation order in the reformational tradition, his rather startling claim that the putative "structural," "collective," and "verbal" senses of his analysis can be correlated, respectively, with the "coherence," "totality," and "origin" of Dooyeweerd's three "transcendental basic problems" seems rather breathtaking in its audacity. To pick just one of the three, I find it particularly daring, not to say foolhardy, to suggest that the supposedly static structural sense of creation order has any special connection with the dynamic intermodal coherence of which Dooyeweerd speaks in his celebrated transcendental critique of theoretical thought.

Since DeRoo is interacting specifically with *Creation Regained*, it may be useful to contrast his definitions and usage with my own terminology in that work. The attentive reader will notice that the expression "creation order" is generally reserved for the law-side of creation (*CR* 31, 33, 40, 47, 109), and the expression "created order" for the subject-side (*CR* 13, 14, 24, 25, 26, 44, 50, 57, 64, 84). As for "creation," the definition that is given is "the correlation of the sovereign activity of the Creator [i.e. law] and the created order" (*CR* 14). Or again: "we understand creation to be the correlation of law and cosmos (or of 'law' and 'subject,' since the whole created order is *subject* to the overarching law of God)" (*CR* 24; cf. also 25 and 50). This is very different from DeRoo's usage and analysis.

Much of DeRoo's discussion is devoted to what he takes to be the static nature of the "structural" understanding of creation order in reformational thought, and to contrast this with the more dynamic nature of the "verbal" understanding. He often describes "structure" in this sense as "fixed" and "unchanging" (he uses each of these adjectives more than a dozen times). It is this "fixed" and "unchanging" nature of the structural sense that makes genuine culture and development impossible, indeed meaningless. Consequently, the structural sense of creation order must be abandoned (p. 3).

It must be said that this is a bit of a caricature of the idea of "structure" in thinkers like Vollenhoven and Dooyeweerd, and certainly also of my own use of the concept in *Creation Regained*. In reformational philosophy "structure" refers to the law-side of creation, and it is never (as far as I know) described as "fixed" or "unchanging." Dooyeweerd never tires of stressing that the law-order in his thought is *dynamic,* and in that way is different from the classical natural law tradition. The creational law in his view is pregnant with meaning, and the "opening-up process" allows for — indeed calls for — a deepening and enrichment in the way that law is responded to in the unfolding of human culture and civilization through history. Thus in Dooyeweerd's own disciplinary specialty of jurisprudence, the norm for justice opens up its meaning from a strict eye-for-an-eye understanding of crime and punishment to an appreciation of mitigating circumstances as a genuine aspect of doing justice. As for my own usage, I was careful throughout *Creation Regained* to avoid using adjectives like those DeRoo ascribes in such profusion to "structure." Instead, I tended to use the adjective "constant" (e.g. *CR* 3, 59) and the noun "constancy" (*CR* 20, 26, 34, 88) to describe the structural side of creation, terms which have ethical rather than metaphysical connotations. I chose them deliberately to highlight the fact that God's creational law is something that can be relied on, since it is guaranteed by the personal faithfulness of God himself.

What is most obviously missing in DeRoo's account of the reformational understanding of creation order, apart from his failure to properly distinguish between law and subject, is an understanding of the dynamic nature of the relationship between these two inseparable sides of creation in the reformational understanding. Their relationship is a correlation of calling and response, of sovereign invitation and creaturely answer, which turns the very nature of reality into a kind of dialogue with deeply personal resonances. The relationship of creational law to creational subject is not one of iron metaphysical necessity, but one of personal address and authority coming from a loving and sovereign God. That is why *Creation Regained* uses a wide variety of dynamic images to describe that relationship. "The law . . . *impinges on* its creaturely subjects. The law is 'valid' in the sense that it holds, it is in force" (*CR* 62). The law (or the creation order, or creational structure) is said "to 'call out,' to 'appeal'" (*CR* 20, 33, 62), to "knock at the door of our hearts and minds" (*CR* 30), to "teach" (*CR* 33), to "norm" human activity (*CR* 17, 25, 29), to "hold for" the subject (*CR* 35), and to act like a restraining leash (*CR* 60) or a repressed coil (*CR* 62). What the structural creational law does is both to constitute and norm the realities of the created world. As I put it at one point: "Structure refers to the order of creation, to the constant creational constitution of any thing, what makes it the thing or entity that it is" (*CR* 59). Therefore when DeRoo's reformational colleague said to him, "That one you call the 'structural' sense — I had always thought that's just what creation order is" (note 14), it seems to me that he had it exactly right.

DeRoo's alternative to the perceived overemphasis of the "structural" sense of creation order is a renewed retrieval not only of what he calls the "collective" sense, but especially of his "verbal" sense, that is, a fresh appropriation of creation order conceived as God's ongoing active command. Although this is something of an innovation in reformational philosophy, as we noted above, it seems like a proposal worth taking seriously. There are, however, two aspects of DeRoo's proposal that puzzle me. One is that the verbal sense of creation order implies the changeability of that order. As he puts it: "A renewed focus on the verbal dimension of creation order can help provide an account of *changing* creational laws" (my emphasis). See also his reference elsewhere to a "changing creation order" and "changing [or: changeable] creational laws." He does not explain why this proposed changeability should follow from the verbal sense of creation order, and I do not myself see why it should. After all, the classical Christian confession of God's providence, which speaks of his ongoing personal care and government of the world, does not imply either that he is a changeable God, or that his dealings with his creatures are fickle or arbitrary. Moreover, the philosophical implications of a changing creation order are quite momentous, and seems to call into question one of the cardinal distinctive features of reformational philosophy. Is it possible, for example, that the logical law of non-contradiction did not hold at some point in the past, or will not hold at some point in the future? If so, does that not invalidate the very possibility of logically valid argumentation?

The other puzzling feature of DeRoo's proposal is his suggestion that we conceive what he calls the "verbal" sense using the categories of speech-act theory, drawing on the works of Austin and Wolterstorff. The difficulty with this, as I see it, is that speech-act theory is an analysis of the way communication in human language works. To transpose the categories of this analysis to the divine speaking of creational law seems like a particularly striking example of the logical fallacy of *metabasis eis allo genos*.

The foregoing concludes my response to what I take to be the central argument of DeRoo's essay. I turn now to a few further points where I think his discussion raises issues worthy of further comment. Prominent among these is his distinction between "creation mandate" and "redemptive mandate," and the conflation of these which he perceives in *Creation Regained*. It is clear that by the former he means what is also commonly called the "cultural mandate" of Genesis 1:28, which in the Kuyperian tradition has been interpreted as God's command (and/or blessing) to humankind to develop culture. But what does DeRoo mean by "the redemptive mandate," which he uses as though it were a well-known concept? I confess myself baffled. One might suppose that he means the so-called "Great Commission" or "missionary mandate" of Matthew 28:19-20, since the relationship of the latter to the cultural mandate is often discussed in the Kuyperian tradition. But that does not seem to be the case. As best I can puzzle it out, he means by "creational mandate" God's call to obey creational laws before the fall, and the redemptive mandate his call to obey those laws after the fall (see especially note 22). The fact that *Creation Regained* speaks in one breath first of the general responsibility of humanity to obey creational norms and then of our still being held to account, on pain of punishment, to do so after the fall, is considered evidence by him of my "conflating" the two mandates (p. 10). But I must confess that I do not understand this at all. In fact, as DeRoo himself states (p. 10), I explicitly reject any such conflation of the two mandates. Yet the place he refers to (*CR* 15) does not speak of two "mandates" at all, but rather of not confusing God's law in *creation* and his saving acts of grace in *re-creation*.

Another clue to DeRoo's meaning is found in the fact that he seems to correlate his two "mandates" with the two kingdoms of which VanDrunen speaks. In footnote 21 he writes that "VanDrunen also claims that Wolters conflates the redemptive and creational mandates." But VanDrunen does not speak of two "mandates" either. Instead, he criticizes me for not properly distinguishing between what he calls the creational and redemptive *kingdoms*. It would seem then that DeRoo equates the two mandates with the two kingdoms, and that he supports VanDrunen's insistence that the two must be kept distinct.

Another significant issue is the distinction in *Creation Regained* between general and particular laws. In his discussion of this distinction, DeRoo fails to point out that it is actually something of an anomaly from the point of view of traditional reformational philosophy, since Vollenhoven and Dooyeweerd and their followers speak of law only in a general or universal sense. Furthermore, DeRoo goes on to interpret the distinction as being that between a general law and a particular interpretation and application (i.e. positivization) of such a general law, forgetting that such postivization is the work of responsible human agents, whereas the particular law which I had in mind was a specific command issued by *God*, which does not presuppose a reference to a more general law.

In speaking of the laws of creation DeRoo states: "These laws are often understood to be given facts, i.e., the way the world 'is'" (p. 6). Elsewhere, too, he repeatedly speaks of laws in reformational thought as "facts." This is an odd assertion, since laws are never called "facts" in reformational philosophy, and in Dooyeweerd's usage the word "factual" is reserved for the subject-side. Apart from that, it is quite inaccurate to say that laws refer to the way the world "is." The laws hold *for* the world, and may or may not correspond to the actual state of affairs on the subject-side. This is most clearly the case for normative laws that are routinely broken by sinful human beings. The norm for justice is not a "fact" that tells us how the world actually is in reality. This seems to be another example of how DeRoo's analysis suffers from a failure to take into account the complicated and dynamic relationship between law and subject in the reformational understanding of creation order.

In conclusion, let me point out two places where DeRoo quotes texts in a rather misleading way. In the first paragraph of his essay he cites Article 37 of the Belgic Confession as apparent justification for those who believe that "there is no point in trying to reform or redeem culture," a position he equates with the two-kingdom view defended by VanDrunen. As DeRoo cites this article, it states that Christ, when he returns, will "burn this old world, in fire and flame." The impression is created that this confession looks upon the present world as doomed to annihilation, and that there is therefore no value to engage in this-worldly culture, since it will all be destroyed anyway. What he neglects to quote are the words that immediately follow:

"in order to cleanse it." According to this confession (which is one of the doctrinal standards of the Dutch Reformed churches traditionally associated with the Kuyperian tradition), the present world will not be discarded, but *purified*. This casts quite a different light on the significance of this-worldly cultural engagement.

The second text I have in mind is the missionary mandate of Matthew 28:19-20. After explaining how in his view the Christian calling involves "deputization in the strong sense," DeRoo writes in his note 48: "In which case the Great Commission must be understood as the moment of God's authorization of us as deputies, and not merely as God giving us a message to deliver. Hence, the call to 'go make disciples of all nations,' and not to 'go tell people the following message.'" Thus apparently the missionary mandate gives considerable freedom to the proclaimers of the gospel, and does not specify a particular message they must transmit. However, this seems to contradict the actual wording of the mandate, in which Jesus specifies that it involves "teaching them to obey everything I have commanded you." Although DeRoo is no doubt right in pointing out that the disciples are Christ's "deputies" in proclaiming the gospel, with the discretionary human responsibility this entails, I believe he is mistaken in playing this off against the specificity of the gospel message.

These two examples of misleading citation can stand as emblematic of what I take to be DeRoo's overall tendency to paint in broad and rather speculative strokes on a large philosophical canvas, but with insufficient attention to the careful reading of texts. This also applies to his reading of *Creation Regained*. Although I appreciate the fact that his criticisms are directed not so much against that work itself as against a popular misunderstanding of it (see his note 6), I must confess that in my view his own understanding of my book has not always been very accurate. In my judgment his stimulating article is provocative in a positive sense of the word, as well as "scintillating" in the literal sense of the word, throwing off conceptual sparks in every direction. Unfortunately, it is also somewhat deficient in careful analysis and clear argumentation.

The Pilgrimage to Kuyper?
Adolf Schlatter and Abraham Kuyper
on Theology, Culture, and Art

Michael Bräutigam

Considering "theology" and "art," one immediately thinks of the icons and altar pieces of Roman Catholicism and Eastern Orthodox Christianity.[1] The Protestant-Calvinist tradition, in contrast, is usually thought of being unassertive and somehow in denial with regards to the arts. But the Swiss Reformed theologian Adolf Schlatter (1852-1938) and his Dutch contemporary, the neo-Calvinist Abraham Kuyper (1837-1920) do away with this stereotype. This essay explores their insightful views regarding the relationship between theology and art in the Protestant-Calvinist tradition. Before we explore their views in more detail, though, it might be helpful to introduce Adolf Schlatter briefly, particularly his relation to culture and the arts.

---

1. The German and Dutch terms "Kunst" and "kunst" respectively, are usually translated into English as "art." It has to be noted, however, that these terms refer more precisely to "the arts," that is, art in a broader sense, including painting, poetry, drama, music, installations, sculpture, architecture, film, etc. In this essay, we will use the English term "art" in that comprehensive sense. Moreover, with a view to the term "aesthetics," it shall be employed in the broader sense, as, for example, defined by Kelly as "a critical reflection on art, culture and nature." Michael Kelly, ed., *Encyclopedia of Aesthetics* (Oxford: Oxford University Press, 1998), ix. Unlike Kuyper, Schlatter does not use the term "Calvinism" as such, rather preferring expressions such as "Christianity" and "religion." I intend to use "theology" as the umbrella term under which Kuyper's and Schlatter's concepts should fit comfortably.

I. Who was Adolf Schlatter?

While Abraham Kuyper is well known in Reformed theological circles, Adolf Schlatter is less well known.[2] Some years ago, Markus Bockmuehl called Schlatter "brilliant but widely ignored."[3] I think that is still true today. Adolf Schlatter was one of the most influential German-speaking theologians of the late nineteenth and early twentieth century. Schlatter's contribution to New Testament as well as systematic theology, to the church and to society in general, is significant, though unfortunately still neglected.[4] During his career, Schlatter published more than four hundred works in a wide variety of disciplines.[5] As theology professor, Schlatter lectured for a hundred consecutive semesters in Bern (1881-88), Greifswald (1888-93), Berlin (1893-98), and Tübingen (1898-1930), thereby influencing several generations of pastors and theologians. Strikingly, a short listing of some of Schlatter's students reads like the "who's who" of twentieth-century German Protestant theology: Dietrich Bonhoeffer, Karl Barth, Rudolf Bultmann, Erich Seeberg, Paul Althaus, Paul Tillich, Ernst Käsemann, and Otto Michel.

Adolf Schlatter was born in 1852 — some fifteen years after Kuyper — in St. Gallen, Switzerland, into a family with a strong Reformed heritage.[6] Growing up in the context of the Swiss Revival movement, Schlatter was

---

2. For a short introduction to Schlatter's life and theology see Peter Stuhlmacher's essay in Martin Greschat, ed., *Theologen des Protestantismus im 19. und 20. Jahrhundert II* (Stuttgart: Kohlhammer, 1978), 219-40. Robert Yarbrough has translated Werner Neuer's short biography, *Adolf Schlatter: A Biography of Germany's Premier Biblical Theologian* (Grand Rapids: Baker Books, 1995). Werner Neuer's magisterial Schlatter biography is, unfortunately, still untranslated: *Adolf Schlatter: Ein Leben für Theologie und Kirche* (Stuttgart: Calwer Verlag, 1996).

3. Markus Bockmuehl, *This Jesus: Martyr, Lord, Messiah* (Downers Grove: InterVarsity, 1994), 218, n1.

4. For some reasons for this neglect see Mark Noll's "Foreword" to *Adolf Schlatter: A Biography of Germany's Premier Biblical Theologian,"* 7-8, and Ernst Käsemann, "Neutestamentliche Fragen von heute," in *Exegetische Versuche und Besinnungen* II (Göttingen: Vandenhoeck & Ruprecht, 1964), 11-31.

5. His literary output ranges from linguistics, church history, archaeology, dogmatics, and philosophy to scholarly commentaries and devotional works.

6. His parents, though both devout Christians, were confessionally divided. While his mother was loyal to the reformed state church *(Landeskirche),* his father was disillusioned with the liberal tendencies in the Swiss *Landeskirche* and consequently broke with it, joining a free evangelical church. The parental division clearly left a mark on Schlatter, who, for the rest of his life, took an ecumenical perspective, trying to emphasize the unifying elements of the Christian tradition.

confronted with an opposing movement in school. The aftermath of the Aufklärung and German Idealism was palpable and did not stop at the door of the classroom of religious education. Schlatter developed a passion for all kinds of art from an early age. Among the family's friends, and a regular guest at the Schlatter home, was the poet Meta Heusser-Schweizer (1797-1876), mother of Johanna Spyri (1827-1901) who would become famous with her novel *Heidi*.[7] Young Adolf used the facilities of the rich St. Gallen library and admired the art treasures of the impressive St. Gallen Monastery. From his childhood, Schlatter was particularly fascinated by literature and poetry. As a young schoolboy, he read Greek and Roman poetry in the original languages;[8] as a twelve-year-old he collected a handwritten 150-page collection of German and Latin poems,[9] while also writing his own poetry.[10] Later in life, when he had the opportunity, he traveled to Florence several times and marveled at the beautiful art displayed in its many museums and galleries.[11] In one of his autobiographical accounts, Schlatter remembers,

> When the sisters showed some giftedness for drawing, it was keenly cultivated. Sure enough, I was not endowed with any productive talent. However, when the Swiss art exhibition came to St. Gallen, each and every picture was beheld with heartfelt devotion.[12]

Around the time when Kuyper founded *De Standaard* and launched his political career, Schlatter took up his studies in theology, first in Basel (1871-

---

7. Schlatter summarizes his personal recollections in his unpublished manuscript "Idealismus und die Erweckung in meiner Jugend," 40-41 (c. 1926, Adolf-Schlatter-Archive, Inventory D 40, No. 1025, see transcript by Albert Bailer, No. 769; page indications are to the transcript, Landeskirchliches Archiv Stuttgart, Germany).

8. For example, Homer, Sophocles, Euripides, Ovid, and Virgil (see Neuer, *Adolf Schlatter*, 40).

9. This collection, written down between 1864 and 1865, is the oldest document from Schlatter's estate (Neuer, *Adolf Schlatter*, 35). Schlatter particularly enjoyed Johann Wolfgang von Goethe's works, as he saw in Faust the most convincing argument for the futility of the Enlightenment theology with which he was confronted in school and later at the university. Schlatter says that Faust is the "superior opponent of the *Aufklärung*," for "Faust does not know what to do; the only thing he accomplishes is that he crushes Gretchen" (*Religion/Christianity*, M.B.; Schlatter, *Die Philosophische Arbeit seit Descartes* [Stuttgart: Calwer Verlag, 1959], 101). Unless otherwise noted, all translations are my own.

10. See Neuer, *Adolf Schlatter*, 87.

11. Neuer, *Adolf Schlatter*, 265, 487.

12. Schlatter, *Erlebtes. Erzählt von D. Adolf Schlatter* ([Berlin, 1924], 5th ed., Berlin: Furche-Verlag, 1929), 125.

73), and then in Tübingen (1873-74).[13] He was subsequently ordained as a minister in the Swiss Reformed state church and worked as a parish minister for several years.[14] While Kuyper was establishing the Free University in Amsterdam in 1880, Schlatter began his academic career in Bern as a private lecturer. Eight years later, Schlatter was called to Greifswald, where he became one of the main proponents of the positive Greifswald school that aimed to counterbalance the influence of Ritschlian theology in the German Protestant faculties.[15] Together with Herrmann Cremer, Schlatter founded and co-edited the theological journal *Essays for the Furtherance of Christian Theology*.[16]

In 1893, the Prussian ministry of culture established a new chair for systematic theology at the University of Berlin in order to counterbalance the predominantly liberal faculty, represented by the influential Adolf von Harnack.[17] The call to the so-called "penal professorship" *(Strafprofessur)* in opposition to Harnack was issued to Schlatter as a representative of a more conservative theology. Five years later, in 1898, when Kuyper delivered his Stone Lectures on Calvinism in Princeton, Schlatter accepted the call to the University of Tübingen where he would live and teach for the rest of his life, nearly four decades, until 1930. At the apex of his career in the southern German university town, Schlatter not only focused on theology, but also on culture and the arts. He was president of the Tübingen YMCA for several years,[18] where he aimed to kindle an interest in the arts among his students.[19] Among Schlatter's friends were many from the cultural scene, such as the church musician and theologian Richard Gölz (1887-1975) and the painter Wilhelm Steinhausen (1846-1924).[20] Schlatter once was deeply moved by a speech delivered by Steinhausen, "The Picture of Christ in the

---

13. Where he profited, first and foremost, from Johann Tobias Beck's (1804-78) teaching.

14. Schlatter served in the parishes of Kilchberg and Neumünster (1875-76), and Kesswil (1877-80).

15. See Eckard Lessing, *Geschichte der deutschsprachigen evangelischen Theologie von Albrecht Ritschl bis zur Gegenwart,* Band 1: 1870 bis 1918 (Göttingen: Vandenhoeck and Ruprecht, 2000), 43-49, 116-21.

16. *Beiträge zur Förderung christlicher Theologie* (*BFChTh;* from 1897 onwards).

17. The so-called *Apostolikumsstreit,* initiated by Harnack's critical publication in the *Christliche Welt* (see Neuer, *Adolf Schlatter,* 292-93).

18. From 1912; he handed the chair over to his son Theodor seven years later.

19. In this context, Schlatter lectured on architecture and composed aesthetical meditations (for instance on Michaelangelo's David; see Neuer, *Adolf Schlatter,* 543).

20. Neuer, *Adolf Schlatter,* 665-67.

Visual Arts." Schlatter reportedly said with tears in his eyes, "With what kind of reverence does this artist speak of the Jesus of the Scriptures; if only the same could be said of our theologians."[21]

Schlatter also had a keen interest in politics, though unlike Kuyper, he never became a full-time politician. In his public speeches, Schlatter continually encouraged Christians to take an active part in politics, even insisting that political engagement is mandatory for Christians.[22] Schlatter argued that the apolitical attitude of many Christians was against nature, irreconcilable with both the Christian belief in creation and Jesus Christ's command of love.[23] From 1926 onwards, Schlatter was personally active in the political and social movement *Christlich-sozialer Volksdienst* (Christian social service for the people).[24] The political situation in Germany then changed for the worse. The rise of National Socialism, culminating in Hitler's seizure of power *(Machtergreifung)* in 1933, concerned Schlatter deeply. He vehemently opposed the National Socialists' ideology, criticized their hijacking of the church with the *Deutsche Christen,* and was highly suspicious of the *Führerkult*[25] that was slowly but steadily gaining ground in Germany. At an early stage he raised his concerns publicly as a speaker[26] and writer,[27] and was later personally involved in the Württemberg church struggle *(Kirchenkampf)* during which he published several statements arguing for a clear independence of the church from the state.[28] *Do we know Jesus? (Kennen wir*

---

21. Neuer, *Adolf Schlatter,* 517-18.

22. See for instance his speeches "Nationalismus und Christentum" (10/1926) and "Was fordert die Lage unseres Volkes von unserer evangelischen Christenheit?" (18/02/1929). See Neuer, *Adolf Schlatter,* 679-87, for details.

23. See his *Die christliche Ethik,* 3rd ed. (Stuttgart: Calwer Vereinsbuchhandlung, 1929), 135-42, and *Das christliche Dogma,* 2nd ed. (Stuttgart: Calwer Vereinsbuchhandlung, 1923), 402-8.

24. Schlatter's political and social involvement for the good of the state moved the King of Württemberg to award Schlatter the *Ehrenkreuz des Ordens* and to ennoble him — an honor of which Schlatter, however, rarely made use (Neuer, *Adolf Schlatter,* 460).

25. See his essay, "Die neue deutsche Art in der Kirche" (1935).

26. "Der Dekalog der Träger unseres Volkstums" (13/07/1933), "Menschengemeinschaft — Gottesgemeinschaft" (16/10/1933). Consult Neuer for Schlatter's view on National Socialism *(Adolf Schlatter,* 725-45).

27. See his published essay "Wird der Jude über uns siegen? Ein Wort für die Weihnachtszeit" (Velbert: Freizeiten-Verlag, 1935).

28. "Das Evangelium und das Bekenntnis" (1934) and "Grenzen der kirchlichen Gemeinschaft" (1935). As the *Kirchenkampf* grew more intense, he had to witness his son Theodor's displacement as dean of Esslingen and could not prevent the repeated house arrests of his friend and fellow countryman, Bishop *(Landesbischof)* Theophil Wurm (1868-1953).

Jesus?) was Schlatter's challenging question to the National Socialists and the German population in his last publication in 1937.[29] Knowing Jesus, his work and demands, was according to Schlatter the only answer for the precarious anti-Christian atmosphere in Germany at that time. On May 18, 1938, Schlatter died, eighteen years after Kuyper, in his home in Tübingen, on the threshold of the Second World War.

Reflecting on Schlatter's life and work, one can see that there are obviously fascinating similarities between the biographies of Adolf Schlatter and Abraham Kuyper. Here, we have two Reformed theologians, both parish ministers, university professors, speakers, authors, politicians, and social activists, who with their lives and their diverse interests and activities set an example of theological and cultural engagement, combining theory and practice, always with the perspective of the whole of human experience and for the good of the "little people" *(de kleine luyden),* as Kuyper would have said.

II. Adolf Schlatter's Ethical-Motivational Approach to the Arts

Though Schlatter once wrote that he would not make the pilgrimage to Kuyper in Amsterdam,[30] they used a similar palette of colors when painting a picture of the relation between theology and the arts. Adolf Schlatter's ultimate goal was to arrive at a unified, holistic understanding of all reality.[31] He rejected any fragmentation of human life into separate, isolated areas. Throughout his works, one can see how Schlatter aims to eliminate any dualisms in theology, church, and society:[32] it was his objective to unify the

---

29. *Kennen wir Jesus? Ein Gang durch ein Jahr im Gespräch mit ihm* (Stuttgart: Calwer Vereinsbuchhandlung, 1937).

30. "I forbade myself the pilgrimage . . . to Abraham Kuyper in Amsterdam." *Erlebtes. Erzählt von D. Adolf Schlatter,* 97.

31. One can detect here Johann T. Beck's influence on his student Schlatter. See Neuer, *Adolf Schlatter,* 68-71; Schlatter, "Becks theologische Arbeit," *BFChTh* 8:4 (1904): 25-46; and Michael Beintker, "Johann Tobias Beck und die neuer evangelische Theologie," *Zeitschrift für Theologie und Kirche* 102 (2005): 230.

32. See his essay, "Die Furcht vor dem Denken" (in *BFChTh* 4:1 [1900]: 3-48), which is directed against Carl Hilty's separation of faith and scientific theology (see Neuer, *Adolf Schlatter,* 413-14). In his speech, "Was ist heute die religiöse Aufgabe der Universitäten?" (in *BFChTh* 5:4 [1901]: 61-79), Schlatter criticizes the unhealthy separation of the realms of theory (university) and practice (church). In his essay "Atheistische Methoden in der Theologie" (in *BFChTh* 5 [1905]: 228-50), Schlatter opposes wrong dualisms that try to drive a wedge between science and theology ("heathen head" vs. "pious heart").

realms of theology and the church, science and religion, reason and revelation, nature and grace, theology and culture, theology and the arts. As "[u]nity is God's characteristic,"[33] according to Schlatter, so also is the product of his creative activity, namely, all of reality, a unified whole — "What God has united man must not divide."

In the pursuit of this holistic approach, Schlatter was clearly influenced by the works of Catholic theologian Franz von Baader (1765-1841).[34] In 1875, Zurich minister Edmund Fröhlich (1832-98) introduced Schlatter to the works of Baader, which had a considerable impact on Schlatter's theological thought. Kuyper was studying Baader's works around the same time as well.[35] As J. Glenn Friesen and Lieuwe Mietus point out, Kuyper was introduced to Baader's thought through the works of J. H. Gunning Jr. (1829-1905) and of Chantepie de la Saussaye (1818-74).[36] Both Schlatter and Kuyper owe a great deal to Baader in their rejection of the dualistic tendencies of German Idealist philosophy. Friesen explains that Kuyper "identifies in Baader . . . the opposition to dualism,"[37] and Schlatter adds, "how valiantly does Baader obey the norm that demands from us the unity, and does there-

---

33. Schlatter, *Dogma*, 369.

34. Franz von Baader (1765-1841) was himself influenced by St. Martin (1743-1803). For an extensive treatment of Baader's influence on Schlatter's theological and philosophical thinking, see Imgardt Kindt, *Der Gedanke der Einheit: Adolf Schlatters Theologie und ihre historischen Voraussetzungen* (Stuttgart: Calwer Verlag, 1978), 62-122; see also Neuer, *Adolf Schlatter*, 103-7. Baader's works were published as *Franz von Baader's sämmtliche Werke*, 16 vols., ed. Franz Hoffmann, Julius Hamberger, et al. (Leipzig: Bethmann, 1851-60; reprint Aalen: Scientia, 1963).

35. Kuyper had read Baader by 1871, since he recommended to a friend, "Lees hem [Baader] opnieuw, gij moet het doen" ("Read him [Baader] again, you must do it"). Leo Mietus, *Gunning en Kuyper in 1978: A. Kuypers polemiek tegen Het Leven van Jezus van J. H. Gunning Jr.* (Brochurereeks nr. 28, Velp: Bond van Vrije Evangelische Gemeenten in Nederland, 2009), 69. Kuyper must have continued to read Baader, since he refers to him in his works as late as 1892. See Glenn Friesen's essay "The Mystical Dooyeweerd Once Again: Kuyper's Use of Franz von Baader," *Ars Disputandi* 3 (2003) [http://www.ArsDisputandi .org], section 1). I am indebted to Glenn Friesen, who pointed me to the connection between Kuyper and Baader, and who was prepared to engage with me in personal correspondence on several questions pertaining to their relationship.

36. See Friesen, "The Mystical Dooyeweerd Once Again: Kuyper's Use of Franz von Baader," and Mietus, *Gunning en de theosofie: Een onderzoek naar de receptie van de christelijke theosofie in het werk van J. H. Gunning Jr. van 1863-1876* (Gorinchem: Narratio, 2006). De la Saussaye's works were published between 1857 and 1870, and Gunning's works in 1866 and 1876.

37. Friesen, "The Mystical Dooyeweerd Once Again," 2-3.

fore not allow for a neglect of nature in theology."[38] Baader's holistic understanding of reality is echoed by Kuyper's emphasis on Calvinism as a *Weltanschauung* and Schlatter's theological *Richtung auf das Ganze*. The task of theology is, therefore, a task with an all-embracing perspective, tracing back the creative activity of God in the whole of creation. Schlatter writes,

> The territory that the theological task has to stride across ranges over the whole revelatory work of God. That endows it with a direction to the whole [*Richtung auf das Ganze*]. . . . The notion of God [*Gottesgedanke*] contains the clause that all being stands in relation to God and that it visualizes in some way his power and will. There is, for that reason, nothing that is unimportant to the one who is faced with the question for God.[39]

Though theology and art are separate spheres, they belong together — "all branches of the arts are at home in Christianity," says Schlatter.[40] What is more, theology, as an all-encompassing science, has a special role to fulfill in relation to the arts, that is, it has to set certain norms for the evaluation of art.[41] Says Schlatter,

> The task of Christianity is, to begin with, to provide . . . protection against the destructive side effects of the arts, in that it . . . sets norms. The arts therefore are faced with a limit. . . . Yet, we cannot do without this limitation of the arts, without which we would destroy everything, both the . . . church and the arts.[42]

Christian ethics and the arts constitute, therefore, from Schlatter's perspective, an inseparable unit, which explains why the main discussion of the subject of art is found in his ethical opus, *The Christian Ethics*. In applying theological-ethical norms to the arts, Schlatter arrives at a threefold distinc-

---

38. Schlatter, "Die Entstehung der Beiträge zur Förderung christlicher Theologie und ihr Zusammenhang mit meiner theologischen Arbeit zum Beginn ihres fünfundzwanzigsten Bandes," *BFChTh* 25:1 (1920): 50.

39. Schlatter, *Dogma*, 13.

40. Schlatter, *Ethik*, 369.

41. Schlatter deals with the arts in his *Ethik* (351-60; 369-73), *Dogma* (124-47), and *Aus meiner Sprechstunde*, 3rd ed. (Bethel: Verlagshandlung der Anstalt Bethel, 1952), 95-96. In both his ethical and dogmatic works, Schlatter treats the arts under the category of feelings/happiness ("Die Seligkeit" in *Ethik* and "Das Fühlen und die Seligkeit" in his *Dogma*), which shows that for Schlatter, the arts are closely related to human experience, i.e., emotions and religious feelings.

42. Schlatter, *Ethik*, 371.

tion in relation to art: "sinful art," "true art," and "pure art."[43] There is, first, on the lowest level, sinful art. Art is sinful, explains Schlatter, when it aesthetically glorifies *(verklären)* sin.[44] This, for instance, is the case in a sinful depiction or description of erotic desires. Schlatter points to the danger of a "dulling" *(Abstumpfung)* regarding sin. According to Schlatter, sinful art is in a sense similar to the Christian penitential sermon *(Bußpredigt)*, though without any gospel presentation.[45] Sinful art, Schlatter claims, is prone to become a substitute for religion when art is pursued merely for the sake of art, without any reference to God: "Where the notion of God is hollow, art can easily become a substitute for religion."[46] Schlatter's main problem with sinful art, however, is that instead of providing an ethical impulse to resist sin (which should be the task of art), it often arouses and intensifies sinful desires.[47] On a higher level, there comes next what Schlatter calls "true art" *(wahre Kunst)*.[48] True art depicts pure beauty, without causing sinful (erotic) desires. "True art," says Schlatter, "is only concerned with the generation of beauty";[49] it merely relates to our aesthetic pleasures. The highest level of art, according to Schlatter, is "pure art" *(reine Kunst)*.[50] Pure art is similar to true art in that it elicits aesthetic pleasures, yet it does so with a far higher quality and intensity, as this art also glorifies God. The glorification of God is in fact a central characteristic of pure art, says Schlatter: "Pure art occurs when the eye is open for the glory of Jesus and his cross."[51] The main feature of pure art, therefore, is the life-changing ethical impact it has on human beings.[52] That is why I call Schlatter's concept an "ethical-motivational" approach.

Schlatter's insistence on an ethical component of the arts lives on in the

---

43. Schlatter, *Ethik*, 370-71, 356, 372.
44. Schlatter, *Ethik*, 370.
45. Schlatter, *Ethik*, 370-71.
46. Schlatter, *Dogma*, 128. Kuyper likewise advised against the religious-like pursuit of art for art's sake. Heslam argues that this is one of the main reasons why Kuyper included "art" in his *Lectures on Calvinism*. Peter S. Heslam, *Creating a Christian Worldview: Abraham Kuyper's Lectures on Calvinism* (Grand Rapids: Eerdmans, 1998), 200.
47. "As the poet, through the artistic form, glorifies the condemnable [*das Verwerfliche*], he brings home to us that his perspective does not breed enmity, nor does it establish the will, through which we separate ourselves from evil, but rather brings about the experience, through which we enjoy the aesthetic . . . composition of the picture." Schlatter, *Ethik*, 370.
48. Schlatter, *Ethik*, 356.
49. Schlatter, *Ethik*, 356.
50. Schlatter, *Ethik*, 372.
51. Schlatter, *Ethik*, 372.
52. Schlatter, *Sprechstunde*, 96.

approaches of Nicholas Wolterstorff, John W. de Gruchy, and Calvin G. Seerveld. Together they emphasize that art is not merely for aesthetic pleasure and to the glory of God, but also significantly contributes to the process of cultural and societal transformation. In his *"functional* approach to art,"[53] Wolterstorff for example argues that art per se moves us, equips us for action. This is not a role it has to aspire to, but something that is distinctively intrinsic to art. "Works of art equip us for action," says Wolterstorff, "[a]nd the range of actions for which they equip us is very nearly as broad as the range of human action itself. The purposes of art are the purposes of life."[54] "Artists," writes John W. de Gruchy, "are not passive onlookers, but potentially agents of social transformation by being true to their vocation as artists."[55]

The prime examples of pure art are, according to Schlatter, the Gospels.[56] They are pure art, not only by reason of their inherent aesthetic beauty, but also by reason of their ability to impel individual men and women to ethical action, which ultimately glorifies God. Pure art is therefore bound up with a religious, ethical imperative, as only pure art endows us with a motive, an incentive for concrete action. That is why, adds Schlatter, the arts should not only present a direct copy of nature, but should go a step further: "they should not keep us in our present state of affairs, but move us towards new goals."[57]

III. Abraham Kuyper's Calvinistic Perspective on the Arts

With Schlatter, Kuyper was no friend of dualisms and pursued a coherent, all-embracing worldview instead.[58] According to Kuyper, the most useful instrument in the formation of a holistic, harmonious understanding of real-

---

53. Nicholas Wolterstorff, *Art in Action: Toward a Christian Aesthetic* (Grand Rapids: Eerdmans, 1980), x; emphasis original.

54. Wolterstorff, *Art in Action,* 4.

55. John W. de Gruchy, *Christianity, Art and Transformation: Theological Aesthetics in the Struggle for Justice* (Cambridge: Cambridge University Press, 2001), 200.

56. Schlatter, *Ethik,* 358.

57. Schlatter, *Ethik,* 372.

58. Kuyper notes that "[o]ne supreme calling must impress the stamp of *one-ness* upon *all* human life, because one God upholds and preserves it, just as He created it all (*Lectures on Calvinism* [Grand Rapids: Eerdmans, 1931], 54; emphasis original). For a biographical account of Kuyper's life see Frank Vanden Berg, *Abraham Kuyper: A Biography* (Grand Rapids: Eerdmans, 1960), and James E. McGoldrick, *Abraham Kuyper: God's Renaissance Man* (Darlington: Evangelical Press, 2000).

ity is Calvinism. In his *Lectures on Calvinism,* Kuyper introduces Calvinism as a *Weltanschauung,* a "life-system." "Calvinism," notes Kuyper, "made its appearance, not merely to create a different Church-form, but an entirely different form for human life, to furnish human society with a different method of existence, and to populate the world of the human heart with different ideals and conceptions."[59] In his speech on "Calvinisme en de kunst," Kuyper highlights that "Calvinism is the dominant direction for life [*het leven beheerschende richting*]" that thirsts for harmony, for a homeostasis between nature and spirit, soul and body, present and future.[60] *Lectures on Calvinism* touches on the different spheres of human social life, religion, politics, science, and art.[61] While on the one hand Kuyper argues for the sovereignty of these spheres *(Soevereiniteit in eigen kring)* — an important concept on Kuyper's agenda — he insists at the same time that they are united and related to each other, as they all have their origin in God and are under God's sovereignty.[62] "Unity," Kuyper underlines, "is only found at that point where it springs from the fountain of the Infinite."[63]

This principle of unity as proceeding from the Divine can now be applied to religion and the arts.[64] While religion and art are distinct, separate, and sovereign spheres, they are united in that they both have their origin in the sovereign God. While Kuyper makes clear that there is no such thing as secular art, for art has always been strongly influenced and intertwined with

---

59. Kuyper, *Lectures on Calvinism,* 17.

60. Kuyper, *Het Calvinisme en de kunst* (speech delivered at the Free University of Amsterdam, 20/10/1888, Amsterdam: J. A. Wormser, 1888), 39-40.

61. Kuyper suggests three major sovereign spheres, namely the state, the society, and the church, each of which, in turn, contains other sovereign spheres. Art belongs to the second, the social sphere. See Kuyper, *Lectures on Calvinism,* 79, 90, and his essay "Sphere Sovereignty (1880)," in *Abraham Kuyper: A Centennial Reader,* ed. James D. Bratt (Grand Rapids: Eerdmans, 1998), 461-90.

62. "Calvin therefore does not estrange art, science, and religion, from one another; on the contrary, what he desires is that all human life shall be permeated by these three vital powers together. There must be a *Science* which will not rest until it has thought out the entire cosmos; a *Religion* which cannot sit still until she has permeated every sphere of human life; and so also there must be an *Art* which, despising no single department of life adopts, into her splendid world, the whole of human life, religion included" (Kuyper, *Lectures on Calvinism,* 163; emphasis original).

63. Kuyper, *Lectures on Calvinism,* 150.

64. Kuyper examines the relationship between theology and art in his *Lectures on Calvinism* (142-70) and in his speech, "Het Calvinisme en de kunst." For an interpretation of Kuyper's views on art, see Heslam, *Creating a Christian Worldview,* 196-23, and Jeremy S. Begbie, *Voicing Creation's Praise: Toward a Theology of the Arts* (Edinburgh: T&T Clark, 1991), 84-105.

religion, he emphasizes that the two spheres are distinct. "Religion and Art have each a life-sphere of their own," notes Kuyper; they "demand an independent existence."[65] Art, says Kuyper, is an "independent branch that grows from the trunk of our life itself, even though it is far more nearly allied to Religion than to our thinking or to our ethical being."[66] "Every maestro is a king in the Palace of Art," as Kuyper puts it, "not by the law of inheritance or by appointment, but only by the grace of God. And these maestros also impose authority, and are subject to no one, but rule over all and in the end receive from all the homage due to their artistic superiority."[67] With the help of Calvinism, Kuyper can see the whole world as proceeding from God, the eternal source, subjected under God's sovereignty. God alone is sovereign over all spheres of life, including culture and the arts. As far as the relationship between religion and art is concerned, Kuyper is, more than Schlatter, keen on emphasizing the separateness of the two spheres.

Through his Calvinistic spectacles, Kuyper can disregard the dualism between "Christian art" and "secular art." All art, whether being produced and enjoyed inside or outside the church, flows from God through common grace.[68] "*Kunstvermogen*," the ability to create art, argues Kuyper, "is in man no separate function of the soul but an unbroken (continuous) utterance of the image of God."[69] "That artistic ability, that art-capacity, as such, can have room in human nature, we owe to our creation after the image of God."[70] Quoting Calvin, Kuyper affirms: "All the arts come from God and are to be respected as Divine inventions."[71] From the fact that we as human beings are created in God's image follows both our human ability to produce art (*kunsttalent*) and our ability to enjoy art.[72] God is sovereign, gracious, generous, and impartial in the distribution of artistic gifts, says Kuyper.[73] As

65. Kuyper, *Lectures on Calvinism*, 148.
66. Kuyper, *Lectures on Calvinism*, 150.
67. Kuyper, *Lectures on Calvinism*, 95.
68. For the important concept of common grace in Kuyper's thought see his "Common Grace (1902-4)," in *Abraham Kuyper: A Centennial Reader*, 165-201. This Calvinistic differentiation between common [*algemeene*] and particular [*bijzondere*] grace was, according to Kuyper, fundamental to the liberation of the arts from its ecclesial tutelage in the Netherlands (see *Lectures on Calvinism*, 157-58, and "Het Calvinisme en de kunst," 21, 39).
69. Kuyper, *Lectures on Calvinism*, 142 (see also "Het Calvinisme en de kunst," 15).
70. Kuyper, *Lectures on Calvinism*, 156.
71. Kuyper, *Lectures on Calvinism*, 153.
72. Kuyper, "Het Calvinisme en de kunst," 14.
73. "If God is and remains sovereign, then He also imparts these artistic gifts to whom He will" (Kuyper, *Lectures on Calvinism*, 155).

both believers and unbelievers are recipients of artistic talent, this gift is therefore to be attributed to common grace, and not particular grace.[74] "Calvinism," argues Kuyper, "has taught us that all liberal arts are gifts which God imparts promiscuously to believers and to unbelievers, yea, that, as history shows, these gifts have flourished even in a larger measure outside the holy circle."[75] Kuyper adds that the "highest art-instincts are natural gifts, and hence belong to those excellent graces which, in spite of sin, by virtue of common grace, have continued to shine in human nature, and that God remains Sovereign to impart it, in His good pleasure, alike to Heathen and to Christian nations."[76] The real artist behind every human artistic product is therefore God himself.[77]

Like Schlatter, Kuyper is convinced that art is "to glorify the name of Almighty God."[78] "In all Liberal Arts," Kuyper asserts, "in the most as well as in the least important, the praise and glory of God are to be enhanced."[79] Art exists — and has to be produced, pursued, and enjoyed — to the glory of God. In this sense, art is very special, set apart, as it were, from the other spheres.[80] Kuyper contends,

> To this end He has ordained for this humanity all sorts of life-utterances, and among these, art occupies a quite independent place. Art reveals ordinances of creation which neither science, nor politics, nor religious life, nor even revelation can bring to light.[81]

Art has a unique place for Kuyper, as it points to a higher reality,[82] to the kingdom of glory *(rijk der Heerlijkheid)*.[83] "Art reveals to us a higher reality

---

74. Kuyper, *Lectures on Calvinism*, 160. See also "Het Calvinisme en de kunst," 15.
75. Kuyper, *Lectures on Calvinism*, 160.
76. Kuyper, *Lectures on Calvinism*, 161.
77. Kuyper, "Het Calvinisme en de kunst," 15-16.
78. Kuyper, *Lectures on Calvinism*, 162. Kuyper writes, "Wherever man may stand, whatever he may do, to whatever he may apply his hand, in agriculture, in commerce, and in industry, or his mind, in the world of art, and science, he is, in whatsoever it may be, constantly standing before the face of God, he is employed in the service of his God, he has strictly to obey his God, and above all, he has to aim at the glory of his God" (53).
79. Kuyper, *Lectures on Calvinism*, 153.
80. Heslam offers three historical reasons why Kuyper allowed for a strong independence of the arts (in contrast to other spheres like science or politics). See Heslam, *Creating a Christian Worldview*, 216-17.
81. Kuyper, *Lectures on Calvinism*, 162-63.
82. Kuyper, *Lectures on Calvinism*, 153.
83. Kuyper, "Het Calvinisme en de kunst," 16.

than is offered by this sinful world," he says.[84] Art must therefore not only copy nature, but also "produce a beautiful world that transcends the beautiful of nature."[85] This is, for Kuyper, "the heart of the matter."[86] Consistent with his Calvinistic cosmic scope, Kuyper insists that art points to the renewal of all things in the eschaton: "Art has the mystical task of reminding us in its productions of the beautiful that was lost and of anticipating its perfect coming luster."[87] In a similar fashion, Jeremy Begbie maintains, "Art which truly bears the imprint of the Spirit will thus not so much hark back to an imagined paradise, as anticipate within space and time, provisionally but substantially, the final transfiguration of the cosmos."[88]

Kuyper, as we can see, went a long way toward redeeming Calvinism's negative reputation for banishing the arts from its field of vision.[89] With his holistic, Calvinistic approach, Kuyper provides a theological framework for aesthetics: all kinds of art have their source in God. As a unique and special sphere, art reflects back on its source, thereby glorifying God, reaching above itself to a higher reality.

IV. Implications, Further Questions, and Solutions?

In this brief survey of Schlatter's and Kuyper's thoughts on the relationship between theology and the arts, we can see that while their approaches are closely related, each has its own distinctive features. Schlatter, with his theology directed to the whole *(Richtung auf das Ganze),* and Kuyper, with his Calvinistic agenda as a "life-system," provide an integrative framework for a holistic understanding of reality. To a certain extent, their common trajectory can be traced back to the influence of Franz von Baader's philosophical-theological writings. Rejecting any dualisms, they both, in theory and in practice, tie together the different spheres of the academy, church, culture, and the arts, and point to their common root and destiny, standing under the common grace and the sovereignty of God. In the light of an increasing fragmentation of theology, church life, and society, these two great poly-

---

84. Kuyper, *Lectures on Calvinism,* 154.
85. Kuyper, *Lectures on Calvinism,* 154.
86. Kuyper, *Lectures on Calvinism,* 154. See also "Het Calvinisme en de kunst," 16.
87. Kuyper, *Lectures on Calvinism,* 155.
88. Begbie, *Voicing Creation's Praise,* 228.
89. For a recent examination of Calvinism's relation to art see Susan Hardman Moore's essay "Calvinism and the Arts," *Theology in Scotland* 16:2 (2009): 75-92.

maths demonstrate the possible benefits of paying heed to their example of cultural engagement and civil courage — always with an all-embracing perspective.

Reformed theology had for too long subscribed to a Cartesian cognitive bias that Schlatter and Kuyper were happy to correct. With their broad vistas, these two scholars brought the arts out of neglect and back into the focus of the attention of Reformed theology, inspiring and stimulating subsequent generations of artists and art critics. Kuyper's return to the arts certainly paved the way for the later contributions of Hans R. Rookmaaker,[90] Francis Schaeffer,[91] and Nicholas Wolterstorff.[92] However, Schlatter and Kuyper both talk as theologians, not as artists, more as art theoreticians than practitioners, but as art lovers nevertheless.[93] The two theologians suggest stimulating frameworks for a general aesthetics that has its focal point in the glory *(Herrlichkeit, Heerlijkheid)* of God. In particular, they suggest aesthetical (Schlatter and Kuyper), moral (Schlatter), and transcendental (Schlatter and Kuyper) criteria for aesthetics.

Yet, ultimately, one discovers that both Schlatter and Kuyper remain on the (comparatively safe) theoretical level in their approaches. On the practical level of application, it seems that major questions remain unanswered. But this is by no means simply a disadvantage, as it creates space for our concluding reflections. In what follows, I wish to explore further two particular reflections: first, the question of ethical requirements for art on a general level, and second, the issues that arise on an individual level.

First, then, I turn to the ethical requirements for art, as suggested by Schlatter. One wonders whether Schlatter goes too far with his ethical requirements for pure art. Does art indeed have to carry an ethical-motivational imperative? Is the mere enjoyment of the aesthetic nature of "true art" itself not sufficient? If one followed Schlatter in this direction, would one not run the risk of ending up with an inflation of moral-ethical criteria? Hans R. Rookmaaker's suggestion of six norms for the arts (truth, honor, righteous-

---

90. Rookmaaker, *Modern Art and the Death of a Culture* (London: Inter Varsity Press, 1970).

91. Schaeffer, *Art and the Bible: Two Essays* (Downers Grove: InterVarsity Press, 1973).

92. Wolterstorff, *Art in Action*.

93. Heslam points out that Kuyper's lecture "is more about religion than art. At every stage it is clear that religious and theological concerns, rather than artistic ones, dominate the argument" (Heslam, *Creating a Christian Worldview*, 220). Like Schlatter, Kuyper was also a keen admirer of art and passed down his knowledge to his students in several lectures (Heslam, *Creating a Christian Worldview*, 197).

ness, loveliness, excellence, and praise) illustrates this danger of inflation.[94] One might also ask how to break down these moral-ethical requirements in detail. Would this imply that one is to restrict one's enjoyment of, for example, Rembrandt's "Return of the Prodigal Son," so that one gains a motivational impulse to turn back to God, or, like the father, one would grant forgiveness to one's debtors?[95] With regards to music, shall one exclusively turn to music with a moral-spiritual dimension, such as the Psalms, hymns, or Bach chorales? But what of the ethical significance of abstract art? Would abstract painter Piet Mondrian (1872-1944) be able to exert a similar motivational impetus? What about the nihilism of Kurt Schwitter's Dadaistic poems or John Cage's chance music? Should these artworks be rejected, counted as less artistic because one sees, at first glance, no moral-ethical value in them?

Unlike Schlatter, it appears that Kuyper is rather hesitant to formulate special criteria for the evaluation of the arts.[96] Attributing the arts to common grace, would Kuyper then say that all art "automatically" glorifies God? Does Mozart's "Magic Flute" glorify God in the same way as a cantata by Bach? What about an artist who intentionally decides to produce art that is not to the glory of God? Would one not then have to distinguish between artistic ability in the process of the creation of the work, which still glorifies God, and the finished artistic product, which can be sinful and, maybe, not to the glory of God? It might be helpful to distinguish, therefore, between the spiritual state and motif of the artist and the ethical-moral quality of her output.

On a similar note, what kind of criteria could one apply in order to decide which art points to a "higher reality" — a requirement of transcendence that both Schlatter and Kuyper want to establish? Is the realist Hopper in this sense inferior to the surreal Dalí? In which ways can or does art point to a "higher reality"? One must scrutinize whether this criterion is useful in the first place, or whether it is a dated relict of Romanticism. Philip Benedict notes that one detects in Kuyper's works "a tendency to interpret works of art in Hegelian or ro-

---

94. Rookmaaker, *Modern Art and the Death of a Culture*, 234-43.

95. Kuyper, *Lectures on Calvinism*, 165.

96. Kuyper is certainly more straightforward when he argues for a distinct Christian influence on the spheres of science, politics, etc. Heslam observes this neglect of concrete application in Kuyper and suggests how Kuyper's criteria could have looked like: the arts have to be "free from political and ecclesiastical control, because God has placed the stamp of his glory on all created things . . . in obedience to classic norms, because of common grace; attentive to the significance of the commonplace and the ordinary, because of the doctrine of election" (*Creating a Christian Worldview*, 222).

mantic idealist ways as manifestations of a larger guiding spirit."[97] While it is certainly true that both Kuyper and Schlatter are influenced by romantic ideas, especially with their common criterion of transcendence, they were convinced that their God was not the abstract dynamic spirit of romantic Goethe or Hegel's Idealist Geist coming to self-consciousness, but theirs was the concrete God who was in Jesus Christ. Both Kuyper and Schlatter would therefore not go as far as Anthony Monti does in his natural theology of art. While they would agree with Monti that all kinds of art are theological by their very nature (in that they proceed from God through common grace), both Schlatter and Kuyper would rather be hesitant to see in them an almost pantheistic "real presence" of God, as Monti does.[98]

The answer, I think, cannot be the promotion of a separate Christian art movement that focuses on pure, true art, as Rookmaaker, for example, has advocated.[99] "Art within the limits of religion alone" would be contrary to the credo of the two holistic theologians. On the contrary, both Schlatter and Kuyper emphasize that Christian artists and art lovers are to produce and contemplate art within the context of a secular culture. Johann Sebastian Bach was comfortable being the court organist and concertmaster at the ducal court in Weimar as well as being the Cantor and Musikdirektor of Leipzig's principal churches. The holistic perspective Schlatter and Kuyper adopt is that the arts, as a whole, work towards a renewal of human culture and society. One is thus left with the question of which artist or art achieves this renewal in an ideal way.

This is, moving to the second and final question, I think, where one is challenged on a personal level. "Art confronts us," says Wolterstorff, "with the need for critical discernment"[100] — and, I would add, on the personal, individual level. As individuals with a redeemed conscience, endowed with

---

97. Benedict, "Calvinism as a Culture? Preliminary Remarks on Calvinism and the Visual Arts," in *Seeing beyond the Word: Visual Arts and the Calvinist Tradition*, edited by Paul Corby Finney, 19-45 (Grand Rapids: Eerdmans, 1999), 23.

98. All "works of art," Monti points out, "are complex metaphors that convey the 'real presence' of God, even when not labeled as such." Monti, *A Natural Theology of the Arts: Imprint of the Spirit* (Hants: Ashgate, 2003), i.

99. See Rookmaaker, *Modern Art and the Death of a Culture*, 67, 71, 75, 228-52. Rookmaaker's call for a distinct Christian art movement would probably not have met Kuyper's and Schlatter's approval. For a contemporary critique of Rookmaaker's approach see Daniel A. Siedell, *God in the Gallery: A Christian Embrace of Modern Art* (Grand Rapids: Baker Academic, 2008), 154-66.

100. Nicholas Wolterstorff, "Afterword," in *Sounding the Depths: Theology through the Arts*, ed. Jeremy S. Begbie (London: SCM Press, 2002), 229.

Christian liberty and freedom, under the guidance of the Scriptures and the Holy Spirit, we are called prayerfully to decide, and responsibly to determine, case by case, which art glorifies God and motivates individuals to perform the good deed.[101] For Karl Barth it was Mozart;[102] for C. S. Lewis it was Wagner;[103] for me it is Bach; for others it might be Stravinsky, or even John Coltrane. There is sometimes the strange desire to shift one's responsibility regarding matters of conscience to higher institutions, i.e., the church. But the introduction of ecclesial taboos with a view to the arts is certainly not the answer, as I am sure Schlatter and Kuyper would agree. One certainly does not want to repeat the crimes of the past in declaring certain pieces of art, or whole art movements, as "degenerate" (*entartete Kunst*). Any such dualisms are anything but helpful. Daniel A. Siedell in his recent book *God in the Gallery* argues in a balanced manner:

> The whole earth is indeed full of God's glory . . . , and modern and contemporary artistic practice can reveal this presence even with work that is not explicitly religious or spiritual or, in fact, even work that might seem at first glance to contradict our assumptions about God's presence in the world. But we are called to penetrate the surface of things, revealing how all things hold together in Christ, even if this is not immediately apparent.[104]

Conclusion

Theologians are called, as Jeremy Begbie insists, to approach the arts with "responsible respect."[105] It is a sphere of its own, but one intricately con-

---

101. The Westminster Confession's rendering goes like this: "God alone is Lord of the conscience, and hath left it free from all the doctrines and commandments of men [which are in anything contrary to his word, or beside it if matters of faith and worship]" (*Westminster Confession* 20.2; cf. Calvin, *Institutes*, III.19). Kuyper underlines the individual's liberty of conscience (*Lectures on Calvinism*, 107-8).

102. Mozart enthusiast Barth asserts that Mozart sure "has a place in theology, especially in the doctrine of creation and also in eschatology. . . ." Mozart, writes Barth, "did not produce merely his own music but that of creation, its twofold and yet harmonious praise of God." What particularly fascinated Barth was that Mozart's music somewhat dialectically "includes a Yes and a No." Karl Barth, *Church Dogmatics*, III/3, 298-99.

103. C. S. Lewis reports that he "had tasted heaven" when first encountering Richard Wagner's *Ring der Nibelungen* (see Anthony Monti, *Natural Theology of the Arts*, 160).

104. Siedell, *God in the Gallery*, 164-65.

105. Jeremy S. Begbie, "Introduction," in *Sounding the Depths: Theology through the Arts*, 10.

nected with the realm of theology. Holistic theologians Adolf Schlatter and Abraham Kuyper carefully suggest guidelines for the appreciation and evaluation of the arts. However, we are challenged over and over to apply their concerns to individual works of art. Living in the already/not-yet tension, theologians, composers, and painters will remain imperfect in this day and age, as will the readers, listeners, and beholders of their works. As they all are God's creatures, however, Schlatter and Kuyper point out, they still reflect the glory of their Maker and in all their frailty they are enabled to produce and enjoy art to the glory of God and toward a renewal of human culture and society.

Theology and Architecture:
Calvinist Principles for the Faithful Construction of Urban Space

Matthew Kaemingk

> *Profound, creative, grace filled spiritualities produce grace filled environments; banal, impoverished, alienated spiritualities produce alienating environments.*
>
> Timothy Gorringe

American architects serve a guild of homebuilder with a particularly focused aesthetic telos: more. More square-footage, more speed, more efficiency, more uniformity, and more profit. Urban planners, finding themselves in a similar situation, are asked by the cities they serve to follow the guiding principle of speed. Squeezing out parks, sidewalks, promenades, and public markets, planners often find that their days are all too often dedicated to adding more high-speed arterials and freeways, as well as parking lots for all the cars traversing them. Christians active in these fields sometimes despair that their faith offers little in the way of historical or theological resources for resisting these more desiccated aesthetic forces in their homes and cities. This essay intends, in some small way, to begin the process of remedy.

Augustine, famously commenting on the politics of the earthly city, argues that each city will organize its political affairs around its deepest love. One can easily imagine unique political structures designed to serve the demands of war, market growth, radical equality, or individual pleasure. This essay will be Augustinian in spirit, in that it will seek to explore how a city's physical structure and design reflects its deepest loves and, more specifically, how a deep and primary love for God might develop a robust architectural imagination that can go beyond the contemporary urban aesthetic of growth and speed.

While it is true that Calvinists lack a vigorous tradition of action and reflection in a number of artistic mediums, the field of urban architecture and planning is not one of them. This essay will seek to demonstrate that, while there is no surviving record of architectural commentary from John Calvin himself, many of his theological descendants found in his commentaries, sermons, books, and pastoral practices an abundance of aesthetic and structural resources uniquely equipped for a theological reflection on the constructed spaces of home, market, and city. This essay will outline four distinct and insightful historical moments of Calvinist architectural reflection in sixteenth- and seventeenth-century France, nineteenth-century Holland, and twentieth-century South Africa and America. Throughout my analysis, I hope to briefly explore how each of these four architectural moments and themes are developed under the influence of, and often with direct reference to, the theology, anthropology, ethics, and creational aesthetics of John Calvin himself.

A few clarifying remarks are in order. First, it is of course true that the majority of Calvinist architects have never imagined that their Genevan roots could inform their craft at all. This essay will not argue otherwise. That said, it will seek to demonstrate that Calvinists who have sought to make a deep connection between their technique and their theology were rewarded with a fertile conceptual stockpile in the life and work of John Calvin.

Second, nowhere in this essay will I consider the field of Reformed church architecture, for two reasons. First, this subject has already been well examined in a number of fine historical, theological, and liturgical studies of Calvinist worship spaces. Second, as this paper will demonstrate, when Calvinists thoughtfully apply their theological imagination to the more negotiated public spaces of streets, marketplaces, housing developments, and government buildings, a number of fascinating theological, ethical, and aesthetic insights can be gleaned for the contemporary Christian architect.

Third, I will nowhere argue that "Calvinism" constitutes a distinct, recognizable, or universally coherent architectural style comparable to, say, Gothic or Bauhaus. Rather, I will demonstrate that its distinct theological vision contains a number of aesthetic and ethical principles that have deeply informed structures across a wide variety of cultural contexts.

I. Constructive Iconoclasm

Catharine Randall's historical analysis of Huguenot architects in sixteenth-century France constitutes some of the earliest recorded architectural reflections in the history of Calvinism. According to Randall's account, this early guild of Calvinist architects sought to creatively render Calvin's theological emphasis on the radical transcendence of God and the utter finitude and fallenness of humanity into subversive architectural form.

Randall begins her historical account by examining the rapid spread of Calvin's teachings through the urban and middle classes of sixteenth-century France. According to Randall, his thought found a particularly friendly audience with the French merchant, artisan, and architectural communities. So pervasive was the Calvinist presence in architecture in sixteenth-century France "that it is difficult today to find architectural manuals penned by Catholic contemporaries or to view buildings erected by major Catholic architects."[1] While it is true that the vast majority of upper-class French patrons remained Catholic, they relied almost completely on Calvinists to design their gardens, mansions, markets, public spaces, palaces, and even cathedrals.

There are numerous historical and sociological reasons for Calvinism's flourishing among the French architectural guilds, but one intriguing factor Randall explores in detail is the "architectonic" nature of Calvin's theological project itself. She points to the Calvin's *Institutes of the Christian Religion* as a veritable blueprint of the Christian faith shot through with the heavily architectural language and rhetoric of structure, balance, boundaries, foundations, supports, simplicity, and beauty. Calvin's opposition to words such as license, caprice, error, and confusion would have found a welcome audience with an architectural community shaped by the values of stability, precision, and order.

Dreaming of structures that reflected Calvin's theo-aesthetic principles of simplicity, balance, and humility, Huguenot architects found themselves serving a French Catholic clientele who, in their opinion, lacked all three. French Catholic structures from this period reflect a high degree of material opulence, aesthetic excess, and political, cultural, and economic dominance. Such structures often contained a primary structural focal point overwhelming the space, creating a sense of imminent completion and human power — surely anathema to Huguenot sensibilities. And yet, while French

---

1. Catharine Randall, *Building Codes: The Aesthetics of Calvinism in Early Modern Europe* (Philadelphia: University of Pennsylvania, 1999), 2.

Catholic patrons held the purse strings, Calvinist architects were careful to have the last structural word. In her historical and architectural analysis Randall systematically demonstrates how Calvinist architects would "subvert from within: to inscribe, via representational reconfiguration and code, their distrust of the hierarchy on the very buildings commissioned to attest to Catholic authority."[2]

Throughout her work Randall demonstrates how Calvinists subversively mocked and undermined the architectural pretensions of the elite they served through the creative use of various structures and symbols. She describes how Calvinists would sneak multiple focal points into their buildings to communicate their own theological visions of human finitude, fallenness, and incompletion. Calvinists would literally cut biblical passages into the sides of their buildings whose texts intimately questioned the ostentatious walls on which they were inscribed. According to Randall, they would purposely lessen the urban profiles of imperial statues and bridges in Paris for two very Calvinist reasons. First, they hoped to humble royal pretensions of limitless power, imminent completion, and monarchical divinity. Second, convinced that all public life was sacred and that the city was filled with the priesthood of all believers, they sought to liberate urban sightlines from imposing imperial structures so that its citizens might enjoy the glory-filled banality of a city filled with the daughters and sons of God.

One might paradoxically label this early Calvinist witness as a moment of "constructive iconoclasm." Rather than tear the buildings down in a destructive and revolutionary fervor, these Calvinists creatively subverted and re-formed architectural idolatries from within, witnessing to an alternative aesthetic telos. A contemporary Christian architect striving to remain faithful to her aesthetic and ethical principles amid a sea of pressure to compromise might find an important encouragement and witness in the life and work of these early Huguenot designers. Continued analysis into the work of these early Calvinist architects could provide an important historical, theological, and architectural resource.

II. Local Craftsmanship

The second architectural theme receives distinct attention in the work of the Calvinist pastor, journalist, and politician Abraham Kuyper. In the Dutch-

---

2. Randall, *Building Codes*, 2.

man's first major public address in 1869 Kuyper railed against what he believed to be modernity's "curse of uniformity." Having rejected the transcendence and unique unity of God alone, modernity, according to Kuyper, was actively seeking to construct an imminent unity and uniformity for itself on earth. This imminent search for uniformity threatened to destroy the local particularity, identity, diversity, and beauty of Dutch life in the name of a universal reason, science, and bureaucratic control. These modern forces of uniformity could already be seen in politics, academics, religion, fashion, and even architecture.

In discussing these "modern forces of uniformity" Kuyper makes a specific and extended reference to housing developments surrounding the old city of Amsterdam. He sets the dull uniformity of the new suburbs over against the wild pluriformity of the old center city. The results of Kuyper's architectural juxtaposition are particularly prophetic for the century and a half of suburban developments that would follow. "What is it," Kuyper asks, "in the architectural styles of our old Dutch cities that so charms the visiting stranger?"

> What else but the infinite variety in width and narrowness, the looseness of twists and curves, the pointed and obtuse angles of even our most elegant canals . . . every dwelling is the fulfillment of a personal dream, the precious product of quiet thrift, based on a personal plan and built slowly from the ground up. Those tufted, tiered, triangular, and shuttered gables were not symmetrically measured with a level but reflected, every one of them, the thinking of a human being, the whimsicality of a somewhat overconfident heart. This motley collection of houses bespeaks a city full of architects. . . .[3]

Kuyper contrasts what he sees as the personal care, craftsmanship, and wild diversity of the old city to the fiercely uniform housing developments encircling Amsterdam. In these "modern" suburbs,

> There is not a gable to be seen which in any way violates the absolute symmetry to which door and window have been fitted. Precisely those straight streets and rectangular corners, those utterly level gables and standardized houses make the modern outgrowths of our cities fatally exhausting and boring. You have to number the streets and count them out so as not to

---

3. James D. Bratt, ed., *Abraham Kuyper: A Centennial Reader* (Grand Rapids: Eerdmans, 1998), 26.

get lost in so featureless a collection of houses. Better: not houses but blocks of tenements that make you think of institutions of mercy or army barracks rather than of the homes of free citizens.... All the poetry of our cities vanishes ... before long all diversity has been removed from Holland's cities.[4]

Romantic melodrama aside, Kuyper is evincing a distinctly Calvinist anthropology that pervades his entire corpus. Convinced that all people have been created in the image of God with unique callings, Kuyper is convinced that individuals and families should have the freedom to express themselves architecturally by designing their own living spaces. He is objecting to what he interprets as a modern architectural imposition that effectively denies the particularity, identity, and creativity of the family as a sovereign cultural sphere. This God-given architectural freedom is therefore seen as a vital component of the creative integrity and sovereignty of the family sphere. With these anthropological principles in mind, Kuyper casts modern architecture, with its emphasis on uniformity, efficiency, predictability, and profit, as a threat to the innate creativity and particularity of the Dutch people. In Kuyper's architectural jeremiad one hears distinct echoes of Calvin's own conviction that a city's design should faithfully reflect "the spirit and manners of the inhabitants"[5] and not be unilaterally imposed from without. Kuyper's Calvinist vision of a more localist form of architecture that could structurally celebrate the particularity and diversity of unique families, communities, and cultures as distinct aesthetic expressions of the glory of God presents an important prophetic witness to a contemporary architectural guild that all too often is ruled by the values of uniformity, efficiency, and profit.

III. Architectural Justice

The third architectural theme is embodied in the aesthetic reflections of the African Calvinist John de Gruchy. In his work *Christianity, Art, and Transformation: Theological Aesthetics in the Struggle for Justice*, de Gruchy puts his Reformed aesthetic tradition in conversation with Africa's colonial and postcolonial architecture. According to de Gruchy, the buildings, streets, and cities of Africa not only reflected, but actively reinforced, the colo-

---

4. Bratt, ed., *Abraham Kuyper: A Centennial Reader*, 26.
5. John W. de Gruchy, *Christianity, Art, and Transformation* (Cambridge: Cambridge University Press, 2001), 45.

nizer's program of racial control, oppression, and dehumanization. From the very beginning,

> Colonial town planning in British Africa (Salisbury, Lusaka, Nairobi, and Kampala) assumed that the cities were the domain of white settlers and administrators. While an Indian market might be permissible on the periphery, Africans had no right to be in the city, and were forced to live in reservations or have their movements strictly controlled. . . . The black townships lie far beyond the peripheries of the city, symbolizing the outsider status of the indigenous inhabitants and migratory labourers.[6]

For the ruling elite the structures of the town were tools — even weapons. De Gruchy uses Langa, a temporary housing settlement in South Africa, as a prime example of this program of structural marginalization. Lange, he writes, "was planned and built . . . with social control in mind . . . designed to make [migrant workers] recognize their status as outsiders welcome only for their labour."[7] Throughout his theological examination of colonial architecture and urban planning de Gruchy unleashes a prophetic critique against architectural forms of oppression and marginalization, declaring that to "deprive people willfully of beauty and intentionally create such ugliness is from a Christian perspective nothing less than a sin in its most cynical form."[8]

De Gruchy did not need to look far for the theological language to condemn this architectural injustice; his own Reformed tradition provided him with plenty. As has been well documented, the just treatment of Geneva's marginalized refugees was central to the public theology of John Calvin. Calvin believed that Geneva's poor were "God's messengers to check on the faith and charity of their neighbors."[9] He had harsh words for those who would seek to ignore or deny their common bond with the poor in their community. "If they were able," Calvin writes of Geneva's rich oppressors, "they would have a sun all to themselves in order to say that the others have nothing in common with them . . . they would change the whole order of God and nature so they could swallow everything."[10] Ac-

---

6. de Gruchy, *Christianity, Art, and Transformation*, 185-86.
7. de Gruchy, *Christianity, Art, and Transformation*, 172-73.
8. de Gruchy, *Christianity, Art, and Transformation*, 88.
9. Fred W. Graham, *The Constructive Revolutionary: John Calvin and His Socio-Economic Impact* (Richmond, VA: John Knox Press, 1971), 69.
10. Graham, *The Constructive Revolutionary*, 68.

cording to Calvin, every citizen of Geneva had a responsibility to consider whether the specific work of his or her hands was "good and profitable to the community."[11]

Echoing Calvin's calls for social responsibility in each and every vocation, de Gruchy argues that, "Irrespective of how they may understand their role, architects share the same political responsibility as any other citizen. What they do is not ideologically neutral."[12] Again and again, de Gruchy asserts that architects are an essential element within African society. Pointing to Calvin's distinct and wide-ranging interest in urban order, justice, and harmony, de Gruchy argues that it would be no surprise if Calvin's reported interest in Genevan town planning and sewage systems may indeed have come "out of his concern for the well being of social life."[13]

De Gruchy's extensive theo-architectural reflections in postcolonial South Africa serve as a important witness to contemporary Calvinist architects of the social responsibility their particular vocation bears for their cities and communities. A Calvinist architect is not an island but lives and works in solidarity with the community she serves. As Calvin wrote, all Christians must repeatedly ask themselves if their vocation is "good and profitable to the community."

IV. Urban Delight

In *Until Justice and Peace Embrace,* Calvinist philosopher Nicholas Wolterstorff attempts to re-imagine Reformed ethics in light of the biblical theme of shalom (a rich eschatological coexistence of justice, beauty, relationship, and delight). Wolterstorff argues that the Hebrew prophets' eschatological vision of shalom has the potential to both complement and inform the Calvinist desire to serve and glorify God in all areas of social, political, cultural, and aesthetic life. Wolterstorff argues that Reformed social ethics should seek not only justice and equity in public life, but delight and beauty as well.

Wolterstorff dedicates an entire chapter of his shalom-centered ethics to an examination of the deep connection between ethics and aesthetics. Traditionally, philosophers interested in such questions focus their analysis on

---

11. Graham, *The Constructive Revolutionary,* 80.
12. de Gruchy, *Christianity, Art, and Transformation,* 178.
13. de Gruchy, *Christianity, Art, and Transformation,* 176.

Theology and Architecture

traditional "works of art," but Wolterstorff turns away from these more traditional mediums and chooses to concentrate on the ethics and aesthetic of urban architecture instead. Why?

> I have very intentionally avoided taking that [traditional art] path, because I am profoundly convinced that if we are concerned that our fellow human beings should find some sensory refreshment in their lives, then it is the city that we must first of all pay attention to, and not those isolated objects that we call works of art. I say this as one who loves the arts intensely; yet I have nothing but abhorrence for our modern practice of constructing cities that are deserts of aesthetic ugliness and then sprinkling about within them as small oases our concert halls, museums, etc., in order to salve an aching conscience.[14]

According to Wolterstorff, modernity's aesthetic teloi of efficiency, power, profit, control, and speed produce impoverished living spaces that actively frustrate a city's ethical obligation to cultivate shalom. Wolterstorff attacks modern forms of urban architecture and planning yet again in his work *Art in Action: Toward a Christian Aesthetic*.

> The tragedy of modern urban life is not only that so many in our cities are oppressed and powerless, but also that so many have nothing surrounding them in which any human being could possibly take delight. For this state of affairs we who are Christians are as guilty as any. We have adopted a pietistic-materialistic understanding of man, viewing human needs as the need for a saved soul plus the need for food, clothes, and shelter. True shalom is vastly richer than that.[15]

Wolterstorff's harsh words for the urban aesthetics of modernity are quite similar to his critique of modern Calvinist aesthetics. Wolterstorff argues that too many modern Calvinists have wrongly interpreted their tradition to be marked by cold command and obedience, and as a result their theological aesthetic is marked primarily by a bland frugality and a bare utilitarianism.

Such paltry aesthetics, according to Wolterstorff, not only fail to reflect the biblical call for shalom and delight; they also fail to reflect the aestheti-

---

14. Nicholas Wolterstorff, *Until Justice and Peace Embrace* (Grand Rapids: Eerdmans, 1983), 131.
15. Nicholas Wolterstorff, *Art in Action* (Grand Rapids: Eerdmans, 1980), 82.

cally rich vision of the beloved Genevan himself. Modern Calvinists, he argues, all too often fail to remember that their ethical obedience was always meant to spring from a disposition of gratitude and delight at the beauty of God's work in Christ and creation. To make his point, Wolterstorff directs his readers back to the gratuitous aesthetic language of the *Institutes*, where Calvin reflects on the gifts of creation and specifically God's desire — even command — for aesthetic delight. Calvin writes,

> Now then, if we consider for what end God created food, we shall find that he consulted not only for our necessity, but also for our enjoyment and delight. . . . Has the Lord adorned flowers with all the beauty which spontaneously presents itself to the eye, and the sweet odor which delights the sense of smell, and shall it be unlawful for us to enjoy that beauty and this odor? What? Has God not so distinguished colors as to make some more agreeable than others? . . . In short, has he not given many things a value without having any necessary use?[16]

Wolterstorff could easily have added numerous additional texts from the *Institutes* to make his case for the importance of beauty in Calvin's theology of creation. The passages below are striking in their depiction of the creator as both an architect and designer. God, Calvin writes, "has so wonderfully adorned heaven and earth with an unlimited abundance, variety, and beauty of all things as could possibly be, quite like a spacious and splendid house, provided and filled with the most exquisite and at the same time most abundant furnishings."[17] In a passage from Calvin's commentary on 1 Peter the architectural analogy reveals itself again: "God the maker of the world has not left the human race in a state of confusion, so that we live after the manner of beasts, but has given them, as it were, a building regularly formed, and divided into several compartments."[18]

According to Wolterstorff, this Calvinist appreciation of creational diversity and architectural delight "belongs to the shalom that God intends for each of us," so that "it becomes a matter of responsible action to help make available, to ourselves and others, the experience of aesthetic delight. It be-

---

16. Wolterstorff, *Until Justice and Peace Embrace*, 131-32.
17. John Calvin, *Institutes of the Christian Religion*, ed. John T. McNeill, trans. Ford Lewis Battles (Louisville: Westminster John Knox Press, 2001), 180.
18. Gordon Spykman, "Sphere Sovereignty in Calvin and the Calvinist Tradition," in *Exploring the Heritage of John Calvin*, ed. David E. Holwerda (Grand Rapids: Baker Book House, 1976), 198. Taken from Calvin's Commentary on 1 Peter 1:12-17.

comes a norm for action; not of course the only norm, but certainly one among others."[19]

Any careful reader of Calvin's theology can recognize Wolterstorff's prophetic critique of modern urban aesthetics as being shot through with the rich aesthetic sensitivities of the Reformer himself. In both Wolterstorff and Calvin one hears a stark repudiation of all urban forms that degrade the profound and mandated beauty of the creation and imago Dei. A final quotation from the *Institutes* drives home the point: "Away, then, with that inhuman philosophy which, while conceding only a necessary use of creatures, not only malignantly deprives us of the lawful fruit of God's beneficence but cannot be practiced unless it robs a man of all his senses and degrades him to a block."[20]

V. Conclusion

Architecture, like no other artistic medium, holds a pervasive power to shape the theological, ethical, economic, political, and aesthetic imagination of a society. Calvinism's deep concern for the health and flourishing of public life led Calvinists time and again to reflect on the theological significance of architecture under the reign of God. Their constructive iconoclasm, love for craftsmanship and diversity, and prophetic critique of architectural injustice, uniformity, and banality all serve to confirm de Gruchy's claim it was none other than "architecture that was destined to be the art form of Protestantism." For those "imbued with the spirit of the Reformation," according to de Gruchy, "true piety was not to be found in the monastery but in the marketplace and the home, amidst the ordinary things and events of life."[21]

This vibrant theological tradition of architectural reflection represents an important resource for contemporary Christian considerations of architectural theory and practice. Christian architects and urban planners hoping to serve faithfully in their cities are by no means the first to think about the pluriform issues involved in the connection between faith and the built environment. They would do well to consider the witnesses of those who have gone before them.

Contrary to a number of public theologies on the market today which

---

19. Wolterstorff, *Art in Action*, 168-69.
20. Calvin, *Institutes*, 721.
21. de Gruchy, *Christianity, Art, and Transformation*, 46.

see the vocation of the pastor or politician as the most vital to the moral and cultural health of society, the Calvinist public theology displayed above argues that all cultural vocations, including that of architecture, can contribute to the health and well-being of society in important ways. From its beginnings Calvinists have recognized the unique and vital role Christian architects and urban planners play in society. In a world of strip malls, freeways, housing tenements, and suburban sprawl, the Christian architect's calling to these four architectural themes of humility, craftsmanship, justice, and delight will not be an easy one. Yet if Timothy Gorringe is right in saying that a society's streets, marketplaces, and houses reflect its deepest loves and spiritual quality, perhaps working for the beauty of our cities is a calling we all share.

Calvinism, Necessity, and the Death of Tragedy

John De Soto

*Is there a man who does not fear
this, does not shrink to hear
how my place has been ordained,
granted and given by destiny
and god, absolute?*[1]

*You have seen a terrible death
and agonies, many and strange, and there is
nothing here which is not Zeus.*[2]

This is the terror of necessity.[3]

*O, fate is always hard and destiny hopeless,
Equally evil when she rages and when she forbears.*[4]

---

1. Aeschylus, *Eumenides*, in *Aeschylus I*, ed. David Grene and Richmond Lattimore, trans. Richmond Lattimore (Chicago: University of Chicago Press, 1953), 389-93.
2. Sophocles, *The Women of Trachis*, 1276-78, in *Sophocles II*, ed. David Grene and Richmond Lattimore, trans. Michael Jameson (Chicago: University of Chicago Press, 1957).
3. Euripides, *Trojan Women*, 616.
4. Seneca, *Medea*, 431-32.

Classical tragedy begins in, is resolved by, or passes through necessity. The analects at the head of this paper attest to the effectual and dreadful operation of this necessity; further, they suggest a kinship between tragic necessity and the Calvinist doctrine of predestination, according to which God's decretive will is the cause of all things: God's will, like fate, is always effectual, and as it actually reprobates as well as elects, God's will is also dreadful. Yet despite their formal symmetries, divine election and fatal necessity do not stand in continuity with each other. Whereas tragic personae are subjected to the vicissitudes of an impersonal necessity, Calvinist predestination seeks a salvific election worked out in love by the living God. When the first Calvinists took up and read classical tragedies, they saw the tragic vision from a Christological perspective, and they beheld the necessary hope of predestination.

The title of this paper requires a brief explanation. First, *Calvinism*: agreeing with Richard Muller that Calvin considered himself a teacher of "the church's doctrine, not his own,"[5] and wishing to respect Calvin's eponymous forfeiture, by *Calvinism* I mean a theological-historical heuristic whose contours were expounded principally by John Calvin, but were shared by his coevals.[6] Second, *necessity* refers to the relationship between a cause and its effect such that the cause always entails a certain effect.[7] Finally, the *death of tragedy* is an amphibology: tragedy dramatizes death, and tragedy itself died — it ceased to be performed. Both of these meanings are relevant to my paper, and after reviewing them I will consider the intersection between Calvinism and tragedy.

The Perseverance of the Tragic

Tragedy has lain moribund more often than it has thrived in its *conatus*. The genre flourished in democratic Athens, where the theater was a civic and re-

---

5. Richard A. Muller, *The Unaccommodated Calvin: Studies in the Foundation of a Theological Tradition* (Oxford: Oxford University Press, 2002).

6. I.e., fellow reformers who were neither Catholic, Lutheran, nor Anabaptist. Jerome Zanchi, Theodore Beza, Peter Martyr Vermigli, John Knox, and Pierre Viret are all accordingly Calvinist.

7. This relationship can be expressed logically as one of entailment, i.e., $p \Rightarrow q$, where an effect q is the implication of cause p. See David Widerker, "Two Forms of Fatalism," in *God, Foreknowledge, and Freedom*, ed. John Martin Fischer (Stanford: Stanford University Press, 1989), 97-110.

ligious institution financed by state liturgies and attended by the Athenian public.[8] Athens staged tragedies during two annual festivals in honor of Dionysus, the City Dionysia and the Lenaea. These tragedies were partly musical (the choral sections were sung) and entirely poetic (all of the lines were spoken in metrical verse).

Of the surviving Greek tragedies (those from Aeschylus, Sophocles, and Euripides), the drama centers on pity and suffering, lament and loss, sacrifice and guilt, blame and reconciliation. Necessity — whether *aisa, anankē, moira,* or *to peprōmenon* — is treated variously and obliquely. Sometimes the gods command destiny, other times destiny commands the gods;[9] for humanity, the effect is the same. As Bernard Williams observes, tragic necessity (what he calls "supernatural necessity") structures the world so that "what you do will make no difference to the eventual outcome, or will even help to bring about what you try to prevent."[10] As such, tragic necessity drives all mortals toward their inexorable end — death, the "pitiless day" (*nēlees ēmar*) in Homeric epithet.[11] Yet while the pertinacious warriors of the *Iliad* and *Odyssey* strive to "ward off" (*amunein*) their pitiless day, the characters of tragedy (many of them erstwhile epic heroes or those otherwise caught in the aftermath of the Trojan War) tend to capitulate to lamentation. In *Prometheus Bound*, Prometheus explains why: "I caused mortals to cease foreseeing fate. . . . I caused blind hopes to dwell within them" (250, 252). Once fate is made visible, as it inevitably is in death, the blind hopes of epic poetry disappear and are replaced by lamentation, regret, doubt, mourning, wailing — the poetics of Greek tragedy.

This poetics enjoyed its *floruit* in the fifth century, though new works were composed into the Hellenistic period. Later, the genre was imitated and appropriated by the Romans, who adapted its rhythm and meter to Latin sensibilities. Later still, tragedy was encoded in the rituals of the Christian church: the "liturgy" of the Dionysian festival was reclaimed in the Christian eucharist (a mystery and spectacle wherein Christ's death is revealed);[12] in

---

8. For my historical survey of Greek tragedy, I am indebted to Robert Garland, *Surviving Greek Tragedy* (London: Duckworth, 2004).

9. Cf. Aeschylus' *Suppliants*, 673, and Euripides' *Iphigenia in Tauris*, 1486.

10. Bernard Williams, *Shame and Necessity* (Berkeley: University of California Press, 1993), 141.

11. See the *Iliad* IV.484, XI.484, XIII.514, XV.375, XVII.511, XXI.57, etc.; *Odyssey* VIII.525 and XI.17. Cf. *Iliad* IX.250, XVI.836, XXI.374, etc.

12. "He [the Master] commanded that the sacrificial offerings and liturgical [*leitourgias*] rites be performed not in a random or haphazard way, but according to set times

the *Kyrie Eleison,* tragic pity was petitioned of God; and hymnody was sung by the chorus of congregants to its heavenly audience. All of these activities were performed in reference to the supreme tragedy of the cross, which was recounted in the *lectio.* The four Gospels act as messenger speeches that proclaim the (evangelical) death of the (divine) protagonist. Once the Gospels' tragedy is finished, however, it is transfigured: Christ dies on a cross *for the sins of the world,* but is then resurrected to everlasting glory.

The evangelical subversion of tragedy creates in Christianity a deep ambivalence toward tragic poetics, and the early Christians' response to the theater admits of no consensus. Tertullian rejects tragedy on the grounds that the theater is "privatum consistorium inpudicitiae."[13] In his *Exhortation to the Greeks,* Clement of Alexandria wavers between Tertullian's disgust of and a *Realpolitik* respect for the tragedians and their art: after condemning the "mad revels of the Bacchic rite,"[14] he extols Euripides' impious ridicule of the gods.[15] Apollinarus the Elder, according to Socrates Scholasticus, wrote Christian tragedies in defiance of Emperor Julian's anti-Christian legislation.[16] Augustine called tragedy (and comedy) the "most inoffensive" of stage plays.[17]

An existential urgency lay behind Christian opposition to tragedy: the church was vying with the theater for public attendance. Yet as the government of the Western Roman Empire disintegrated, the Latin *oikoumenē* became deprived of much of its own cultural heritage, and the *agōn* eventually went to the church.[18] When the monk Salvian attacked the theater in the fifth century, high dramatic art was nearly extinct in the western provinces. Scribes in the Eastern Roman Empire continued to copy classical texts, and perhaps did so with little interruption until the fall of Constantinople;[19] yet

---

and hours." Clement of Rome, *First Letter of Clement* 40:2, in *The Apostolic Fathers I,* ed. and trans. Bart D. Ehrman (Cambridge: Harvard University Press, 1999). See also *1 Clement* 41:1.

13. *De Spectaculis,* 17. Cited in *Tertullian,* trans. T. R. Glover (Cambridge: Harvard University Press, 1977). Tertullian refers to Seneca the Younger as *"saepe noster"* (*De Anima* 20), but Seneca belongs to the Christians as a Stoic philosopher, not as a playwright.

14. Clement of Alexandria, *Exhortation to the Greeks,* 1, in *Clement of Alexandria,* trans. G. W. Butterworth (Cambridge: Harvard University Press 2003).

15. Clement of Alexandria, *Exhortation to the Greeks,* 7.

16. *Historia Ecclesiastica,* 3.16.

17. *De Civitate Dei contra Paganos,* II.8.

18. R. A. Markus, *The End of Ancient Christianity* (Cambridge: Cambridge University Press, 1990), 172-74.

19. See Garland, *Surviving Greek Tragedy,* 80: "Virtually nothing is known about the survival of Greek tragedy in Constantinople and its outriders from the sixth to the ninth centuries."

where it remained, it seems that tragedy was primarily or exclusively text, not performance.[20] The church did make further appropriations of theater: liturgical dramas, morality plays, farces, satires, mimes, and "dramatic homilies"[21] replaced tragedy, which had become one of the many cultural casualties of the Early Middle Ages.[22]

Howsoever and insofar as tragedy had died, in sixteenth-century Europe it was born again. Once Constantinople fell, the texts transmitted by refugee scholars — which included the tragedies of Aeschylus, Sophocles, Euripides, and Seneca — became midwives of the European Renaissance. The humanists revived this body of work, performing the tragedies that they read, edited, and translated. New works were written as well: Theodore Beza's *Abraham Sacrifiant* (1550) gave the French language a drama in the classical style; English tragedy was inaugurated at the court of Queen Elizabeth with a performance of *Gorboduc* (1561);[23] and Jacapo Peri composed his *Dafne* (1597) as a reconstructed Greek tragedy, inventing opera thereby — the afterbirth of the Italian *rinascita*.

The Terror of Necessity: Tragic Predestination

The rediscovery and renewal of classical drama formed a historical homology in the Protestant Reformation. Agitation for religious reform began to convulse Europe in a great performance piece of ecclesiastical contest, political reversal, and social crisis. Beza's *Abraham Sacrifiant* shares in this milieu, for it is a "moyen de propagande" as well as a play.[24] Especially in its textual residue, the Reformation reads as a tumultuous City Dionysia. The *agōnes* of Luther and Erasmus, the stichomythic exchanges between Calvin and Westphal, *Tridentum ex machina:* in the Reformation, history becomes a tis-

---

20. Alan Sommerstein, *Greek Drama and Dramatists* (London: Routledge, 2002), 4.

21. George La Piana, "The Byzantine Theatre," *Speculum* 11:2 (1936): 176.

22. A notable exception is the *Christos Paschon*, a tragic pastiche that served as a link between classical antiquity and the Renaissance. See La Piana, The Byzantine Theatre," 171-211.

23. See Sara Ruth Watson, "'Gorboduc' and the Theory of Tyrannicide," *The Modern Language Review* 34:3 (1939): 355-66.

24. Marguerite Soulié and Jean-Dominique Beaudin, eds., *Abraham Sacrifiant: Tragedie Françoise* (Paris: Honoré Champion Éditeur, 2006), 7. Beza eventually abandoned the *jouissance* of his humanist poetics — principally his *Juvenilia* — and wholly involved his learning in the controversies of the Reformation.

sue of dramatic episodes, an interval between two epochs whose tragic conclusion is the Peace of Augsburg *(cuius regio, eius religio* is analogous to the compromise of democracy that concludes the *Oresteia)* and whose tragic sequel is the devastation of the Thirty Years' War.

The Reformation formed into a theater of the polemic in part because its principal actors were educated as humanists.[25] Although the reformers of the sixteenth century were acquainted with the *littera humaniores,* God was the dominant subject of their discourse, and every other discipline served their theological principle. The reformers' dispute over predestination was only one of many logomachies. Classical tragedies merely explored the effects of necessity; Calvinism, on the other hand, had resolved necessity in God himself: God, according to Calvin, was the *prima causa* who determines all things that come to pass.[26] More severely:

> Before the first man was created, God in his eternal counsel had determined what he willed to be done with the whole human race. In the hidden counsel of God it was determined that Adam should fall from the unimpaired condition of his nature, and by his defection should involve all his posterity in sentence of eternal death. Upon the same decree depends the distinction between elect and reprobate: as he adopted some for himself for salvation, he destined others for eternal ruin. While the reprobate are the vessels of the just wrath of God, and the elect vessels of his compassion, the ground of the distinction is to be sought in the pure will of God alone, which is the supreme rule of justice.[27]

Because they insisted that the sovereign will of God determined all things, the Calvinist reformers faced accusations from all quarters.[28] Charges of ab-

---

25. See Pierre-François Moreau, "Calvin: fascination et critique du stoïcisme," *Le stoïcisme au XVIIᵉ et au XVIIIᵉ siècle,* ed. Pierre-François Moreau (Paris: Albin Michel, 1999), 51-64.

26. Calvin, *Institutes* II.xvii.1.

27. John Calvin, "Articles Concerning Predestination," in *Calvin: Theological Treatises,* ed. J. K. S. Reid (Philadelphia: The Westminster Press, 1954). Following Augustine (to this as to so many other *topoi*), the Calvinists averred that because of the sin of Adam, humanity had become a *massa damnata* (*De Civitate Dei* XXI.12). Cf. John Calvin, *Concerning the Eternal Predestination of God,* VIII.5.

28. The opposition was later taken up by Arminius and continues to this day. For example, see David Bentley Hart, *The Beauty of the Infinite* (Grand Rapids: Eerdmans, 2003). He comments that in the doctrine of double predestination "[o]ne ancient Augustinian misreading of Paul's ruminations upon the mystery of election had, at last, eventuated in fatal-

surdity, blasphemy, and calumny began with Calvin's enemies — Pighius, Bolsec, and Velsius — but in time Calvin's friends formed their own doubts. Bullinger worried that Calvin's doctrine of predestination made God "the author of sin."[29] Melanchthon thought that the "Genevan battles over Stoic necessity" were a symptom of the madness of the times.[30] Calvin himself was disturbed by the scope of God's reprobation: "Decretum quidem horribile, fateor."[31] Aroused to pity and fear, Calvin responded to divine predestination as to a tragedy. Reprobation, in its formal effect, becomes indistinguishable from the necessity of tragic fate.

Melanchthon's accusation of Calvinist Stoicism, which was independently laid by others,[32] could be supported by inculpatory evidence: Calvin's

---

ism. . . . Theology was subjected to the abysmal sublimity of a god of absolute arbitrary will" (134). Calvin's answer to this charge is found in his *Commentary on Genesis* 25:29: "Since God is the Creator of the world, he is . . . in such a sense, the arbiter of life and death, that he cannot be called to account; but his own will is . . . the cause of causes. And yet Paul does not, by thus reasoning, impute tyranny to God, as the sophists triflingly allege. . . . But whereas He dwells in inaccessible light, and his judgments are deeper than the lowest abyss, Paul prudently enjoins acquiescence in God's sole purpose; lest, if men seek to be too inquisitive, this immense chaos should absorb all their senses." Hart's own words are compromised, or at least corroborate Calvin's, when he later states, "God is the infinity of being in which every essence comes to be, the *abyss of subsistent beauty* into which every existence is outstretched" in *Commentary on Genesis*, ed. Alister McGrath and J. I. Packer (Wheaton: Crossway Books, 2001), 245.

29. Calvin, CCXC, "Letter to Bullinger." See Cornelius Venema, "Heinrich Bullinger's Correspondence on Calvin's Doctrine of Predestination, 1551-1553," *The Sixteenth Century Journal* 17:4 (1986): 435-50. The Reformation debates over predestination reveal a Christian preoccupation with denying that God is the "author" of sin. Cf. Vermigli's *An Deus Sit Author Peccati*; Beza's *The Life of John Calvin*, pp. 53 and 65; Philip Schaff, *History of the Christian Church*, Vol. VII: *Modern Christianity: The Swiss Reformation* (New York: Charles Scribners' Sons, 1898), 261; Robert Kolb, "Nikolaus von Amsdorf on Vessels of Wrath and Vessels of Mercy: A Lutheran's Doctrine of Double Predestination," *The Harvard Theological Review* 69:3/4 (1976): 325-43.

30. See Barbara Pitkin, "The Protestant Zeno: Calvin and the Development of Melanchthon's Anthropology," *The Journal of Religion* 84:3 (2004): 345-78. Beza remarks that, during Calvin's controversy with Bolsec, "Even Melanchthon himself . . . notwithstanding he had expressly before this period subscribed to Calvin's book against Pighius [this treatise was in fact dedicated to Melanchthon], yet some thought he pointed to the ministers in Geneva, as if they were introducing a stoical fate" (Beza, *The Life of Calvin,* 53-54).

31. Calvin, *Institutes* III.xxiii.7.

32. Cf. Vermigli in *De Providentia*: "Some will say that we are reviving the opinion of the Stoics concerning fate; that is false. They defined their fate as the necessity of the connection of causes, and said that it overruled even God himself. We teach that God governs all things and uses them to his glory" (*Providence*, in *Philosophical Works: On the Relation of*

first publication was a commentary on the *De Clementia* of Seneca the Younger. Yet even before his career as a reformer, Calvin was critical of "Stoic necessity." According to Pierre-François Moreau, "il semble critiquer Sénèque au nom même de la doctrine de la nécessité que celui-ci défend."[33] Once he took up the cause of the Reformation, Calvin actively and constantly denied allegations of Stoicism.[34] Yet while he and other reformers placed divine predestination in opposition to fate, Zanchi eagerly sought out affinities between the two. In what Augustus Toplady styled *An appendix concerning the fate of the ancients*, Zanchi rehabilitates the "fatalists of antiquity" for the express purpose of corroborating his doctrine of predestination.[35] Zanchi mainly examines Stoic philosophy, but at one point he turns to tragedy:

> Excellent is that of Sophocles (Aj. Flagell.): "I am firmly of the opinion that all these things, and whatever else befall us, are in consequence of the Divine purpose; whoso thinks otherwise is at liberty to follow his own judgment, but this will ever be mine."[36]

Perhaps Zanchi did not want the context to detract from his main argument, but the quotation from *Ajax* is more foreboding than it appears. Sophocles placed these words in the mouth of Teucer, who has just seen the corpse of his son; shortly before the passage quoted by Zanchi, Teucer exclaims, "O face painful to look upon and full of cruel boldness, what a full crop of sorrows you have sown for me in your death!" (1004-1005). Whatever Zanchi's rehabilitation accomplishes, it does not mitigate the dread of "Divine purpose." How could it do so? Death makes fate visible.

Under the tragic condition, lamentation is a natural reflex of human psychology. "Would that the hull of the Argo had never reached the land of

---

Philosophy to Theology, trans. and ed. Joseph C. McLelland [Kirksville: Truman State University Press 1996], 176-96).

33. Moreau, "Calvin: fascination et critique du stoïcisme," 53.

34. See, for example, *Institutes* I.xvi.8 or *The Secret Providence of God:* "Fate, named by the Stoics, is that which is necessary from the various and complicated labyrinth of causes that in some manner restricts God himself. By contrast with this, I define predestination ... as the free counsel of God by which he governs the human race and every single part of the universe according to his immense wisdom and incomprehensible justice" (*The Secret Providence of God,* ed. Paul Helm, trans. Keith Goad [Wheaton: Crossway Books, 2010], 62).

35. Zanchi, *Absolute Predestination* (Lafayette, Ind.: Sovereign Grace Publishers, Inc., 2001), 123.

36. Zanchi, *Absolute Predestination,* 123. The quotation is from *Ajax,* 1036-39.

Colchis through the dark blue Symplegades," says the Nurse in *Medea*, "nor ever had fallen in the glens of Pelion the fir-tree to furnish oars for the hands of men who for Pelias set forth for the Golden Fleece!" (1-5). The Nurse wishes that the Argo had never been built because she views the ship as a determinative cause of Medea's misfortune. If the Argo had not been built, Medea would never have boarded the ship, fled from her home, murdered Pelias, been abandoned by Jason — the Nurse, in short, wishes for a counterfactual so that history would not have progressed as it did. Her optative is one of regret, a tragic optative that is unable to alter what has already come to pass, and her very grammar forces the recognition of despair.

In her grief, the Nurse merely avers the past's ineluctable succession of events, the eternal inviolability of which constitutes divine predestination. Looking at the Nurse's lamentation, Calvin sees a confusion of cause and responsibility. He remarks that the Nurse "accuses neither [Medea's] shameless passion, nor the allurement of Jason, but complains that a ship had been built in Greece."[37] The Nurse resigns herself to a fatalistic hermeneutics. People so resign themselves in order to shirk responsibility, as when a guilty man "seeks pretexts of extenuation in remote causes." Lost in a modal fantasy, such a man "ridiculously forgets himself."

Perfect Love Casts Out Fear: The Perseverance of the Saints

In his locus on predestination, Vermigli recounts a contemporary tragedy:

> In our time a certain man in Italy named Francesco Spiera felt within himself that God had imposed this evil [reprobation] on him, but in my judgment this happened to induce fear in other people. After he had known the truth of the Gospel and confessed it openly, when brought before the papal legate in Venice he publicly recanted it. Later he was seized with a grave wound of conscience and convinced himself that he had sinned against the Holy Spirit. By this means he was thrown into such great despair that he would never afterward accept any consolation, although famous and pious men attended him, exhorting him to have hope in Christ and his death. He used to say that these things served well when

---

37. Calvin, *Secret Providence*, trans. James Lillie (New York: Robert Carter, 1840). Here Calvin's motive is to exonerate God's absolute sovereignty: "though God in his own way hardens hearts, yet everyone is justly responsible for his own hardness, because everyone is hardened by his own wickedness."

spoken of others, but to him they did not count, for he saw with absolute certainty that he had sinned against the Holy Spirit, and there was no remedy left to deliver him from damnation. He remained in this despair until he died.[38]

Beza, Calvin, and Zanchi recognized the humanity of tragedy; here Vermigli recognizes the tragedy of humanity. Vermigli's passage is a record of how sin has made tragedy immanent. "In our time," Vermigli begins, and this period extends beyond the upheaval of the Reformation — "our time" is the deictic present of the fallen world's *saeculum,* and in our time, tragedy inheres within the human condition. The tragedy of Francesco Spiera, Vermigli concludes, served a pedagogical end: "Through this man, by a singular and unusual dispensation, God wished to frighten others away from such evil and impiety."[39] Believer and reprobate alike may be frightened, but the believer is frightened "away from" the reprobate, being alienated from the reprobate's alienation and impelled toward "Christ and his death."

When considering the tragedy of the reprobate, Calvin sees a mirror of eternal destruction.[40] For the believer, the reprobate become a deterrent to sin; but reprobation, *qua* mirror, invites the possibility of an alienating self-reflection, a *Verfremdungseffekt* among the reprobate wherein they "ridiculously forget" themselves. According to Calvin, "our happiness consists in our cleaving to God . . . there is nothing more miserable than to be alienated from him."[41] The distinction of the *duplex cognitio Dei,*[42] the twofold knowledge of God, schematizes the difference between the believer, who has the eye of faith, and the reprobate, who is blinded with unbelief. While God is *simplex* (according to Vermigli *simplicissimus*[43]), the sin of Adam has com-

---

38. Vermigli, *Locus on Predestination* 2.33. Cited in *Predestination and Justification: Two Theological Loci,* trans. and ed. Frank A. James III (Kirksville: Truman State University Press, 2003).

39. Vermigli, *Locus on Predestination* 2.33.

40. Calvin finds "mirroring" in creation, marriage, judgment, redemption, reprobation, etc., but for him, the reprobate alone act as a mirror of eternal destruction. Cf. Calvin's commentary on Colossians 3:6.

41. Calvin, *Commentary on Colossians* 1:20. In *The Epistles of Paul the Apostle to the Galatians, Ephesians, Philippians, and Colossians,* ed. David W. Torrance and Thomas F. Torrance, trans. T. H. L. Parker (Grand Rapids: Eerdmans, 1965).

42. See *Institutes* I.ii.1.

43. Vermigli, *Visions: How and How Far God May Be Known,* in *Philosophical Works: On the Relation of Philosophy to Theology,* trans. and ed. Joseph C. McLelland (Kirksville: Truman State University Press, 1996), 138-54.

plicated our knowledge: in "the present ruin of the human race," Calvin writes, no one will "perceive God to be either a father, or the author of salvation, or propitious in any respect, until Christ interpose to make our peace."[44] We first understand God "simply [simpliciter] as a Creator, and afterwards as a Redeemer in Christ."[45] This creator-God, so understood, is as indifferent as tragic fate to the present ruin of the human race. Vermigli adduces the end of recognizing only the first half of the *duplex:*

> [A]nyone ... endowed only with human wisdom and helped only by the light of reason ... when it comes to extreme dangers ... will lose heart, be filled with despair, and certainly judge that he must bend to natural necessity. He will bewail his lot, blame his destiny, and finally will accuse the terrible powers of the stars, "O my unhappy situation, O my miserable kind of life, O my unbearable desperation!"[46]

This is the mode of tragedy, and humans will blame destiny because of their destination: death. Tragedy clarifies the problematic of death so that lamentation, in its impotence, is figured forth as humanity's essential Being-toward-death.

Tragedy offers no escape from death because no one escapes death. Afflictions are visited upon the righteous and the unrighteous alike; repentance delivers none from the grave. The *duplex cognitio Dei* relativizes man's unhappy condition: it consoles him with hope while reminding him that this life leads to death by way of suffering. Calvin performs a further rhetorical shift away from tragedy: the human condition began, not in an always already tragic fall, but in Eden, where man was "placed as in a theater, that he, beholding above him and beneath the wonderful works of God, might reverently adore their Author."[47] Eden was a Sabbath's theater of the divine majesty, and this dramatic simile was not destroyed by the sin of Adam, only inflected: because of sin, the cosmic theater had become provisionally tragic.[48] Tragic

---

44. *Institutes* I.ii.1.

45. *Institutes* I.ii.1.

46. Vermigli, *Strasbourg Oration*. Cited in *The Peter Martyr Reader,* ed. John Patrick Donnelly, S.J., Frank A. James III, and Joseph C. McLelland (Kirksville: Truman State University Press, 1999), 55-66.

47. "Preface," in Calvin, *Commentary on Genesis,* ed. Alister McGrath and J. I. Packer (Wheaton: Crossway Books, 2001).

48. Again Calvin: "For it is true, that this world is like a theater, in which the Lord presents to us a clear manifestation of his glory, and yet, notwithstanding that we have such a spectacle placed before our eyes, we are stone-blind ... it is only with the eye of faith that we

lamentation looks backward at an irrevocable past and forward to a final death; Christian hope seeks assurance in the certainty of a divinely ordained future from eternity past, looks to the inevitability of death — and then looks beyond this necessity toward an eternal reward. Therefore Vermigli can write, "In a way, we are performing a comedy: although it has a tumultuous beginning and middle, yet it has a happy end and concludes with applause. But the wicked perform a tragedy: although it may appear to be great and elevated at the beginning, yet it has a mournful and tearful ending."[49]

To believe that we are performing a comedy requires faith — the tragedy of Francesco Spiera is not the necessary consequence of Calvinist theology, though Calvinism may create the conditions for his kind of anxiety and his final despair — and to persevere through the tumultuous beginning and middle requires Christ, who is "for us the bright mirror of the eternal and hidden election of God . . . we contemplate by faith the life which is represented to us in this mirror."[50] Yet when we contemplate this life, we are again confronted with suffering. As Vermigli observed above, believers are impelled toward "Christ and his death." Even as Christ submitted to death, so those who are united to Christ in baptism are baptized into his death. Calvin remarks that salvation is based on the election of God, and that "by the same celestial decree, the afflictions, which conform us to Christ, have been appointed."[51] The eternal death of reprobation is, like evil, a privation, and divine election is a privation of this privation: divine election is redemptive. The *duplex cognitio Dei* discerns the suffering in election so that both suffering and election connect "as by a kind of necessary chain . . . our salvation with the bearing of the cross."[52]

---

can behold him," *Commentary on I Corinthians* 1:21, in *The First Epistle of Paul the Apostle to the Corinthians*, ed. David W. Torrance and Thomas F. Torrance, trans. John W. Fraser (Grand Rapids: Eerdmans, 1960).

49. Vermigli, *In Epistolam S. Pauli ad Romanos . . . Commentarii* (Basel: P. Perna, 1558), 8:28. "Res piorum abibunt in melius: impiorum vero in exitium. Nos quodammodo agimus Comoediam: quae quamvis habeat turbulenta initia, & media tamen fine laeto, & plausu concluditur. Impii autem agunt Tragoediam, quae quamvis magnifica, & elata videatur ab initio, tamen exitum habet funestum, & lachrymabilem."

50. Calvin, *Concerning the Eternal Predestination of God*, ed. and trans. J. K. S. Reid (Cambridge: James Clarke & Co., 1961; Louisville: Westminster John Knox Press, 1997), VIII.6. Cf. Calvin, *Institutes* III.xxii.1, where Christ is the "bright mirror of free election."

51. Calvin, *Commentary on Romans* 8:28. Cited in *The Epistles of Paul the Apostle to the Romans and to the Thessalonians*, ed. David W. Torrance and Thomas F. Torrance, trans. Ross MacKenzie (Grand Rapids: Eerdmans, 1960).

52. Calvin, *Commentary on Romans* 8:28.

Instead of ignoring or denying mortal necessity, the Calvinist reformers sought its source. And while this source may have elicited from them those two tragic emotions, pity and fear — such is the beginning of wisdom — the reformers were confident that, in Christ, one could face the dread that pervaded the postlapsarian world, even the *decretum horribile*. For in Christ, the very image of God and bright mirror of free election, the love of God is perfected.

The Correlation between Creation and Culture in the Theology of Abraham Kuyper and Colin E. Gunton

William Baltmanis Whitney

Introduction

What role does the doctrine of creation play in conceptualizing a theology of culture? How does a robust understanding of the created order lend itself to an affirmation of a wide range of human activities that we may classify as culture? To answer these questions, I will examine how two theologians, Abraham Kuyper and Colin E. Gunton, correlate creation and culture in their own theologies.[1] Even though Gunton and Kuyper never knew each other and lived in different contexts, there exists a great commonality between them in how they understand the created order, and how this understanding influences their conception of culture and the arts. I will explore insights from both Kuyper and Gunton regarding culture and will demonstrate how creation has an intrinsic relation to how one conceives a theology of culture. I will also demonstrate how this dialogue between these two theologians has potential to yield several insights that will help contribute to a contemporary Reformed account of culture.

1. Kuyper, Creation, and Culture

For our purposes, the first major theme in Kuyper's understanding of creation to consider is his notion that there is a "unity, solidity, and order" in

---

1. A distinction should be made between "creation" as the divine act of creation, and "creation" as created reality. The use of the term "creation" in this essay refers to the latter of these distinctions, i.e. the created reality.

creation that is established by God.² Broadly speaking, this emphasis on the unity and order of creation contributes to other significant aspects of Kuyper's theology, most notably his understanding of Calvinism as a coherent life system. However, Kuyper's stress on the order of creation also enables him to uphold the importance of human action within the world — and this includes the human activities of culture and the arts.

For Kuyper, if there is an order and unity to creation, then this also means that the world can be explored and investigated. Or said another way, since God created a world that is unified and ordered in a certain way, humans have been given the ability to investigate and explore the patterns found in creation. If the created realm did not have a pattern or order, the human enterprise of science could not take place. Kuyper uses two words, *discover* and *develop*, to describe this activity of human exploration:

> And for our relation to the world: the recognition that in the whole world the curse is restrained by grace, that the life of the world is to be honored in its independence, and that we must, in every domain, discover the treasures and develop the potencies hidden by God in nature and in human life.³

For Kuyper, this discovery has potential to shed "light on the glories of the entire cosmos in its visible phenomena and operations," and there is nothing either in the life of nature or in human life that does not "present itself as an object worthy of investigation."⁴ In addition to this, Kuyper emphasizes that art has the unique ability to help humans produce and develop something beautiful that "transcends" nature. This is why Kuyper can say,

> So also it is the vocation of art, not merely to observe everything visible and audible, to apprehend it, and reproduce it artistically, but much more to discover in those natural forms the order of the beautiful, and, enriched by this higher knowledge, to produce a beautiful world that transcends the beautiful of nature.⁵

Here, we find that art observes the natural realm, helps with discovery of the "natural forms" that are beautiful within creation, and also, according to Kuyper, amplifies these patterns or forms that are found in nature. Kuyper

---

2. Abraham Kuyper, *Lectures on Calvinism* (Grand Rapids: Eerdmans, 1931), 115-16.
3. Kuyper, *Lectures on Calvinism*, 31.
4. Kuyper, *Lectures on Calvinism*, 126.
5. Kuyper, *Lectures on Calvinism*, 154.

argues that God has ordained all sorts of "life utterances" for humans, but art reveals these ordinances of creation in a unique way that science and politics cannot.[6]

Yet what is most interesting about Kuyper's stress on the unity and order of creation is how he relates it to present human action. If creation has a unity and order, then this order compels humans to act in a certain way towards the creation. Since the world is a unified and ordered whole, made by a good Creator, emphasis is placed on serving God in the world, instead of being removed from the world. Culture and the arts can be affirmed as good activities because they represent ways that God has ordained and enabled humans to explore the order and unity of creation. Kuyper notes that order is inherent within creation, and he relies on his understanding of common grace to describe how humans are able to discover these wonders of creation in light of the reality of sin.[7]

Consequently, for Kuyper, if the world has a certain form and structure to it, then human investigation and exploration of the world is not only possible, it is a normal human activity that enhances how humans understand creation. While these human activities or "life-utterances" are diverse, these good human activities include enjoying creation, investigating the created realm, and developing the order of creation. However, the most crucial point to recognize is how the structure of the created realm naturally lends itself to a certain form of human activity for Kuyper, so that humanity (whether redeemed or not) relates to the created realm in a certain way. This human action involves art, but it also includes all manner of human activities that we can call culture, i.e. what humanity makes within the created realm.

1.1. The Correlation between Creation and Salvation

The second major aspect in Kuyper's doctrine of creation that has ramifications for his theology of culture is how he correlates creation and salvation. As Kuyper sees it, an understanding of salvation that stresses a spiritual realm

---

6. Kuyper, *Lectures on Calvinism*, 163.
7. Common grace is God's movement to allow human culture to develop despite the reality of sin. For Kuyper, common grace is God's restraint of the power of sin so that "civic virtue, a sense of domesticity, natural love, the practice of human virtue, the improvement of the public conscience, integrity, mutual loyalty among people, and a feeling for piety leaven life." "Common Grace," in *Abraham Kuyper: A Centennial Reader,* ed. James D. Bratt (Grand Rapids: Eerdmans, 1998), 181.

over and above the material world creates a division between the life of nature and the life of grace.[8] For him, a dualistic conception of redemption has too intense a "contemplation of celestial things" while neglecting to "give due attention to the world of God's creation."[9] Thus, any view of salvation that divorces the spiritual from the material has an "exclusive love of things eternal but has been backward in the fulfillment of its temporal duties."[10]

Just as Kuyper advocates for conceiving the created order in a non-hierarchical way, he also understands that salvation must not deal exclusively with the soul but also must emphasize the importance of the body. For Kuyper this comes from the singular vision of wanting to advocate for the interpenetration of the spiritual and material realms. Van Egmond observes that Kuyper's intention is to "give full weight to bodiliness and the world" and how humans come into contact with the world through their body."[11] By highlighting the importance of the material world and elevating the body to a place of importance, Kuyper is able to strengthen his proposal that human action in the world through culture and the arts is an aspect of the elect's calling.

Kuyper's emphasis suggests a correlation between soteriology and the doctrine of creation. Kuyper sees that if salvation only concentrates on the otherworldly, or the spiritual/eternal realm (individual salvation out of the world), it runs the corresponding danger of neglecting the material world and the body. Conversely, if salvation includes a non-hierarchical view of the world, i.e., one in which the spiritual is not elevated over the material, then human activities in the present life have a greater degree of significance and value.

The significance of this cannot be stressed too heavily for our understanding of culture. If one's theology does not effectively relate soteriology and creation, then a view of salvation emerges that disregards or places less importance on the material world as being part of God's good creation. Any theology that de-values the material creation will have more difficulty making sense of the significance of human activity engaging with the material, created realm. Here, we find that Kuyper goes beyond Calvin by broadening and reinterpreting the scope of the doctrine of election to emphasize human action within the temporal realm.[12] To be elected means that one has a duty

---

8. Kuyper, *Lectures on Calvinism*, 118.

9. Kuyper, *Lectures on Calvinism*, 118.

10. Kuyper, *Lectures on Calvinism*, 118.

11. A. van Egmond, "Kuyper's Dogmatic Theology," in *Kuyper Reconsidered: Aspects of His Life and Work* (Amsterdam: VU Uitgeverij, 1999), 89.

12. C. van der Kooi, "A Theology of Culture: A Critical Appraisal of Kuyper's Doctrine

to take part in shaping and developing creation through the activities of science, politics, and the arts.

1.2. Observations

David Fergusson has recently noted that the doctrine of creation has often been treated as a preamble to other areas of systematic theology and has been isolated from other doctrinal loci.[13] As we turn to Kuyper, we find that a key feature of his theology is that he does not treat creation in isolation from other doctrines, but rather demonstrates the relation between creation and other significant theological loci. Furthermore, it is Kuyper's relation of creation to other doctrinal loci that enables him to develop his theology of culture. Kuyper moves beyond a mere appreciation of the created realm, and while he affirms the value and goodness of human cultural activity in the world, he also emphasizes how one should engage the created realm through exploration, discovery, and development.

This remains a highly significant point, because it is Kuyper's theology of creation that enables him to make a conceptual link between dogmatics and ethics. This is most clearly seen in his linking of salvation and creation that portrays a vision of human activity — a life where humans are called to honor God through culture.[14] How one understands the value and importance of the material world, in addition to how one sees calling or election, ultimately shapes one's ethics. Thus, the influence of Kuyper's doctrine of creation upon his soteriology also enables his doctrine of election to have a worldly orientation that ultimately undergirds his theology of culture. For Kuyper, to be a creature in God's world means that one engages this world in a particular way through a wide range of human activities — and these include the realm of human culture and the arts.

2. Gunton's Theology of Creation and Culture

For nearly three decades, the Reformed minister and professor Colin E. Gunton (1941-2003) was a prominent voice in contemporary theology, espe-

---

of Common Grace," in *Kuyper Reconsidered: Aspects of His Life and Work* (Amsterdam: VU Uitgeverij, 1999), 109.

13. David A. S. Fergusson, *The Cosmos and the Creator: An Introduction to the Theology of Creation* (London: SPCK, 1998), 1.

14. C. van der Kooi, "A Theology of Culture," 101.

cially in the area of trinitarian studies. Although research on Gunton's work has mainly revolved around his conception of the Trinity, Gunton's engagement with culture and the doctrine of creation are prominent features of his theology that have received less attention. Gunton, like Kuyper, stresses the order and unity of creation and the relation between salvation and the doctrine of creation. His focus on a trinitarian doctrine of creation enables him to highlight the relational aspects of the entire created order and human action within culture.

2.1. *The Logic of Creation, Salvation, and the Created Realm*

Gunton argues that creation has an "intrinsic logic" and observes that there is a beauty, order, and purposefulness in the created realm that speaks for itself.[15] He stresses that the created order does not point to the existence of God per se but shows intrinsic patterns of rationality. I understand this point to be very similar to Kuyper's understanding of the unity and order of creation. Science, Gunton observes, as the "study of the created order in its own right, is a proper human activity, as are technology, art and the other human activities we call culture."[16] In short, Gunton argues that God has created a world that has its own reality, and this reality is worth studying:

> The temporal shape of God's acts of creation has important implications, particularly for our understanding of the status of matter. Rather than diminishing the importance of the material world, its importance in itself is . . . to be established: it, and not some higher "spiritual" world, is the object of God's actual willing. The fact that the act of creation is directed to the establishment of things whose rationale is their shaping as beings in time and space demonstrates the importance of the created world in and for itself.[17]

In addition to this, Gunton also argues that the doctrine of creation and redemption should be more closely correlated. For Gunton, salvation occurs in and with the material world, not apart from it, and redemption is what he calls the "perfecting" of the created realm. This process, the "perfection" of creation, is the movement by the Son and by the Spirit where creation (both

---

15. Colin E. Gunton, *The Triune Creator: A Historical and Systematic Study* (Grand Rapids: Eerdmans, 1998), 234.
16. Gunton, *The Triune Creator*, 87.
17. Gunton, *The Triune Creator*, 84.

human and non-human) is made into what it is supposed to be. For Gunton, salvation is bound up with the doctrine of creation, and salvation represents a forward movement of growth that is cosmic in scope:

> There is in the Bible no redemption, no social and personal life, apart from the creation. It is therefore reasonable, especially in light of Old Testament witness to the creation, to hold that the Bible as a whole is concerned with the future of creation, particularly in view of the evidence ... from the Synoptic Gospels of Christ as Lord of creation. But the fact that it is Israel and Jesus who are at the centre of God's action in and towards the world means that it is the personal that is central, the non-personal peripheral. That does not rule out the ecological concern, but it cannot be of independent interest.[18]

For Gunton, any soteriology that suggests that humans are saved apart from the created order neglects biblical portraits of salvation that discuss the redemption of humans and the world together. Creation in the beginning implies that there is a projected end, and both humans and non-human creation are part of this eschatological goal of redemption. Gunton's intention is to give due weight to this salvific proposal. Thus, for Gunton, redemption is less about a point where one is "converted" and more focus is placed on process — a process where creation is restored to achieve a status greater than it even had in the beginning. What is interesting to note here is that Gunton, like Kuyper, places emphasis on the restoration of the entire creation, instead of focusing on election as the salvation of a limited number of souls for heaven, as the traditional doctrine of election has suggested.

Even though Kuyper and Gunton operated in different contexts, and worked out their theologies of culture under different circumstances, Gunton shares some important commonalities with the Neo-Calvinist tradition. In my estimation, Gunton's views on creation and culture follow Neo-Calvinist themes, and here we have examined how Gunton also emphasizes the order of creation and the relation between salvation and redemption. He, like Kuyper, draws corollaries to what this means for human action within creation. This is particularly interesting when we consider that Gunton claimed he was not "familiar" with Neo-Calvinism.[19] However,

---

18. Colin E. Gunton, *Christ and Creation* (Carlisle, England: Paternoster Press, 1992), 33-34.

19. Colin E. Gunton, "Foreword," in Jeremy S. Begbie, *Voicing Creation's Praise* (London: T&T Clark, 1991), xi-xiii.

while Gunton was not familiar with Neo-Calvinism, his emphasis on the intrinsic logic of the created realm and the correlation between salvation and creation moves him to stress the importance of human action in the present through cultural activities. While Gunton does not stress the Kuyperian notion of election as "calling," through Gunton's emphasis on the importance of the material world, and the relationship between human and non-human creation, he still stresses the essential nature of humans engaging with the world through culture.

2.2. The Particularizing Action of the Spirit and the Perfecting of Creation

Some of Gunton's most unique insights regarding culture build upon the "intrinsic logic" of creation and the relation between redemption and creation. Human action in and through culture is the way for the creation to reach its intended destiny, as well as the way that human life is offered up to the Triune God. The important point for Gunton is that humans have a role in enabling creation to become what it is supposed to be through human activity. For Gunton, one of the roles of the Spirit is to bring freedom within the structures of creation. In this way, the Spirit frees human action within the world to achieve a certain destiny that it would not have been able to achieve on its own. In short, creation needs human interaction so that it is fit for habitation. Gunton also calls this action "perfecting." He points out that all "derives from the divine creating and providing action. . . . The human creature is the one through whom the whole of the created order . . . is enabled to speak."[20]

For our discussion here, it is also necessary to note that through the Spirit, God makes possible in the present the things that are promised for the end.[21] In this way, the eschatological Spirit creates "authentic human reality in the here and now," and allows humans to be themselves.[22] The Spirit particularizes human personhood in a distinct fashion and creates community. This is not primarily a community that is saved out of the world; it is a community saved within the world and for the world, since the Spirit works

---

20. Gunton, *The Triune Creator*, 197.
21. Colin E. Gunton, *Enlightenment and Alienation* (Grand Rapids: Eerdmans, 1985), 103.
22. Gunton, *Enlightenment and Alienation*, 103.

to bring things to reality in the world. While the world is "very good," it still is in need of being perfected by faithful human action.[23] Furthermore, this role that humans have in making creation what it is intended to be is humanity's participation in the life of the Triune God. This human perfecting is not done by human action alone, but relies upon the work of the Spirit, who vivifies and inspires humans for this work.

Gunton's favorite illustration of human participation in perfecting the created order is one of a garden (he was an avid gardener). In a garden, human interaction in tending, pruning, and caring for the plants makes the environment more beautiful. Just as the plants in the garden reach a greater potential with human influence, the various realms of human activity have the possibility of actualizing the true beauty and wonder of creation. He also points out that in the beginning Adam and Eve were put in the garden to care for it, and in this way, the garden needed human interaction. This is why Gunton can say that the non-human creation actually needs the human creature in order for it to become what it is intended to be. Therefore, if both persons and things, "for all their crucial ontological differences, alike receive the shape of their being from the particularizing Spirit, we can no longer . . . treat matter as merely the intrinsically meaningless object of our instrumentality, as tends to be the way of both modernism and late modernism."[24]

The advantages of Gunton's understanding of "perfecting" the created order through human and divine agency are threefold, and each ultimately impacts how one understands culture. First, the notion of perfecting focuses on human action in the present, and avoids the idea that Christians should remain separate or isolated from culture. Second, there is a redemptive quality to this perfecting, so that humanity is able to participate in God's overall plan to bring creation to its ultimate destiny. This also places value on the human activities of culture, because it is something that God uses over and through time so that creation may become what it is intended to be. Gunton reminds us that God did not have to give humans the freedom to participate in his activity, but it is part of God's gracious action that is bestowed upon humanity. Third, an understanding of how human action influences the created order has the possibility of affirming a range of disciplines without depriving persons or culture of their particularity and distinctiveness. For

---

23. Colin E. Gunton, *Father, Son and Holy Spirit: Towards a Fully Trinitarian Theology* (London: T&T Clark, 2003), 90, 110.

24. Colin E. Gunton, *The One, the Three and the Many: God, Creation and the Culture of Modernity* (Cambridge: Cambridge University Press, 1993), 207.

Gunton, the Spirit makes things what they are intended to be in both particularity and distinction.[25] Gunton reminds us that true culture is the achievement of instances of the "good, the true and beautiful in anticipation of the eschatological completion of all things."[26] Here, divine and human action must be held in proper relation — the Spirit enables truth, beauty, and goodness to be realized in his creation, and to speak of culture means to speak of humanity being enabled by the Spirit to shape the creation towards what it is intended to be.[27] Thus, we find that Gunton broadens some of these Neo-Calvinist themes in his own unique direction — specifically in relation to the work of the Spirit and the perfecting of the created order.

3. Evaluation

Having established the basic relationship between creation and culture in both Kuyper and Gunton, I propose, by way of conclusion, to sketch four elements that have potential to contribute to a contemporary Reformed account of culture.

First, my focus in this essay has been to draw attention to how a theology of the created realm has ramifications for one's conception of culture. Since the doctrine of creation has often been treated in isolation from other doctrines, it is a topic that deserves careful consideration — especially when we attempt to understand culture from a theological perspective. Yet it is essential to recognize that the doctrine of creation plays a significant role for both Kuyper's and Gunton's theology of culture. If there is a crisis of belief that the created realm is good and something worthy in and of itself, this will dramatically impact the human enterprises that we know as culture.[28] Gunton's work is careful to note the significance of the material, created realm and how it impacts human action within the creation, while Kuyper emphasizes that the order and unity of creation means that the activities of science, politics, and art are worthwhile ventures. As we consider what a Reformed account of culture might look like, I suggest that a robust theology of creation enables us to place greater value and significance on human cultural action.

25. Gunton, *The One, the Three and the Many*, 177.
26. Gunton, *The Christian Faith*, 50.
27. Gunton, *The Christian Faith*, 50.
28. See further: Colin E. Gunton, *The Christian Faith: An Introduction to Christian Doctrine* (Oxford: Blackwell Publishers, 2002), x.

For both Kuyper and Gunton, the doctrine of creation is intrinsically related to the arts, because beliefs about the created order also determine how we interact and relate with the created order. Both Kuyper and Gunton remind us that as humans discover truths about the created order, they have the ability to further articulate the beauty and logic of creation — and this manifests itself in human activities that we may call culture.

Both Kuyper and Gunton show their perceptivity in recognizing how art and aesthetics are ways to gain knowledge of the world. Humans are not detached from their environment — we do not determine truth by attempting to remain neutral, but are creatures that are intimately related to and affected by what we encounter and touch. In this way, the artist has the ability to express emotions and feelings through a particular medium that are true and accurate depictions of the human experience in a way that scientific and empirical calculations cannot. Furthermore, because of the value of the created realm, humans should act in a certain way toward the created realm, and this includes all the human activities of shaping and forming culture. This is a useful connection primarily because it helps us to conceive the relation between dogmatics and ethics: rather than separating the two, our understanding of the value of the created order prompts us to uphold the value of creation in our actions towards the human and non-human creation. In this way, Kuyper's and Gunton's doctrines of creation move us to consider ethics, and help us consider the importance and value of human action.

Second, I propose that the intersection of redemption and creation is a vital link for conceptualizing a theology of culture. In sum, if the created order is merely the stage where salvation takes place, instead of the very thing that is saved, then human activity within the material world is often relegated to a place of secondary importance. As we have seen, both Kuyper and Gunton rightly perceive that there has been the tendency in other "theologies" to see the material world as less important than the spiritual. As a result, salvation is construed as "being out of this world rather than in and with it."[29] Gunton adapts this theme from Irenaeus, while Kuyper emphasizes it with his notion of election as "calling." However, the focal point for both of them is a robust soteriological vision that places value on human activities within the created world, including the arts. If we take Kuyper's comments seriously about how the arts illuminate our world, then aesthetics and the arts have an important place in our society. Gunton's notion of perfecting moves this forward in a direction that demonstrates how humans (em-

---

29. Gunton, *The Triune Creator*, 168.

powered by the Spirit) make the created order into what it is intended to be while also being transformed in the process.

Third, there is merit in Gunton's emphasis on the role of the Spirit in the transformation or "perfecting" of culture. A prominent feature of this is Gunton's elaboration of how the Spirit particularizes, transforms, and enables creation to be what it is intended to be through the human activity of culture. In my estimation, this is not in conflict with Kuyper's view, but remains a further extension of it. The world's fundamental goodness is established through Christ, who gives structure to creation, and humanity has the ability to transform the world as they are enabled through the Holy Spirit. Gunton urges us to reconsider human activities within the created realm in light of the work of the Son and Spirit in creation. Thus, Gunton's notion of perfecting broadens Kuyper's proposal of culture in a helpful direction by drawing attention to the particular way that humans participate with God in culture. The emphasis on perfecting enables Gunton to call attention to the synergy of human and divine action and its role in developing the created order.

As we recall, one of the aspects of Kuyper's understanding of creation is the unity of the created world — and this unity allows humans to discover and develop the order that is present within creation. Gunton notes that the Spirit allows particular aspects of culture to be what they are intended to be in their distinctiveness — and this broadens Kuyper's notion of development in a helpful direction. On this account, the Spirit works to allow various aspects of culture to become what they are supposed to be through human discovery and development. The Spirit working in this way also explains how there can be a diverse array of particular cultural activities. The Spirit's role of perfecting provides a meaningful way to speak of the integration of art and culture and to see cultural activity as significant. While Kuyper affirms that science, art, politics, and architecture all have their place as activities within the created order, Gunton reminds us that the role of the Spirit allows the particular activities of culture to become what they are distinctly supposed to be. (Unfortunately, I do not have space here to outline how this might also help us conceive of the relation between the spheres in Kuyper's understanding of sphere sovereignty.) For Gunton, it is not only the work of humanity to discover the created realm, but also the Spirit working in humanity to make these particular human discoveries distinct from other activities. Moreover, this perfecting of the Spirit through human action in and through culture and art are ways for the creation to reach its intended destiny.

Gunton's insight not only affirms human activity in the world but also allows for unity of culture that in turn allows for an interrelationship of disciplines, that is, an understanding of culture that sees the value of and relation between theology, science, and art. At the same time, this permits a particularity and distinctiveness of the various human activities within the cultural realm — creation's true beauty emerges in the complexity and diversity of the created order. Since modernity has tended to homogenize culture, Gunton reminds us how the Spirit allows particular things to become what they are in their own way. This means that science, art, politics, and architecture all have their place, because they each show how humans interact with the created world in a variety of ways while also reflecting the diversity of the world that God has created. Unless there is an understanding of the material world in all of its "particularity," we will never understand how science relates to morality, and morality to art.[30] Gunton sees that theology can develop a competence of its own as it interprets the reality of the world in which we live.[31]

If we understand that the Spirit works in humanity to perfect the created realm, then aesthetics and the arts also have distinct place not only to speak truths about creation, but also to play a part in changing or transforming culture. In this way, culture has a part to play in the social cultivation of human patterns of thinking, feeling, and behaving.[32] Moreover, if we consider that conversion is a journey marked by a "series of transformations" that happen as one is embedded in one's culture, then it is also possible to understand that the Spirit uses the realm of the aesthetic to help us discover truths about the world and ourselves that contribute to our transformation as persons.[33] As humans discover these truths about the created order, they have the ability to articulate the beauty and logic of creation. There is a redemptive quality to this perfecting, so that humanity is able to participate in God's overall plan to bring creation to its ultimate destiny. This does not mean that every human action in culture is redemptive action, but it does mean that the Spirit does speak and move through elements of human culture as both human and non-human creation are redeemed over time. This places value on the human activity of culture because it is some-

---

30. Gunton, *The One, the Three and the Many*, 51.
31. Colin E. Gunton and Paul Brazier, *The Barth Lectures* (London: T&T Clark, 2007), xx.
32. See further: Joel B. Green, *Body, Soul and Human Life: The Nature of Humanity in the Bible* (Grand Rapids: Baker/Paternoster, 2008), 91.
33. Green, *Body, Soul and Human Life*, 38.

thing that God uses over and through time for creation to reach eschatological perfection. Furthermore, Gunton reminds us that God did not have to give humans the freedom to participate in his activity, but it is part of God's gracious action that is bestowed upon humanity. Moreover, this notion of perfecting also has the potential to strengthen Kuyper's view of election as "calling." We find that Kuyper goes beyond Calvin by broadening the scope of the doctrine of election to emphasize human action within the temporal realm.[34] For example:

> Whoever believes in election knows that he has been chosen for something, that this is a spiritual calling, and that, as a divine calling, it may require the dearest sacrifice. At the same time it is a calling that guarantees success. Since God is the sovereign who calls him, he does not hesitate, does not weigh the pros and cons, but takes hold of the job and perseveres.[35]

As Willem van der Schee notes, "Kuyper stresses the point that every elected person is called to his specific task, his calling, something specifically to be done by him in God's Name."[36] While Kuyper rightly calls to attention that election includes human action in the present, there is little explanation of how humans participate in the action of God within culture. Gunton emphasizes how the Spirit's action through culture is one aspect of how God works to bring creation to completion. This does not supplant, but rather gives greater explanation to how art, as Kuyper says, is "a most serious power in our present existence" and stands in "close relation with the principal variations of our entire life."[37] With a pneumatological emphasis, one can see how art and culture are part of the Spirit's larger work of "making new" the whole creation. What Kuyper typically refers to as common grace, in Gunton's view, can be seen as the work of the Spirit bringing creation and culture to its intended end as humans participate in the action of God in the world. The pneumatological emphasis of Gunton helps contribute to a contemporary Reformed account of culture by giving a framework for under-

---

34. Willem van der Schee, "Kuyper's Archimedes' Point: The Reverend Abraham Kuyper on Election," in *Kuyper Reconsidered: Aspects of His Life and Work* (Amsterdam: VU Uitgeverij, 1999), 109.

35. Abraham Kuyper, *Het Calvinisme, oorsprong en waarborg onzer constitutioneele vrijheden* (Amsterdam: B. van der Land, 1874), in James D. Bratt, ed., *Abraham Kuyper: A Centennial Reader* (Grand Rapids: Eerdmans, 1998), 309-10.

36. Willem van der Schee, "Kuyper's Archimedes' Point: The Reverend Abraham Kuyper on Election," 109.

37. Kuyper, *Lectures on Calvinism*, 151.

standing how human participation within culture is a dynamic process that is guided, illuminated, and vivified by the Holy Spirit. This emphasis also sheds light on how humans, guided by the Holy Spirit, participate with God in shaping and transforming the created realm.

Fourth, Gunton's pneumatological emphasis gives clarity to how humans participate in the action of God within the created order (his conception of "perfecting") — and this should be seen as related to his trinitarian account of God's action in the world. Broadly speaking, Gunton's trinitarian focus upholds the unity of God and safeguards against the tendency to separate God's being from his action. While Kuyper does not explicitly separate the act of God from the being of God, there is the tendency, as van der Kooi notes, to see the various forms of God's acts as different "compartments."[38] "The question," van der Kooi asks, "is whether Kuyper's theology does not suffer from a too sharp division of the various doctrines.... [T]he compartmentalizing of his theology likewise appears in the considerable depth of the distinction between the zone of God as the agent of creation and Jesus Christ, the Incarnate Word, as the agent of salvation."[39]

In order to counter this tendency that is found in Kuyper, we would be wise to take into account all of the interrelated actions of the Triune God within the realm of culture. More specifically, developing a theology of culture informed by the work of the Son and Spirit keeps us from the tendency to reduce all the action of Christ as the Incarnate Word to individual salvation. For Gunton, God, in his very nature, is constantly involved in the created world through the Son and Spirit, and this means that to speak of the Trinity means to speak of God's action towards creation. Or, said another way: who God is in his movement and relations towards the created order is who God is in his eternal being.[40]

The relation of the doctrine of the Trinity to the doctrine of creation remains one of the hallmarks of Gunton's theological contributions — but this also influences how we understand elements of culture. To consider culture apart from the work of the Son and Spirit leads to "distinctions within the work of God" and ultimately threatens to ignore the unity of God.[41] On this account, art and culture may display a rationality and wisdom because of the christological and pneumatological dimensions at work within the

---

38. C. van der Kooi, "A Theology of Culture," 99.
39. C. van der Kooi, "A Theology of Culture," 99-100.
40. Gunton, *The Christian Faith*, 101.
41. C. van der Kooi, "A Theology of Culture," 100.

created realm. It is important to note that when we consider the work of both the Son and Spirit within the created order, we move away from the tendency to conceptualize the action of God in various compartmentalized realms within creation, as is sometimes seen in Kuyper. Consequently, art and culture do not remain discontinuous from God's action in the world, but are also related activities when we consider how Christ and the Spirit use these activities to redeem and transform culture through human action.

The doctrine of creation provides the dimension by which one may understand the action and being of the Triune God, i.e. the movement of the Son and Spirit within space and time towards both human and non-human creation. For Gunton, since the being and action of God are inseparable, the Trinity and doctrine of creation are also inseparably related. The unity between God's being and God's action in the world helps us consider how the work of the Son and Spirit, along with human participation within the realm of culture, is a movement of God to bring the entire creation to its intended *telos*. An emphasis on how the Father, Son, and Spirit are all related and involved in creation gives greater clarity to the christological and pneumatological dimensions within the creation and their ramifications for culture.

We have seen how the work of the Spirit makes each particular human activity what it is distinctly supposed to be, and how Gunton highlights the action of the Father, Son, and Holy Spirit as the Triune God is involved in the human activity of culture. Highlighting the work of Christ and the Spirit reminds us that human activity of culture is not only what humans are elected for (Kuyper), but also that culture may operate in transforming both human and non-human creation (Gunton). Thus, Gunton enlarges Kuyper's understanding of the significance of culture and the arts, that is, to see human involvement in the created realm as actually playing a part in shaping and transforming creation into what it is called to be. Moreover, if we are to move towards a more robust Reformed account of culture, I suggest that due consideration must be given not to separate God's being from God's action within creation and culture. In order to do this, I have suggested that greater emphasis needs to be given to how the work of the Son and Spirit are involved and related *(perichoresis)* not only in the created realm, but also more specifically in the human activity of culture. Gunton's insights move us in this direction — from a view of culture that supports discovery of the created realm to a trinitarian view of culture that conceives how humans take part in participating in God's work in the world through cultural activity. In fact, this is why Gunton states that trinitarian theology enables one to rethink "the topics of theology and culture" rather than simply "offering a privileged view of the being of God."[42] In short, our response to culture should always be consistent with what we know about God's purposes, being, and action in creation.[43]

4. Conclusion

As I write this in the context of the United States I recall the particularly difficult relationship that evangelical American Christianity has had with culture, which has largely stemmed from Fundamentalism's reaction against modernity.[44] The evangelical suspicion towards science (particularly Darwinism), along with the lack of constructive theology in how to approach the arts, has left many Christians in America with few resources to draw upon for positively engaging culture. Fundamentalism's influence on the American scene has further encouraged a separatist attitude towards culture among many evangelical Christians, and has posited a soteriology that favors the spiritual over the material. The result is that there has been a deficit of theological reflection in how to view human action in the world.

However, as we have seen, both Kuyper and Gunton offer theological descriptions of human activity in the world. They both urge humans to engage with culture, to take pleasure in making music, creating art, and making spaces beautiful, as these activities are good, and at the most basic level they are part of what it means to be a human creature. To recognize our limits as creatures and carry on with normal "human" activities is good and at the very core of what it means to be human.

What has been highlighted in this essay is how the doctrine of creation ultimately does influence how we understand human culture. Thus, how we understand the value of the world and God's action in the world directly relates to how we conceive of the interaction of humans with the created realm and the shaping of creation through human activity. Both Kuyper and Gunton remind us that the created realm presents a reality that has an order

---

42. The relation between the Trinity and the created realm is a prominent theme in Gunton's work but is much too broad to be able to be discussed in further detail here. Colin E. Gunton, *The Promise of Trinitarian Theology* (Edinburgh: T&T Clark, 1997), xxix.

43. See further: William Dyrness, *The Earth Is God's: A Theology of American Culture* (New York: Orbis Books, 1997), 24.

44. See further: George M. Marsden, *Fundamentalism and American Culture*, 2nd ed. (Oxford: Oxford University Press, 2006), 153-70.

and unity since it is from a good Creator. Consequently, truth is accessible in the world through the secular, not because it proves the existence of God, but because God has fashioned a world that will reveal itself to those who study and explore the created order. This human activity of discovering and exploring creation is an essential element of culture. In addition, correlating creation and culture also encourages an ecclesiology that keeps the church from becoming a theological ghetto where Christians remain isolated from culture. For Gunton, a robust doctrine of creation will ultimately impact the behavior of the church and culture, since "the acid test of any cosmological theory . . . or theology is the ethic it generates."[45] Furthermore, both Kuyper's and Gunton's conception of culture distinguishes how Christians may learn from non-Christians, so that truth may be discovered and human life informed and nourished from sources that are not specifically Christian.

Both Gunton and Kuyper are interested in providing a coherent system for understanding life in God's world and affirming engagement in God's world through a wide variety of human activities. Furthermore, the interconnected nature of humans with their world and environment enables us to locate a theology of culture within the doctrine of creation. Both Gunton and Kuyper support Christian engagement in the world because the world is God's — and both operate with a theology that has a positive attitude towards culture.

Overall, how we understand the importance of the material world ultimately impacts what we do with the created world — it matters in the realm of human development, in how we use (and often misuse) the created realm, and in how we understand humans' ability to discover new truths about the world. In short, one's view of culture is dependent upon one's understanding of the created order. The way that the doctrine of creation is construed will have profound effects on human personhood and on how humans interact with the created order through culture. This vision demonstrates how human life is deeply embedded in the social and relational realms in which the human creature finds herself, and these relations are not separated from the context of creation and redemption.

---

45. Gunton, *Triune Creator*, 225.

The Calvinian Eucharistic Poetics of Emily Dickinson

Jennifer Wang

Emily Dickinson was born in 1830, in Amherst, Massachusetts, to a prominent family of the New England Congregationalist community. Although baptized as a child, she was the only one of her family never to seek official membership in the church, which was prerequisite for participation in Holy Communion, from which she was barred her whole life. This exclusion cannot be said to have been forced upon her, as the only qualification was that one had to "satisfy the community that [one] had experienced the forensic grace that justifies the sinner and puts him or her on the road to glory."[1] Indeed, when examined by Rev. Jonathan Jenkins, she was found to be spiritually sound and eligible for church membership had she only chosen to apply. Her choice not to do so was not so much reflective of a lack of belief or rejection of doctrinal tenets as it was of her "revulsion against the need for public proof of conversion and the subsequent obligations of church members to participate regularly in church service."[2] Hers was a time of high anxiety, as membership to Puritan churches was limited to visible saints, and people were thus pressed to provide signs of conversion to the institutional church before being admitted. I will draw out the tension between the frequent use of Calvinist language (e.g., sacrament, covenant, election) and the recurring theme of exclusion from Communion in Dickinson's poetry, which was discovered only after her death. I will suggest

---

1. Jane Eberwein, "'Graphicer for Grace': Emily Dickinson's Calvinist Language," *Studies in Puritan American Spirituality* 1 (1990): 172.
2. Eberwein, "'Graphicer for Grace,'" 176.

that Dickinson attempted to find a surrogate for the Lord's Table in and through her poetry.

In her seminal 1987 paper "Emily Dickinson and the Calvinist Sacramental Tradition," Jane Donahue Eberwein points out the specifically Calvinist character of Dickinson's language, and more specifically, the relation to the peculiar Puritan Congregationalism of her time. Eberwein dispels the prevalent misinterpretation of Dickinson's sacramental language in light of contexts outside the scope of her knowledge and interaction (e.g., imputing to her a use of the Catholic notion of transubstantiation). Nevertheless, she places more emphasis upon providing a corrective to ill-conceived readings than she does to setting forth a positive alternative.

Having abandoned institutional Calvinism, Dickinson in her poetry evinces a commitment to many of its themes, which had been deeply impressed upon her consciousness. As Eberwein summarizes, "the Congregational churches in America adopted the Savoy Declaration of 1658, which defined sacraments as "holy Signs and Seals of the Covenant of Grace, immediately instituted by Christ to represent him and his benefits and to confirm our interest in him, and solemnly to engage us to the service of God in Christ, according to his Word.'"[3] In line with Calvinist theology, the Westminster Assembly's Catechism for New England Puritan children, which Dickinson would have studied, says of the sacraments, "Christ and the benefits of the new covenant are represented, sealed, and applied to believers." Thus, for Dickinson, a sacrament is meant to unite one to God by the covenant of grace, and is a means by which God strengthens one's faith.

For instance, we see Dickinson declaring her faith with confidence.

> Mine — by the Right of the White Election!
> Mine — by the Royal Seal!
> Mine — by the Sign in the Scarlet prison —
> Bars — cannot conceal!
> Mine — here — in Vision — and in Veto!
> Mine — by the Grave's Repeal —
> Titled — Confirmed —
> Delirious Charter!
> Mine — long as Ages steal!

---

3. Jane Eberwein, "Emily Dickinson and the Calvinist Sacramental Tradition," *ESQ: A Journal of the American Renaissance* 34 (1987): 68.

Here we see that Dickinson professes, or rather exclaims, a personal assurance of faith and election in stark contrast to the insecurities of her Puritan contemporaries. Likewise, Dickinson's attitude toward the concrete practice of Communion in her day as is clearly unfavorable.

> I had been hungry all the years —
> My noon had come — to dine —
> I trembling drew the Table near —
> And touched the Curious Wine —
>
> 'Twas this on Tables I had seen —
> When turning, hungry, Home
> I looked in Windows, for the Wealth
> I could not hope — for Mine —
>
> I did not know the ample Bread —
> 'Twas so unlike the Crumb
> The Birds and I had often shared
> In Nature's — dining-room —
>
> The plenty hurt me — 'twas so new —
> Myself felt ill — and odd —
> As Berry — of a Mountain Bush —
> Transplanted — to the road —
>
> Nor was I hungry — so I found
> That Hunger — was a way
> Of persons outside Windows —
> The entering — takes away —

Initially, the poet's attitude is one of felt exclusion from being denied participation at the Table, and thus of the nourishing experience that the elements were purported to offer. It is her outsider-looking-in mentality, compounded by her affirmation of the meal's weightiness, that increases her sense of both lack and desire. When she approaches the elements, she finds that she is no longer hungry, no longer lacking. Her hunger dissipates at the realization of how similar this bread is to the crumb she enjoys among the birds, and that her feelings of hunger were a symptom of exclusion from a table whose contents are actually quite accessible otherwise — a table that cannot claim an exclusive hold on hope. It appears, then, that she neither abandons the signifying elements nor the hope they signify, but simply a particular exclusionary table. She suggests here that Nature, too, has her own sacramental table, one at which the poet feasts on crumbs together with the birds, and that does not disappoint or exclude.

A sacramental view of Nature shows up elsewhere when Dickinson reflects on the covenant promise of eternal life.

> It will be Summer — eventually.
> Ladies — with parasols —
> Sauntering Gentlemen — with Canes —
> And little Girls — with Dolls —
>
> Will tint the pallid landscape —
> As 'twere a bright Bouquet —
> Thro' drifted deep, in Parian —
> The Village lies — today —
>
> The Lilacs — bending many a year —
> Will sway with purple load —
> The Bees — will not despise the tune —
> Their Forefathers — have hummed —
>
> The Wild Rose — redden in the Bog —
> The Aster — on the Hill
> Her everlasting fashion — set —
> And Covenant Gentians — frill —
>
> Till Summer folds her miracle —
> As Women — do — their Gown —
> Or Priests — adjust the Symbols —
> When Sacrament — is done —

The poem begins with the anticipation of summer, which the poet knows to leave only to return again. The cyclical return of the summer is indicated by the "everlasting fashion" of the aster, and is amply proven by the bees' humming of the hymns of their forefathers — the present in continuity with the past. Nature is eucharistic, and her denizens like the "Covenant Gentians" are the elements. As each seasonal liturgy ends, there is a sacramental remembrance of the covenant of eternal recurrence. As Elizabeth Petrino points out, though, there is a tension in that the alignment of summer, women, and priests means that summer's miracle is divested of spiritual meaning just as when the priest folds up the symbolic elements. Thus, in spite of the regularity of summer/sacrament, doubt is cast upon the certainty of the covenant promise once the elements are gone.[4] The flowers that symbolize the eternal stand against the background of the reddening hills, the setting sun.

In this final poem, the other face of Nature is presented more prominently. We see a possibility of discontinuity emerge with the perpetuation of summer's death following autumn, exposing the enticing fraudulence of a belief otherwise. Dickinson still shifts to calling the summer days a sacrament of Communion in which she wishes to participate, bearing witness to the eternal cycle of nature, but the tension between faith and doubt is still present.

> These are the days when Birds come back —
> A very few — a Bird or two —
> To take a backward look.
>
> These are the days when skies resume
> The old — old sophistries of June —
> A blue and gold mistake.
>
> Oh fraud that cannot cheat the Bee —
> Almost thy plausibility
> Induces my belief.
>
> Till ranks of seeds their witness bear,
> And softly thro' the altered air
> Hurries a timid leaf.
>
> Oh Sacrament of summer days,
> Oh Last Communion in the Haze —
> Permit a child to join —
>
> Thy sacred emblems to partake —
> They consecrated bread to take
> And thine immortal wine!

---

4. Elizabeth Petrino, "Late Bloomer: The Gentian as Sign or Symbol in the Works of Emily Dickinson and Her Contemporaries," *The Emily Dickinson Journal* 14:1 (2005): 115.

Rather than rejecting Calvinism wholesale, it is more probable that Dickinson rejected the specific practices of her Puritan Congregational church, which treated partaking of Communion as evidence of moral transformation, a marker of one's piety, rather than as a reception of grace on behalf of imperfect faith. In her poetry, she questions not the substance of her faith but the type of experience of God that her community expected to be outwardly visible. In other words, she alternates between the doubts and certainties that come with being among the faithful. As Eberwein says, many "less predictable spiritual experiences such as Emily Dickinson's" were not validated.[5] However, if we begin with Calvin's conception of the Table as the place where God quickens one's faith, then it also must be the place where the frailty and insecurity of one's convictions are allowed to be present, and where one begs God by faith to shape that faith so that convictions do not dissipate. Considering her doubts about the fulfillment of the sacramental promise in her contemporaries' actual practice of Communion, and her displacement of true eucharistic participation for herself onto nature, I want to suggest instead that Dickinson adopted a kind of inverted Calvinism.

For Calvin, a sacrament is defined as "an outward sign by which God seals on our consciences the promises of his good will toward us in order to sustain the weakness of our faith."[6] In particular, of Communion, he says that "the Lord instituted for his Supper, in order to sign and seal in our consciences the promises contained in his gospel concerning our being made partakers of his body and blood; and to give us certainty and assurance that in this consists our true spiritual nourishment; so that, having such an earnest, we might entertain a right assurance about salvation."[7] In Communion, then, God assures us that we are truly partaking of Christ's body, just as he said at its institution. In turn, it is also given to cause us to know his saving grace and to exhort us to holiness.

As a sign, the sacrament consists of the elements and the invocation of Christ's instituting words. The reality signified is union with Christ, and the substance of the elements does not undergo transubstantiation or consubstantiation. Although neither magical nor transformed in essence, the elements are more than merely symbolic, being pledges of real presence and

---

5. Eberwein, "'Graphicer for Grace,'" 172.

6. John Calvin, *Institutes of the Christian Religion*, ed. John T. McNeill, trans. Ford Lewis Battles, Library of Christian Classics (Philadelphia: Westminster, 1960), 4.14.1.

7. John Calvin, "A Short Treatise on the Holy Supper of Our Lord and Only Saviour Jesus Christ," in *Calvin: Theological Treatises*, ed. J. K. S. Reid (Philadelphia: Westminster, 1954), 144.

thus neither themselves the reality nor merely symbolic of it. Christ's presence is not localized to the elements, but it is offered through them. We repeat the initial promise in the words that instituted the sacrament, aligning our celebration now with the words of the past. The increase of faith and the union with Christ do not happen because the elements themselves are transformed, but because the Spirit lifts up our souls to heaven to feed on Christ's body and be united to him.

In this picture of the joining of Christ with his elect, there is a union between heaven and earth. Tapping into this intuition, Dickinson sacramentalizes Nature, seeking refuge and eucharistic fulfillment there. The signified remains unchanged, and it is precisely that part which she never gives up, always clinging to the hope of divine union by faith, which we hear in her claim, "Mine!" This union is not merely personal, but cosmic in scope, and so with equal fervency she holds on to the unchanging symbols of creation. Her poetry declares parts of nature to be sacramental elements, sealed with a promise of renewal and received by faith, since that promise cannot be found in nature as such.

But how far can this parallel be taken? In Dickinson's eucharistic poetics, one does not consume Nature as one would bread and wine. However, if we think of communing strictly in terms of participation, we see that Dickinson does identify with Nature's children as a guest at her dining table, becoming a sparrow among birds, a child to the summer days. The words of institution, which here correspond to her written poems, as repeatable parts of the sacrament, are distinguished from the material elements themselves.

An inversion of Calvin's semiotics is evident when we recall that sacraments for him are understood as visible words and appendages to the Word. If Dickinson's poetry is a surrogate for Communion, what is its signified? In "It will be summer — eventually," the "Covenant Gentians" are themselves a sign of the promised endurance of Nature. If the Table is a visible word, pointing to the greater reality of the Word, the words of poetry are a sacrament that points to the greater reality of Nature. In the traditional construction, visible symbols are an aid to contemplating the invisible Word, but for Dickinson, written words point to a visible Nature. The relative arrangement of material and immaterial is thus reversed.

The sacrament of the poem acts as a sign and seal of the prior experience of the promise of Nature. Dickinson does not quietly or bitterly accept rejection from the Table, but attempts to find its essence in her poetry as the place where she asks for God to increase her faith and grant her assurance of salvation. Furthermore, she reverses the traditional subordination of the material by discovering a sacramental capacity in Nature. While Calvin values the physical sacrament insofar as it speaks to us of the unseen Word, Dickinson's immaterial poetry only inadequately reaches toward visible Nature in its resplendent fullness. Yet Dickinson's surrogate eucharistic offering, too, is not without its troubles, and even on the lived horizon of her inversion, she bears the indelible mark of Calvinism and all its anxieties in her corpus. While assuming and not doubting her faith, Dickinson's overriding concern is for a faith transformed from an introspective, self-enclosed piety into an open embrace of even the transient world as a divine pledge while we wait for eternity.

Beautiful Harmony:
Kuyper, Dooyeweerd, and the American Musical Avant-Garde

Janet Danielson

Ten years ago, when genome sequencing revealed that humans have 99 percent of their genes in common, a *Time* magazine article waggishly suggested that one gene that would surely turn up is the gene that makes everyone regret that they quit taking piano lessons.[1] Another sure-to-be-discovered gene is the one that makes people certain that the reformer John Calvin had no sense of, or time for, beauty, and habitually fulminated against it. In view of this genetic predisposition (with apologies to Marilynne Robinson for borrowing her strategy of obscuring Calvin's identity by using his French name[2]), I propose that a Dutch philosophical tradition sometimes dismissed as neo-Calvinist was actually influenced by Renaissance humanist Giovanni Covino, sometime visitor to the court of Ferrara, who fulminated against any who would deprive life of beauty:

> Nor can we shun those things which seem more subservient to delight than to necessity. . . . Has the Lord adorned flowers with all the beauty which spontaneously presents itself to the eye, and the sweet odor which delights the sense of smell, and shall it be unlawful for us to enjoy that beauty and this odor? What? Has he not so distinguished colors as to make some more agreeable than others? [. . .] In short, has he not given

---

1. Sarah Vowell, "Instant Piano for the Busy and Lazy," *Time Magazine*, 9 October 2000.

2. Marilynne Robinson refers to Calvin as *Jean Cauvin* in order avoid "the almost comically negative associations of 'John Calvin.'" See Robinson's essay "Marguerite of Navarre," in *The Death of Adam: Essays on Modern Thought* (New York: Houghton Mifflin, 1998), 174-75.

many things a value without having any necessary use? Have done, then, with that inhuman philosophy which, in allowing no use of the creatures but for necessity, not only maliciously deprives us of the lawful fruit of the divine beneficence, but cannot be realized without depriving man of all his senses, and reducing him to a block.[3]

"Covino's" ideas were taken up by Abraham Kuyper (1837-1920): "God in His Revelation always recommends the Beautiful. Even of Christ it is said: Thou art fairer than the children of men."[4] Kuyper considered art to be "a most serious power," asserting that "the beautiful is not the product of our own fantasy, nor of our subjective perception, but has an objective existence, being itself the expression of a Divine perfection."[5]

Kuyper's championing of beauty within a "Covinist" framework was taken up by Dutch philosopher Herman Dooyeweerd (1894-1977), who understood "beautiful harmony" to be the very core of the aesthetic mode of meaning. However, for the "neo-Covs" in generations subsequent to Dooyeweerd, as for most philosophers of aesthetics of the past century, beautiful harmony has been at best a wallflower, more often simply not invited to the dance.[6]

Yet in my field, music composition, there has been a re-embracing of harmony — indeed, of beautiful harmony — undergirded by careful research and philosophical re-conceptualization on the part of some key composers of the American postwar avant-garde, including John Cage (1912-1992) and James Tenney (1934-2006). In this paper I will explore some concepts common to Kuyper, Dooyeweerd, and these musical mavericks: naïve experience, the epoché, the nature/freedom dichotomy, the root, and harmony itself. Having held these concepts in creative tension for some time, I feel that an exploration of the admittedly tenuous links between these disparate and sometimes opposing schools of thought may be fruitful.

Harmony, prior to modernism, was seen as having cosmic significance.

---

3. John Calvin, "On the Christian Life," in *Institutes of the Christian Religion* II.iii.10 (Grand Rapids: Wm. B. Eerdmans, 1975), 31-33.

4. Abraham Kuyper, *The Antithesis between Symbolism and Revelation* (Amsterdam: Höveker & Wormser, 1857), 23, accessed 7 June 2008, OL23278267M.

5. Abraham Kuyper, *Lectures on Calvinism* (Grand Rapids: Eerdmans, 1975), 151, 156.

6. For example, Calvin G. Seerveld, "Dooyeweerd's Legacy for Aesthetics: Modal Law Theory," in *The Legacy of Herman Dooyeweerd: Reflections on Critical Philosophy in the Christian Tradition,* edited by C. T. McIntire (Lanham, Md.: University Press of America, 1985), 64-66.

For the ancient Greeks, harmony — the ordering principle in both the macrocosm of the universe and the microcosm of the human soul — was conceived within a rather static framework of ultimate perfection.[7] The Jewish and Christian cosmos, however, was one of dynamic mediation and ultimate cosmic reconciliation in which harmony modeled the "operation of God."[8] From within this tradition Kuyper understood Christ's creative power as the Word or speech of God, animating both nature and human conscience, thereby guaranteeing a correspondence between what we perceive in nature and what we value as right and good.

> Both this speech of God in nature and this speech of God in our conscience, thanks to our reconciliation in Christ, obtain for us an altogether different sound, increase in clearness and in meaning, and are now heard by the opened ear in a purity, which to our perception unites the life of grace with the life of nature in glorious harmony, and turns the whole world . . . into one mighty revelation of the Father.[9]

Dooyeweerd's student paper on Wagner has strong Kuyperian echoes:

> Let the soul be restored through the second birth, and let the veil be torn from our eyes. With great astonishment, we now see the unity and beauty of all creation. The light of transfiguration breaks through and illumines all of life, which is now deepened to an infinite perspective, and experienced in its marvelous harmony.[10]

For Kuyper and for Dooyeweerd, harmony was a manifestation of ultimate beauty and wholeness, a beauty and wholeness which cannot be contained within the limits of human experience, although its resonance can "break through" to the "opened ear."

James Tenney is known for his spectralist and process-oriented compo-

---

7. Leo Spitzer, *Classical and Christian Ideas of World Harmony* (Baltimore: Johns Hopkins Press, 1963), 11-12.

8. "harmony, n." OED Online, accessed 5 April 2011. http://www.oed.com.proxy.lib.sfu.ca/view/Entry/84303?redirectedFrom=harmony.

9. Abraham Kuyper, *To Be Near Unto God* (Vancouver: Regent College Publishing, 2005), 348-49.

10. Herman Dooyeweerd, "De Troosteloosheid van Het Wagnerianisme" [The Comfortlessness of Wagnerianism], in *Opbouw*, Vol. 2 (1915), 112, my translation. See Glenn Friesen's more recent translation at http://www.members.shaw.ca/hermandooyeweerd/wagnerianism.html.

sitions. A Juilliard graduate and student of Edgard Varèse, John Cage, and Harry Partch, Tenney did pioneering work in computer-generated music as composer-in-residence at Bell Labs in the 1960s. He went on to develop the concept of harmonic space. Tenney approached harmony through phenomenology and Gestalt psychology, and liked to quote psychologist Kurt Koffka's definition of phenomenology: "as naïve and full a description of direct experience as possible." For Tenney, phenomenology "begins with experience . . . and continually returns to experience as both the foundation and final arbiter of knowledge,"[11] bypassing the morass of musical ontology and overcoming the limitations of more culturally-bound musical philosophies. But Tenney was not naïve about the limitations of naïve experience; he realized that naïve experience could not fully account for its connections to its objective correlates, and needed to be confirmed by rational deduction and empirical evidence: "Such considerations are at least as important as 'intersubjective dialogue' in preventing phenomenological descriptions from degenerating into mere exercises in solipsism."[12] What really prevents us, Tenney asked, "from simply projecting — onto the object of our description — some condition that properly belongs to ourselves?"[13]

Dooyeweerd's view of naïve experience, like Koffka's, involves directness and fullness, but is rather more dynamic. In naïve experience, "we experience reality in an indivisible coherence of cosmic time"[14] which refracts like colors through a prism into a diversity of temporal and experiential modes. Each mode in turn ultimately refers to a transcendent fullness of meaning. For Dooyeweerd, naïve experience, though not ultimately foundational, "is the temporal basic layer of all cognition" which makes theoretical insight possible.[15] But the experiencing ego is "determined and limited"[16] by being rooted in a deeper fullness of meaning found in a three-way relation of the self to its divine Origin, its interpersonal community of fellow humans, and its temporal world. In contrast, the "phenomenological attitude" requires that the ego transcend meaning in order to become the "constitutive origin of meaning."[17]

---

11. James Tenney, review of "Music as Heard: A Study in Applied Phenomenology by Thomas Clifton," *Journal of Music Theory* 29:1 (Spring 1985): 200.
12. Tenney, "Music as Heard," 204.
13. Tenney, "Music as Heard," 212.
14. Herman Dooyeweerd, *New Critique of Theoretical Thought*, Vol. III (Philadelphia: The Presbyterian and Reformed Publishing Company, 1969), 29.
15. Dooyeweerd, *New Critique* II, 475.
16. Dooyeweerd, *New Critique* I, 12.
17. Dooyeweerd, *New Critique* II, 489.

So though Dooyeweerd had himself been influenced by Husserl's philosophy, which he said "has indeed penetrated to an a priori level of philosophical thought which had never been seen so sharply in the earlier Humanistic views," its appearance of being unbiased, he argued, was deceptive.[18]

Although Tenney depended upon the rational and the empirical to correct any misperceptions of naïve experience, the rational and empirical are not always reliable. Dooyeweerd points out that the rational always involves some degree of abstraction, which is resisted in the naïve view, and that experiments are not independent of analytical thought.[19] Furthermore, the empirical sometimes delivers less than it promises — for example, in Tenney's definition of musical pitch: "Pitch is a perceptual quality that is somehow synthesized by the auditory system in response to a physical stimulus which, from a certain point of view, is nothing but a periodic variation of amplitude with time."[20]

However, despite its limitations, phenomenology's legitimization of naïve experience offered a rationale for Tenney's acoustic and harmonic research in a particularly chilly climate for harmony. "Faith in the magic power of the old rules of harmony is fast disappearing," wrote composer Paul Hindemith in 1943, prognosticating a future in which "hardly anyone will feel a great desire to spend more time in the acquisition of harmonic knowledge than is absolutely necessary."[21] Cage's teacher Arnold Schoenberg proclaimed in 1949 that he had "establish[ed] the law of the emancipation of the dissonance."[22] Under the covert "cultural cold war" policies of the CIA and the US Army, harmony — at least in the world of American high culture — was considered subversive.[23] Composer Aaron Copland was shamed into giving up the use of harmony and melody in his compositions. But shielded by the discourse of phenomenological investigation in the high-tech bastion of Bell Labs, Tenney's harmonic research was bulletproof.

18. Dooyeweerd, *New Critique* II, 487.
19. Dooyeweerd, *New Critique* I, 561.
20. Tenney, "Music as Heard," 203.
21. Paul Hindemith, *A Concentrated Course in Traditional Harmony*, Book 1 (New York: Schott Music Corporation, 1968), iii.
22. Arnold Schoenberg, "My Evolution (1949)," in *Style and Idea: Selected Writings of Arnold Schoenberg*, ed. Leonard Stein with translations by Leo Black (New York: St. Martin's Press, 1975), 91.
23. Amy C. Beal. "Negotiating Cultural Allies: American Music in Darmstadt, 1946-1956," *Journal of the American Musicological Society* 53:1 (Spring 2000): 105-39. See also Frances Stonor Saunders, *Who Paid the Piper? The CIA and the Cultural Cold War* (London: Granta Books, 1999).

Another important concept for both Tenney and Dooyeweerd is epoché, or bracketing, which Tenney understood as a "suspension of belief in virtually everything,"[24] in favor of a reliance on intuition. Tenney credited composer John Cage with helping clear the ground: "His work encourages us to re-examine all of our old habits of thought, our assumptions, and our definitions."[25] In short, Cage stripped music down to what was essential. Cage is best known for *4′33″*, his famous work for pianist David Tudor in which the pianist sits silent but poised to play for 4′33″, and the "music" consists of only the ambient sounds of the performance space and audience. Tenney situates Cage's approach within a phenomenological programme of renunciations.[26] For Husserl, "The renunciation of the world, the 'bracketing of the world,' did not mean that henceforth the world was no longer our focus at all, but that the world had to become our focus in a new way, at a whole level deeper."[27]

Husserl's strategy of epoché enabled Tenney to avoid pitfalls into which Schoenberg and Hindemith had been led. He could see assumptions in their theories that were every bit as dubious as those they were intended to replace. "Schoenberg talked about the emancipation of the dissonance, so that means it doesn't have to resolve anymore. So that means it's actually the emancipation of the composer from resolving the dissonance."[28] In acoustics, however, Tenney found "a really important area where there's something to learn that is given."[29] Acoustics brackets off the physical aspect of sound and provides empirical evidence about the nature of musical experience.

Dooyeweerd also used the term *epoché*, but in contrast to Husserl, considered it "impossible to eliminate the religious starting-point of theoretical thought."[30] For Dooyeweerd, epoché signified an abstraction from the temporal continuity of the cosmic coherence of meaning,[31] and must start by

---

24. Tenney, "Music as Heard," 200.

25. James Tenney, "John Cage and the Theory of Harmony," accessed online 18 March 2011, www.plainsound.org/pdfs/JC%26ToH.pdf, 4. Also in *Writings about John Cage*, ed. Richard Kostelanetz (Ann Arbor: University of Michigan Press, 1983), 139-61.

26. Tenney, "John Cage," 21.

27. Edmund Husserl, *Phenomenology and Anthropology*, June 1931, trans. Thomas Sheehan and Richard E. Palmer, www.stanford.edu/dept/relstud/faculty/sheehan.bak/.../g-phenan.pdf, 7.

28. Ciarán Maher, "James Tenney on Intention, Harmony and Phenomenology — A Different View of the Big Picture," *Musicworks* 77 (2000): 7.

29. Maher, "James Tenney," 6.

30. Dooyeweerd, *New Critique* II, 74.

31. Dooyeweerd, *New Critique* II, 468-69n1.

eliminating philosophical prejudices.[32] But just what is this cosmic coherence of meaning?

One of Kuyper's great insights was that institutions which arise to ameliorate the effects of the brokenness of the world — such as state, church, and society — each have "sphere sovereignty," a legitimate sovereignty in their own respective spheres. Dooyeweerd elaborated this concept into a dynamic world-structure of diverse, mutually irreducible spheres or modal aspects of meaning. Within this structure, categories such as "substance" and "thing" are replaced by a broader category, "structures of individuality." Unlike substances and things, structures of individuality do not so much "exist" as "function within" the modal aspects of meaning. Dooyeweerd provisionally lists fifteen of these modal aspects, each with its nucleus or kernel of meaning. "Beautiful harmony," for Dooyeweerd, is the nucleus of the aesthetic aspect. A nucleus is multivocal, eluding analysis; rather, its sense unfolds in a diversity of "analogical moments" as seen from the other aspects.[33] Dooyeweerd's insight that the analytical is just one aspect of many, and that in its epoché it abstracts its analytical object from the continuity of cosmic time, militates against the privileging of theoretical thought.

Dooyeweerd's epoché more rigorously identifies possible pitfalls than Husserl's does. In observing the function of an individuality structure within each aspect, we are able to discern absolutizations which we might otherwise overlook. For example, Schoenberg's unexamined allegiance to the absolute claims of history relativized any appeal to the properties of harmony or to the nature of aural perception. And Tenney's reliance on acoustics, though it helped him see through historical constructions, provided a confining platform for the development of any kind of musical aesthetic. Hence much of his music consists of an unfolding process, sometimes of a single harmonic series. Within the physical mode, there is no rationale for melody, so generally Tenney refrained from writing melodic music.[34]

Dooyeweerd distinguished modes of experience from basic orientations or ground-motives, which are directed toward the Absolute, transcending the temporal. If this orientation is misdirected toward a temporal aspect, then dualisms and reductionisms arise. It is important to note that such an

---

32. Dooyeweerd, *New Critique* II, 72.

33. Herman Dooyeweerd, *In the Twilight of Western Thought* (Nutley, N.J.: Craig Press, 1968), 9.

34. Outside of contemporary Western music, music without melody is virtually an oxymoron, except where instruments which can sustain pitch are not used, as for example drumming traditions.

orientation is not necessarily a matter of personal faith, but rather "lies at the foundation of a community of thought,"[35] often outside an individual's conscious awareness. An example is the enlightenment nature/freedom ground motive, in which nature is seen not as the "speech of God" but as something inert whose operations are mechanistically determined, offering infinite possibilities to satisfy the absolute creative freedom of mankind.[36]

As Bruno Latour has recently pointed out, those in the grip of an absolutist dualism have a compelling need to purify — to categorize everything in terms of one or the other sides of the dualism, eliminating any possibility of a real Absolute; it is upon such purification, according to Latour, that the entire project and agenda of modernism depends.[37] Latour's analysis strikingly echoes Kuyper's prescient aphorism: "Modernism is bound to build a world of its own from the data of the natural man, and to construct man himself from the data of nature."[38]

Cage's renunciations can be seen as a kind of ultimate purification. By "letting sounds be" — that is, by refusing to legitimate the human habits and traditions of music-making, he took artistic freedom to its logical extreme. His work can be read as a brilliant exposé of modernist absolutism, revealing what remains when the process of purification is complete:

> The novelty of our work derives therefore from our having moved away from simply private human concerns toward the world of nature and society of which all of us are a part. Our intention is to affirm this life, not to bring order out of chaos nor to suggest improvements in creation, but simply to wake up to the very life we're living, which is so excellent once one gets one's mind and one's desires out of its way and lets it act of its own accord.[39]

Was this nature/freedom dualism operative in Tenney's thought and work? Artistic freedom was an overriding force in Tenney's life and thought: when confronted with evidence that the careers of paragons of artistic freedom like Jackson Pollock and possibly Cage himself were underwritten by the

---

35. Dooyeweerd, *Twilight*, 33.
36. Dooyeweerd, *Twilight*, 47.
37. Bruno Latour, *We Have Never Been Modern* (Cambridge: Harvard University Press, 1993), 10-11, 58.
38. Kuyper, *Lectures on Calvinism*, 11.
39. John Cage, "Experimental Music" (1957), in *Silences* (Cambridge: MIT Press, 1969), 95.

CIA and the American army, he sat in stunned silence for a moment, and then exclaimed, "Well, the CIA finally did something right!"[40] It was also important to him that nature and culture be carefully distinguished: "Some things we work with are culturally determined and some are actually physically, or mathematically determined; and they need to be learned as the basis for possibilities."[41]

Tenney correctly identified the theory of harmony in its present form as mere historical musicology, a set of rules of etiquette derived from "masterworks" from the post-Renaissance European past, and he worked hard to provide something better. Yet behind his call for a theory of musical perception that was aesthetically neutral, culturally general, and quantitatively verifiable — in his words, "a truly scientific theory"[42] — lurks a strategy for guaranteeing the creative freedom of the composer. In Tenney's important paper "John Cage and the Theory of Harmony," he emphasizes Cage's desire for absolute freedom with Cage quotations such as: "My philosophy in a nutshell. Get out of whatever cage you happen to be in."[43] Indeed: but the trick is knowing a cage when you see one.

One final theme common to Tenney, Kuyper, Dooyeweerd, and to harmony itself, is that of the root. For Kuyper,

> It is the central emotion, the central impulse, and the central animation, in the mystical root of our being, which seeks to reveal itself to the outer world.... Art is also no side-shoot on a principal branch, but an independent branch that grows from the trunk of life itself.... Would it not be both a degradation and an underestimation of art, if you were to imagine the ramifications, into which the art-trunk divides itself, to be independent of the deepest root which all human life has in God?[44]

Dooyeweerd saw the character of the entire created cosmos as one of referring and expressing. "Meaning is the being of all that has been created,"[45] including the I as central point of reference which transcends the boundary of time in a regenerated fullness of meaning. This transcendence is made possi-

---

40. In conversation with the author, Vancouver, Spring 2005.
41. Maher, "James Tenney," 6.
42. Tenney, "John Cage," 3, 9.
43. John Cage, *Diary: How to Improve the World . . . Continued, 1971-1972*; quoted in Tenney, "John Cage," 16.
44. Kuyper, *Lectures on Calvinism*, 150, 151.
45. Dooyeweerd, *New Critique* I, 4.

ble through participation in Christ, the new root of the temporal cosmos who reconciles all things to himself, a transcendent central unity of being in which the temporal peripheral diversity of meaning finds its root.

Tenney acknowledged (rather tentatively) a "creative force" beyond his own creativity. Speaking of his role as composer, he said:

> It's not going to happen unless I do it, but it's not about me. I think we're all channels, in a certain sense, for a creative process which already exists in the universe. . . . Biological evolution is a manifestation of a creative process which is inherent in matter, or inherent in the material world.[46]

But a much more specific explication of rootedness is Tenney's magnificent last work, *Arbor Vitae* (Tree of Life) for string quartet, completed only two weeks before his death in 2006. The tonal material of *Arbor Vitae* is derived from a single harmonic series branching up to the 1331st partial. Winter's impressive visual schematic (see p. 112) hardly does it justice; in the sonic *Arbor Vitae*, a rooted plenitude of multidimensional richness and splendor is instantiated in the listener's experience.

Dooyeweerd's suite of experiential aspects starts with number and ends with faith. He considered these to be the two "window aspects" — the aspects which most closely approach the supratemporal. It is tempting to imagine Tenney at the numerical window and Dooyeweerd at the faith window, both in the thrall of a compelling supratemporal vision — or, better, supratemporal symphony.

But the present reality is a situation in which young musicians with enormous creative gifts are given no clear sense of where to direct them. A sense of direction is difficult to provide in a climate in which it has become rude to assume that what is beautiful to you might also be beautiful to others. Beauty, we are told, is unquantifiable, socially constructed, a throwback, elitist, merely subjective. One wonders at some arts events if mundane abasement has become the new transcendent beauty.

Dooyeweerd would argue that the nature/freedom model sets up insoluble antinomies which undermine the coherence and meaningfulness of human experience, including the experience of beauty. He would argue further that the nature/freedom model is every bit as religious as the biblical narrative of creation, fall, and redemption which it intended to replace. Let us compare the nature/freedom paradigm with the biblical narrative musically

---

46. Maher, "James Tenney," 4.

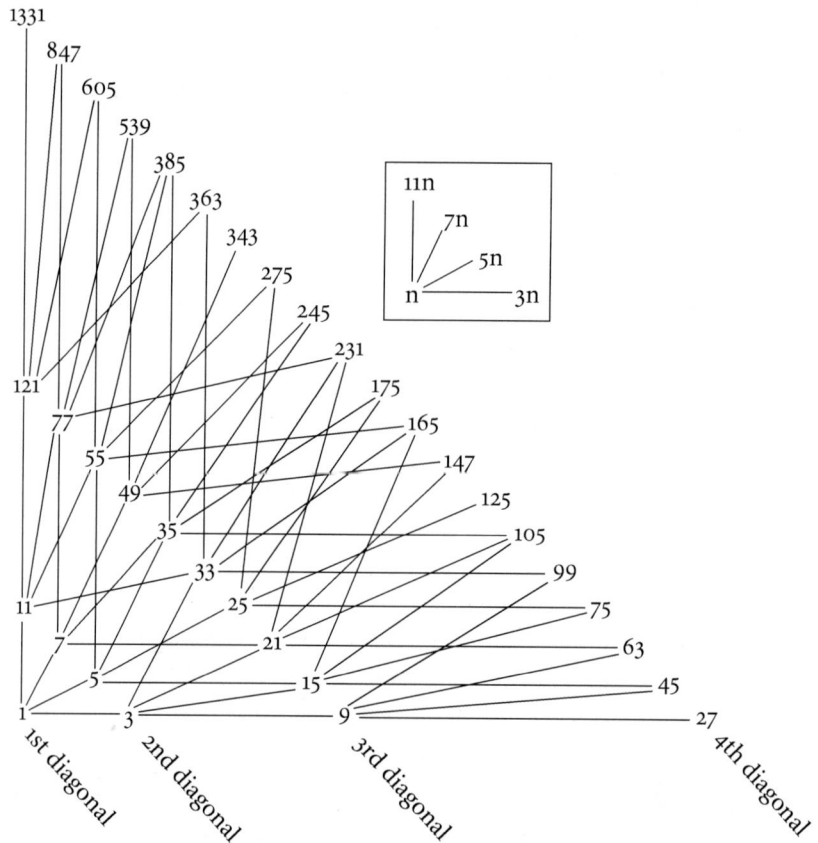

Schematic of James Tenney's *Arbor Vitae* by Michael Winter. The numbers refer to the harmonics of the tone B flat (B flat is 1).[47]

rather than philosophically. The biblical narrative is the one in which "Western," "common practice," or "goal-oriented" music emerged: a kind of music unprecedented on the world scene, featuring simultaneous tones strategically placed so as to give the impression of forward motion towards a resolution. Because James Tenney's music stands outside this "common practice" tradition, it makes a good test case: he does not so much compose in the traditional sense, but rather, he sets up certain conditions under which sounds will interact in interesting ways. Sound is essentially evidence for energy, so

47. Michael Winter, "On James Tenney's Arbor Vitae for String Quartet," *Contemporary Music Review* 27:1 (2008): 134.

it could fairly be said that Tenney's music affords us an experience of the properties and behaviors of energy. But even the term "energy" may be implicated in the reductionist program: during Kuyper's lifetime, it was still assumed by scientists to be a living force *(vis viva)*.[48]

Tenney's *Critical Band* (1988), for large ensemble and tape (or digital) delay, is like a sonic linear accelerator. It starts with a long unison A440, the pitch to which orchestras tune. Very gradually, the instruments diverge from one another in precise increments. The process is slow enough to invite the listener to become an observer in this sonic laboratory; yet in listening, one becomes not only an observer but also a subject of the experiment. In *Critical Band*'s opening minutes, a pure and unified energy activates one specific location on the basilar membrane in our inner ears, where long stereocilia — hair cells — bow and bend in response. Furthermore, to any pure and unified energy excitation, our ears add "otoacoustic" (ear-generated) sound emissions in harmony with the exterior tone. We are usually unaware of these harmonies, but they are measurable in the auditory nerves.[49] Thus each listener also becomes part of the orchestra. It is not easy to endure such a long pure tone; we wait impatiently for some motion or event.

How do we experience this pure A440 from within the nature/freedom model? We may feel pinned down by its immobility, or focus on the shimmering variations of tone color as the various instruments stop for breath and reenter the continuing tonal thread. We may question the freedom of a composer to make a large group of people pay attention to so little, or be grateful that human creativity can offer a rare opportunity to experience energy in such a pure form. We may ponder the nature of unity, or of the origin of the cosmos.

But is it not an opening and deepening of experience to hear in every

---

48. "Descending from the planetary space and firmament to the surface of our earth, we find a vast variety of phenomena connected with the conversion of living force and heat into one another, which speak in language which cannot be misunderstood of the wisdom and beneficence of the Great Architect of nature. . . . Indeed the phenomena of nature, whether mechanical, chemical or vital, consist almost entirely of a continual conversion of attraction through space [gravity], living force [*vis viva*, or energy], and heat into one another. Thus it is that order is maintained in the universe — nothing is deranged, nothing ever lost, but the entire machinery, complicated as it is, works smoothly and harmoniously [. . .] the whole being governed by the sovereign will of God." James Joule, "Matter, Living Force and Heat," in *The Scientific Papers of James Prescott Joule (1884)*, accessed 27 April 2011, http://openlibrary.org/books/OL239730M/The_scientific_papers_of_James_Prescott _Joule272-273.

49. Arthur H. Benade, *Horns, Strings and Harmony* (New York: Doubleday, 1960), 80-81.

pure tone echoes of the Spirit hovering over the face of the waters? Jewish philosopher André Neher's interpretation of creation has strong musical resonances:

> The universe is not a parenthesis within God. He penetrates and permeates it, without however identifying Himself with it. This is the biblical "panentheism," which has rightly been interpreted as the original Hebraic response to the transcendentalism and pantheism of philosophers.... It is the "Word" which effects [God's] entry. In the third verse (of Genesis 1) God speaks and the "Word" is ingrained in the world, becomes incarnate in the thing created. Each new "Word" of God evokes a new phase of Creation. The "Word" of God ... is the Rhythm of Creation.[50]

As *Critical Band* progresses and the tones gradually diverge from a pure unison, we become aware of motion in the form of regular gentle pulsations or fluctuations of amplitude, known as "beats": rhythm is indeed the first audible evidence of the process of divergence from the central root tone.

Toward the middle of *Critical Band,* the gap between tones widens by microtonal increments, moving into a perceptual zone known as the "critical band," from which Tenney's piece takes its name. Simultaneous tones within a range of less than a minor third (the "critical band") generate electrical interference — static — in the auditory nerves, obscuring the individual tones. The sensation, also known as distortion, can be unpleasant, though if it is brief enough it can also provide a sensation of sparkle or buzz. If *Critical Band*'s departure from unison into gentle beats evokes a primordial originating Rhythm, the middle section of Tenney's piece indicates a boundary in human hearing. We simply cannot resolve interference between tones that sound within the auditory critical band. Tenney's provision of the digital delay as a continual reference prevents performers from losing memory of the originating tone and getting lost in the chaos of dissonance. Yet even with the delay system, *Critical Band* demands utmost precision and control on the part of the performers, because they must eventually diverge into consonance. While neither Tenney nor the "neo-Cov" philosophers would be justly served by a simplistic equation of the critical band with the Fall, there is no denying the discomforting effect of the sustained irreconcilable tones in the middle section of *Critical Band,* and the need for a fixed (in this case, nonhuman) pitch reference if harmony is ever to be restored.

---

50. André Neher, "The View of Time and History in Jewish Culture," in *Cultures and Time,* ed. Louis Gardet (Paris: Unesco, 1976), 153-54.

Towards the end of his life, John Cage could see that the ideal of artistic freedom had not effected much positive change in the world. In his 1990 Darmstadt lecture, he lamented that New York had become a city of homelessness and AIDS. He had hoped that the freedom and acceptance he had modeled in his composition would extend to all reality, yet things had become worse, not better. But he said he had found one consolation: "I no longer consider it necessary to find alternatives to harmony. After all these years, I am finally writing beautiful music."[51] He credited James Tenney with revealing to him the true nature of harmony: on his lecture handout was this mesostic:[52]

> alTernatives
> to Harmony
> lifE spent finding them beating my head
> against a wall now haRmony
> has changEd
> its nAture it comes back to you it has no laws
> there is no alternative to it how Did that happen
> first of all james tenneY

In the final minutes of *Critical Band,* the tones eventually glide out of the roughness into a radiant harmony, an audible version of the otoacoustic harmony with which our ears responded to the pure originating tone. The effect is stunningly beautiful. Ciarán Maher reports, "On hearing Tenney's composition *Critical Band* (1988), Cage renounced his fifty-year antagonism to harmony, saying, 'If that's harmony, I take back everything I ever said. I'm all for it.'"[53]

Critical Band demonstrates that a single originating tone slowly diverging into harmony affords us an immediate experience of unity, chaotic disruption, and beautiful reconciliation. Dooyeweerd's essay on Wagnerianism (quoted earlier) connects redemption with the experience of harmony and a direction of love:

---

51. Notes taken by the author at Cage's lecture, Darmstadt, Summer 1990.
52. In the mesostic, entitled "Readymade Boomerang," Cage's phrase, "It has no laws, there is no alternative to it," is almost like a twist of Calvin's formulation, *Deus solus legibus solutus est, sed non exlex* (God alone is not subject to law, but is not arbitrary).
53. Maher, "James Tenney," 7.

But now: let the soul be restored through the second birth, and let the veil be torn from our eyes. With great astonishment, we now see the unity and the beauty of all creation. The light of transfiguration breaks through and illumines all of life, which is now deepened to an infinite perspective, and experienced in its marvelous harmony. Now we search out the essence of things not in themselves, but in their fulfillment. Our lives acquire direction; we now seek the Sun of life, who dawns on the golden horizon, and toward whom all creation now directs itself in great love.[54]

Powerful resonances of this grand narrative enrich and vivify our musical experience, even in an experimental process piece like Tenney's *Critical Band*. They ring true. The boundaries between the physical, the aesthetic, and the transcendent prove to be permeable. Perhaps unsurpassed in its articulation of this unspeakable wonder is George Herbert's poem "Easter":

> Awake, my lute, and struggle for thy part
>   With all thy art.
> The crosse taught all wood to resound his name,
>   Who bore the same.
> His stretched sinews taught all strings, what key
> Is best to celebrate this most high day.
>
> Consort both heart and lute, and twist a song
>   Pleasant and long:
> Or since all musick is but three parts vied
>   And multiplied;
> O let thy blessed Spirit bear a part,
> And make up our defects with his sweet art.[55]

---

54. Dooyeweerd, "Wagnerianism" (1915), 112.
55. http://www.luminarium.org/sevenlit/herbert/easter.htm

From Neo-Calvinism to *Broadway Boogie Woogie:* Abraham Kuyper as the Jilted Stepfather of Piet Mondrian

James D. Bratt

On the face of it, Abraham Kuyper and Piet Mondrian make a most unlikely pair. The Dutch painter is an icon of Modern art, devoted to its program of constant innovation that was intended to call forth a "new man" required for a radically new age. Kuyper, on the other hand, made theological Modernism the target of the early speech that established his reputation, characterizing it as a passing illusion that should be rejected for traditional orthodoxy.[1] Mondrian's relentless simplification of painting down to its bare essentials — straight lines, right angles, and three primary colors — casts the greatest possible contrast to Kuyper's baroque style, indeed, constitutes a fair image of that "uniformity" which Kuyper declared to be "the curse of modern life."[2] There was nothing Kuyper favored more than organic form, the very ideal Mondrian wished to negate with his severe abstractionism. The two would likely agree, however, in identifying religion as their greatest point of difference. Kuyper, the devotee of classic Calvinism, sought to restore the consciousness that all things are subject to the Lordship of Christ. Late in his career he singled out the rising tide of mysticism and spiritualism as eroding that sensibility. Mondrian swam in precisely those waters, joining the Theo-

---

1. Abraham Kuyper, *Het Modernisme: een Fata Morgana op christelijke gebied* (Amsterdam: H. de Hoogh, 1871); English translation: "Modernism: A Fata Morgana in the Christian Domain," in James D. Bratt, ed., *Abraham Kuyper: A Centennial Reader* (Grand Rapids: Eerdmans, 1998), 87-124.

2. Abraham Kuyper, *Eenvormigheid: De Vloek van het Modern Leven* (Amsterdam: H. de Hoogh, 1869); E.T.: "Uniformity: The Curse of Modern Life," in Bratt, ed., *Abraham Kuyper: A Centennial Reader,* 19-44.

sophical Society of Amsterdam at the moment when he decisively broke from his inherited aesthetic toward the radically new.

Yet their life circumstances and aesthetic positions require that we pair these two men anyway: Mondrian was reared in a decidedly Kuyperian household and joined Kuyper's church while undertaking his advanced art studies in Amsterdam, even living with Kuyper's publisher. More importantly, I will argue, even in his Modernist maturity he espoused a set of aesthetic principles that bear remarkable resemblances to those which Kuyper set forth on Calvinist grounds. Both men called upon the artist to delve beneath appearances and project in visible form a universal spiritual truth that would approximate the perfect end of human life. This is not to minimize the substantial differences between their respective visions, nor to argue that his Kuyperian upbringing by itself determined the path to Mondrian's mature aesthetic. It is to say, first, that Mondrian's native Calvinism needs to be added to the catalogue of spiritual influences that are typically adduced to explain the views of this most intently philosophical of Modern artists; and second, that the points of similarity between Kuyper's philosophy of art and Mondrian's are worth extrapolating in some detail. Put briefly: Mondrian's abstract art can be added to the catalogue of the products and inadvertent by-products of Neo-Calvinism. *Broadway Boogie Woogie,* Mondrian's penultimate famous work of art and testament to his love of the New York jazz scene of his day, is what you get if you filter Neo-Calvinism through Cézanne and vent the result in the fresh free air of New York City in the 1940s.

*   *   *

Piet Mondrian was born at Amersfoort in 1872 to a father of the same name who was principal of the local Christian school.[3] In 1880 the family relocated to Winterswijk, near the German border, where Piet Sr. held a similar position and continued his avocation as a good amateur artist. Mondrian pere was a native of The Hague and had been educated there at the school of Guillaume Groen van Prinsterer, Abraham Kuyper's hero, teacher, and sponsor, and thus a main root of Kuyper's neo-Calvinist program. The central

---

3. On Mondrian's childhood and father, see Herbert Henkels, *Mondrian: From Figuration to Abstraction* (Tokyo: Tokyo Shimbun, 1987), 145-52. The family spelled its name Mondriaan, which Piet Jr. shortened to Mondrian upon moving to Paris in 1911. This article observes the latter practice for clarity's sake.

initiative in that program was to create a national network of Christian dayschools; Piet Sr. undertook his career as part of that crusade. He soon became one of Kuyper's collaborators in campaigns to protect Christian schools from hostile public policy or to advance them under fairer conditions. This was the galvanizing issue behind the formation of Kuyper's independent Calvinist Antirevolutionary political party (ARP); Mondrian pere was the head of its incipient Amersfoort chapter. Perhaps the pressure of performing in that role up to Kuyper's exacting standards helped prompt the family's move to Winterswijk, but even there Piet Sr. continued to receive invitations from Kuyper to work on his newspaper or to contribute visuals for ARP promotion and propaganda campaigns. An outstanding effort to this end was a lithograph Piet Sr. executed in 1874, "The Revolution or the Gospel." Designed in collaboration with Kuyper himself, it portrayed the Dutch political scene as a confrontation between two antithetical powers in which God's faithful were called to join the heroic lineage arrayed on the right side of the print over against the chaos laid out on the left.[4] The work combined classical ornament with Victorian flourish in a cause at once religious and patriotic.

Piet Jr. not only grew up in this atmosphere but took to it. Upon declaring his wish to become a professional artist, he followed his father's advice to take exams to qualify as an art educator, then studied on scholarship for two years at the National Academy of Art in Amsterdam. In that period (1892-95) he lived at a residence on Kalverstraat owned by J. A. Wormser, Kuyper's chief publisher.[5] Piet Jr.'s most notable, if barely known, product in these years was not executed at the Academy, however, but for his father's school in Winterswijk: a large (150 × 250 cm) semi-circular painting probably designed to fit over the school's entryway and entitled "Thy Word is Truth." The painting is filled with Christian imagery evoking the circle of life, all of it gathered around a Bible captioned "Romans 5:1." (The words actually inscribed on the page, however, are the text of Romans 8:38-39.[6]) Thus citing the beginning and ending of the Apostle Paul's great essay on justification by faith, the painting is the summa of Christian — particularly of Protestant — piety. Piet Jr. executed it at age twenty-one. Seven years later, now freelancing to keep body and soul together, he carved figures on the new pulpit in the

---

4. Henkels, *Mondrian*, 148-50.

5. Henkels, *Mondrian*, 152-53, 156; J. M. de Jong, "Piet Mondriaan en de gereformeerde kerk van Amsterdam," *Jong Holland* 3 (1989): 21.

6. Henkels, *Mondrian*, 151-52.

English Reformed Church of Amsterdam, located in the Begijnhof. All the while, he was duly registered upon the roles of the Gereformeerde Kerken in Nederland as a full member by profession of faith. Since his father had never taken the step of leaving the National Church for the GKN, Piet Jr. by this measure was more Kuyperian than Piet the elder.[7] In any case, by all evidence the artist known to history as the epitome of high Modernism was once a true Calvinist believer, and painted that way.

By 1910 Mondrian seemed to have left all that behind: he changed in his painting program and he changed in his worldview, those two being deeply connected. His philosophical development has been ascribed to different inspirations: to Theosophy first of all, along with variants on that program; to Platonism and/or neo-Platonism; to German Idealism, with Goethe in the background, Hegel front and center, and Schopenhauer at the end.[8] Typically, Mondrian's Calvinist formation is dismissed in these explanations as a dark and narrow dogmatism that offered no plausibility for belief in a modern age, much less any possibility for artistic growth. Artistically, Mondrian evolved in these years from painting landscapes in the mode of the country's dominant Hague School (in which his uncle and sometime teacher Frits Mondrian was a modest player), to a neo-Impressionism only recently (and barely) acceptable to Dutch taste, to the mystical allegories he executed toward the end of the decade, coincident with his joining the Theosophical Society in Amster-

---

7. Henkels, *Mondrian*, 178; de Jong, "Piet Mondriaan," 22-23.

8. John Milner, *Mondrian* (New York: Abbeville, 1992), 60-79, presents the standard argument regarding Theosophy. Hans Janssen and Joop Joosten, *Mondrian: The Path to Abstraction, 1892-1914* (Zwolle: Waanders, 2002), 65-66, 90, 134, agree, dating the beginning of Mondrian's change to Annie Besant's lecture tour in the Netherlands in 1898 and noting the subsequent modulation wrought by Rudolf Steiner's "anthroposophical" lecture series in The Hague in 1908. Henkels, *Mondrian*, 172, emphasizes the neo-Platonic impulse along with the preparatory impact exerted on Mondrian by his fellow Dutch painter, and sometime mentor, Jan Toorop's conversion to Roman Catholicism around 1905. (Milner, *Mondrian*, fleshes out the Toorop influence, 10-13.) Mark A. Cheetham, *The Rhetoric of Purity: Essentialist Theory and the Advent of Abstract Painting* (New York: Cambridge University Press, 1991), 48-64, argues for the strong influence of German Idealist aesthetics along with Neo-Platonism. John Golding, *Paths to the Absolute: Mondrian, Malevich, Kandinsky, Pollock, Newman, Rothko, and Still* (Princeton: Princeton University Press, 2002), 14-16, notes that Steiner's lectures covered Goethe and Hegel as well as anthroposophy. Hans L. C. Jaffé, *Piet Mondrian* (New York: Harry N. Abrams, n.d.), 41-42, presents the strongest case to date for continuities between Mondrian's mature art and his native Calvinism, while L. J. F. Wijsenbeek, *Piet Mondrian* (Greenwich, Conn.: New York Graphic Society, 1968), 9, 91, posits the influence of Christian mystical traditions as well as the psychology, though not theology, of Calvinism.

dam in 1909. His major career breakthrough came at an exhibition in Amsterdam in 1910, after which his development leapt forward owing to his exposure to cubism during his residence in Paris (1911-1914). Then, while pent up in the Netherlands for the duration of World War I, he synthesized these various currents into his definitive style and set forth what proved to be his lasting philosophy of art in the avant-garde journal, *De Stijl*.[9] To that philosophy as deployed in his characteristic non-representational paintings we will return after a brief tour of the notions of art laid out in the grand man of his childhood, Abraham Kuyper.

*   *   *

Kuyper gave significant attention to the arts — first, as a domain of human activity in its own right, and second, as a force of growing importance in modern society. One of the first non-theological courses he taught at the Free University was on art; the last was on Impressionism. His most concentrated attention to the subject came in coincidence with his campaign to democratize Dutch politics. He launched it with a rectorial address in 1888, one year after a radical expansion of the Dutch electorate. He devoted one of his Princeton lectures to the topic in 1898 during his visit to the ultimate land of democratic ways. He wrapped up his long series extrapolating the theology of common grace on the question of the arts in 1901, just before he took office as prime minister.[10]

Part of his motive in taking up the subject was to prove his thesis that Calvinism embraced "all spheres" of life, the toughest objection to which proposition arose from the arts. On this score Kuyper himself recited — and did not dispute — the litany of Calvinism's aesthetic under-performance: no monumental architecture, little in the way of sculpture, a music long on Psalm-singing and short on everything else, an aversion to nudity in painting,

---

9. Mondrian's artistic evolution after 1909 is recounted, with some variations, in Milner, *Mondrian*, 92-151; Golding, *Paths to the Absolute*, 16-37; and Janssen and Joosten, *Mondrian*, 153-96.

10. Kuyper's three concerted treatments of art are *Het Calvinisme en de Kunst* (Amsterdam: J. A. Wormser, 1888); "Calvinism and Art," in *Lectures on Calvinism* (Grand Rapids: Eerdmans, 1931), 142-70; and the second half of *De Gemeene Gratie in Wetenschap en Kunst* [*GGWK*] (Amsterdam: Höveker & Wormser, 1905), 43-87 (originally a series in *De Heraut*, 16 June–14 July 1901). Kuyper alludes to his early course on aesthetics at the Free University in *Calvinisme en Kunst*, 5; and Johannes Stellingwerff refers to his course on Impressionism in *Dr. Abraham Kuyper en de Vrije Universiteit* (Kampen: J. H. Kok, 1987), 253.

and a virtual prohibition on the theater. Every other world religion has its distinctive aesthetic, Kuyper said; one instantly recognizes Buddhist art and Islamic art, medieval Catholic or Byzantine style. What was Calvinist art? And where was it, especially in an era when art was becoming more available to, and more important for, more people than ever before in history?[11]

Kuyper eventually came around to answering this question, but the material he could adduce as positive evidence proved so modest that he spent most of his time postulating indirect contributions instead. If Calvinism had not produced much art itself, it had created the freedom for others to do so; in diminishing "the sensory" in worship so as to make it properly "spiritual" again, it liberated artists from ecclesiastical control.[12] The Calvinist elevation of everyday life legitimated the body as well as the soul, saw as much virtue in the ordinary mother as in the Madonna, and brought common things into the artist's purview. No accident, then, that Hals, Vermeer, and above all Rembrandt worked in a "Calvinist" context. That the gentlemen in question were hardly champions of the Canons of Dort led to Kuyper's other claim, that the arts are supremely the domain of common grace. It was "Calvinism outside the circle of Calvinists in the stricter sense that pressed its stamp upon our national life," he told his Dutch audience.[13] Likewise, it was the ancient Greeks, bereft though they were of Christ and Scripture, who set the standards for beauty — standards that were "objective" and universal, deriving as they did from God's being "the Deviser and Creator of beauty." The cognitive apparatus of the human race the Creator had apparently turned upon a classical lathe.[14]

Kuyper was too biblical to leave the matter there, however, and so his deeper argument turned back to the first tenet of Calvinism. Election was not just politically but aesthetically democratic, he said. It disclosed to the artist's eye a fellowship of suffering and glory beyond the subject's standing or wealth. In tracing out the works of God in human life, the eye of election "penetrates the depth of misery and grasps for redemption behind the somber impress of pain."[15] An artist could work on such a basis, and virtually the last words in Kuyper's six-year series on common grace urged his followers to do so. The believer "who can understand human life in its wealth of ap-

---

11. On Calvinism's problematic aesthetic past, see Kuyper, *Calvinisme en Kunst*, 8-10, 28-29.
12. Kuyper, *Calvinisme en Kunst*, 20-27.
13. Kuyper, *Calvinisme en Kunst*, 27.
14. Kuyper, *GGWK*, 72.
15. Kuyper, *Calvinisme en Kunst*, 23.

pearances and its manifold struggles as these are to be understood in the light of God's word, and can transfer these impressions to the world of beauty, has translated the Spirit of his God into that life."[16] For concrete examples Kuyper had to go no farther than the shores at Scheveningen, where Jozef Israels and his fellows in The Hague School had for a quarter-century been painting the dignity and fortitude of common people at their daily tasks. This "poetry" of "unvarnished lives . . . [extrapolated] to the wide domain of humanity" fit Kuyper's prescription perfectly, all the more since Israels esteemed the family as highly as did Kuyper. Or he could have invoked the work of the recently deceased Vincent van Gogh, one-time theology student and evangelist to the wretched of the earth who, though losing his formal faith, had caught the anguish and hopes of human life in unexcelled color and motion. Yet Kuyper passed by these and other potential allies, despite certainly knowing of them. He had private correspondence with Israels but made nothing public of his work.[17]

Part of the explanation for this puzzle lies in the very democratic impulse so pronounced in Kuyper during these years. The religious leaders of the day who were encouraging new trends in Dutch art and letters fell on the conservative side of the political spectrum. They could indulge their hobbies, Kuyper argued, because they were comfortable residents of the established order interested in satisfying — and showing off — their fashionable tastes. In consequence, they had no eye for the demoralizing effects that avant-garde productions would have on ordinary people. To transit safely into modern society common folk needed a consolidated system of faith, a consistent Calvinism in culture as much as in politics, not just a personal "spirit of the gospel" to which they could assimilate trendy wares from the cultural marketplace.[18]

This hints at the specific purpose Kuyper posited for art, a purpose that

---

16. Kuyper, *GGWK*, 86.

17. On the Hague School, see John Sillevis and Anne Tabak, *The Hague School Book* (Zwolle: Waanders, 2004), and G. H. Marius's classic, *Dutch Painters of the Nineteenth Century,* ed. Geraldine Norman (Woodbridge, UK: Antique Collectors' Club, 1983 [1908]), 121-208; quotation, 135-36. Kuyper's correspondence with Israels can be found in the Kuyper Archive, Historische Documentatie Centrum, Vrije Universiteit-Amsterdam. On Van Gogh's early popularity in the Netherlands even amid anti-Impressionist opinions, see Janssen and Joosten, *Mondrian,* 74-76, 128; and Milner, *Mondrian,* 10-13.

18. See Roel Kuiper, *Zelfbeeld en Wereldbeeld: Antirevolutionairen en het buitenland, 1848-1905* (Kampen: Kok, 1992), 188-90; and D. Th. Kuiper, *De Voormannen: een sociaalwetenschapelijke studie . . .* (Meppel: Boom, 1972), 245-50.

led him toward a very traditional aesthetic — and a practical dead end. Without comment or question he linked art to "beauty," thus instantly bracketing off a large range of potential Christian, not to mention actual Modernist, productions. True beauty, furthermore, was the earthly shadow of heavenly "glory," and it was this glory — epitomized in the majesty and perfection of God — that Kuyper insisted art try to represent. Granted, the artist deals with earthly appearances, but the human "imagination" at the hands of "genius" could capture the "higher, nobler, richer reality" behind the forms of nature and display it for all to see. This would "add something to human life which it [otherwise] would never have possessed," thus "improving" the material environment and "elevating" the spiritual sense so that people could glimpse more of grace.[19] Art, that is to say, was to be idealistic, didactic, positive, and inspiring, always pointing toward "higher" things. Its ultimate calling, in fact, was to struggle by fits and starts through the limits of human sight in the ordinary world to give something of a foretaste of heaven here on earth.

In alternative aesthetics Kuyper saw only trouble. The cult of art for art's sake just now at its peak he deemed irresponsible; art might be one of his separate "sovereign spheres," but the beautiful could never be isolated from the true or the good. Bohemian Paris, in turn, amounted to an ersatz aristocracy, complete with corruption, petty feuds, and external show masquerading as inward quality. Worst of all was the market mechanism, the allure of "money" or "fame." Kuyper's prime example was theater, evil not in itself but by the base product it had to purvey to make ends meet. To portray the "raw" or the "low," whether on stage, in stone, or on canvas, was to praise the consequences of sin.[20] This raised a particularly troubling specter in an age of dawning democracy, and Kuyper brought out his hoariest polemic against it. The market established the "tyranny of popular sovereignty in the field of art"; against that, Christian artists ought to perform the "priestly service" of holding up a higher standard for emulation. "Our Calvinism thirsts for harmony and calls for balance," he declared, even though his own political and theological commentary drew some of its best insights from exploring the disharmony and unbalances that needed divine redemption.[21]

In sum, Kuyper was utterly logo-centric. The full range of human life

19. For his positive aesthetic, see Kuyper, *Calvinisme en Kunst*, 10-17, and *GGWK*, 52-57, 64-69; "glory," 56, 57; "imagination" and "genius," 62, 73, 76-77; "higher, nobler, richer," 64; "add something to human life," 69.
20. Kuyper, *GGWK*, 73-81; quotations, 73, 79-81.
21. Kuyper, *GGWK*, 74, 76; *Calvinisme en Kunst*, 40.

had to be treated by words on a page, which remained subject to rational controls. Sounds and images pierced right to the soul and so needed stricter limits, particularly in an age of mass culture. When forced to declare what art Calvinism had delivered in its own right, Kuyper typically referred to the Genevan psalms — that is, to canonical texts sung in the context of worship. Beyond that he dilated longest on a writer from the Dutch Golden Age, Jacob Cats (1577-1660), a lawyer, politician, and diplomat who compiled illustrated "emblem books" of rhymed couplets, chiefly on domestic themes.[22] By Kuyper's day this material had long since passed to the status of proverbial lore. A less likely entry into the pulses of modern art is hard to imagine.

Yet I suggest that a far more successful candidate did emerge from his movement, even if by a dialectical process of separation, in the person and work of Piet Mondrian Jr. The movement that most immediately triggered Mondrian's Modernist style was Theosophy in one or another of its adaptations. A picture of Madame Helene Blavatsky, Theosophy's founder, was a permanent fixture in Mondrian's studio, and friends record him taking in the 1908 lectures of Rudolf Steiner, voice of "anthroposophy," from the German embassy in The Hague.[23] Characterized by some as a Westernized morphing of Buddhism, theosophy aimed to synthesize the eternal truths, the hidden wisdom, that lay behind any number of world mystical and esoteric traditions into a worldview and an ethical catalyst for a new phase of ontological evolution. This evolution was key to the vision. If all being was the expression of fundamental forces, all matter the outplay of spiritual dynamics, then human beings had a central role to play on the cosmic scene. By way of recurrent reincarnations they could gain enlightenment — that is, cognizance of the nature and direction of core spiritual forces — and so make evolution more conscious and intentional. The enlightened thus had the privilege and duty to spread their knowledge to others, to help humanity as a whole gain critical consciousness and move forward to their destiny. That destiny was a paradise on earth, where the countervailing forces of time and eternity, individual wills and social collectives, the givens of nature and the constructions of humanity, would unite in harmony, at equilibrium.

There is much here that troubled Kuyper down to his foundations. The

---

22. On Genevan psalmody, Kuyper, *GGWK*, 78; on Cats, Kuyper, *Calvinisme en Kunst*, 31-39.

23. On Theosophy and its role in Mondrian's development, see the literature cited in note 8 above, especially Milner, *Mondrian*, 10-13, 60-79, 118-40. Mondrian's definitive statement of his new program came in two series of essays in the Dutch periodical, *De Stijl*, 1917-18. Henkels, *Mondrian*, mentions the Blavatsky picture in Mondrian's studio, 179.

notion that human beings had the potential to bring in a perfect world Kuyper rejected as a perennial delusion of the race, the one most alluring and therefore toxic in modern times. Then too, theosophy represented exactly the pantheism and its "blurring of the boundaries" which he saw as the essential mark of the fin de siècle and which he bewailed in every one of his major cultural commentaries thereafter.[24] The specter was personal too, for Kuyper's second son, Jan Frederik, who had moved far away to the Dutch East Indies, there "swam in the theosophical murk."[25] In his commentary on the arts in 1912, Kuyper repeatedly associated the mystical and spiritualistic tendencies with artists in particular. Given Mondrian's association with Kuyper's past publisher, and his descent from one of Kuyper's early lieutenants, it is more than plausible that he had Mondrian's course in mind as a prime example of the syndrome.[26]

At the same time, it is hard to miss the functional similarity between the place that the "enlightened" held in Mondrian's new vision and that of the "elect" in his native Calvinism. Both were a select vanguard having a grand role to play in the coming of the perfect future. That most obvious congruence leads on to consideration of other parallels between the two programs — structural congruencies beneath substantive differences, or old bottles of Kuyperian forging containing Mondrian's new wine.

We can begin with Mondrian's ascetic lifestyle. On the Paris scene of the 1920s, Mondrian was an enthusiastic habitué of jazz clubs but otherwise resisted what Kuyper would count as the decadence and false show of the bohemian scene. Mondrian's stark, plain studio became legendary among his peers and collectors, his resistance to fads and gossip proverbial, his dedication to his own program resolute.[27] If selling out to the market was the leading sin against Kuyper's ten commandments for art, then Mondrian was a saint. This is traceable, secondly, to Mondrian's strong sense of the artist's calling. As one of his most astute critics observed, Mondrian's "vocation as an artist he regarded as a ministry, bringing total dedication and unfailing faith

---

24. Kuyper, *De Verflauwing der Grenzen* (Amsterdam: J. A. Wormser, 1892); E.T.: "The Blurring of the Boundaries," in Bratt, ed., *Abraham Kuyper: A Centennial Reader*, 363-402.

25. Kuyper discussed Jan Frederik's situation in letters to Alexander F. W. Idenburg, collected in J. de Bruijn and G. Puchinger, eds., *Briefwisseling Kuyper Idenburg* (Franeker: T. Wever, 1985); *inter alia*, 237, 276, 285, 296, and 323 (quotation).

26. Kuyper refers to theosophy and related "spiritualist" practices in *Pro Rege* (Kampen: J. H. Kok, 1911-12), vol. 1, 104-5, 200-202, 205; vol. 3, 360, 427.

27. Janssen and Joosten, *Mondrian*, "Foreword"; Milner, *Mondrian*, 7; Jaffé, *Piet Mondrian*, 37-38.

to the task that he and his friends were engaged in for the benefit of mankind."[28] These good works, furthermore, were rooted in the equivalent of a religious conversion, a "mental transformation" that the artist had to undergo so as to attain enlightenment. The climactic painting of Mondrian's theosophical journey was a Modernist version of a medieval altarpiece, a triptych depicting exactly the prescribed process of spiritual transformation.[29]

As a result of that inner change, the world of outer appearances was opened up to reveal the true structure of being. Here, on the ontological level, the Kuyperian template appeared again. Perhaps even more to the point, Kuyper and Mondrian shared a common dialectic, echoing a Hegelian original, that posited at the heart of reality a fundamental dynamic of countervailing forces. Mondrian was not shy of calling this a set of "absolute oppositions," a phrase Kuyper used more often than "the antithesis" that his subsequent followers would favor.[30] Indeed, absolute oppositions constitute the most familiar trait of Mondrian's iconic art: all curves straightened out into perfectly vertical vs. horizontal lines that meet always and only at right angles. Mondrian had his own horror at "the blurring of the boundaries," scotching all mixture of tints in favor of the three primary colors only. His mature style thus featured colored planes set off starkly against lines and spaces composed of the closest he could get to non-colors: white, black, and grey. This was the painterly way to capture on canvas the fundamental oppositions in the everyday world: male vs. female, the human-made vs. the naturally given, the eternal vs. the transient, the celestial vs. the terrestrial. Some critics have ascribed this pattern to Dutch national character, its primordial struggle of land against sea.[31] It is just as plausible that it derived from the table-talk of Mondrian's boyhood home, where the *"tegenstelling"* between the gospel and the Revolution was a persistent theme, and the subject of his father's work for Kuyper.

Kuyper did not anticipate — in fact, zealously opposed — resolving the antithesis in a synthetic union between the opposing forces. Here Mondrian might be seen as defying Kuyper's model in that he anticipated that the dynamic rhythm of action and counter-action between primal forces would

---

28. Jaffé, *Piet Mondrian*, 59.

29. Janssen and Joosten, *Mondrian*, 112; Milner, *Mondrian*, 197; Cheetham, *Rhetoric of Purity*, 44-45. The theosophical triptych is "Evolution," 1910-11.

30. Wijsenbeek, *Piet Mondrian*, 94. The themes treated hereafter come up in virtually every treatment of Mondrian's art, making multiplication of references easy, and redundant. I cite only the site of quoted material.

31. Jaffé, *Piet Mondrian*, 46, 48. See also Cheetham, *Rhetoric of Purity*, 42-44.

one day lead to "equilibrium," a state of harmonic unity. But if we look away from the war of the human spirits to the plane of ontological development, we can see a similar pattern in Kuyper's neo-Calvinist concept of the dynamic relationships at the heart of society and historical development — indeed of all being. Kuyper's ontology saw creational givens unfolding over time in myriad particular instantiations, all governed by the norms or laws instituted in the lines of force by the Creator Word. The "principles" at the heart of things — a term some of Mondrian's commentators use to characterize his understanding of the "laws" of being — led for both the theologian and the painter to an end of perfect harmony.[32]

Yet Kuyper always said that the road to that end is long and winding, owing to the fact of sin. Mondrian agreed. In one essay that explicitly invoked Adam and Eve, Genesis and Eden, Mondrian declared that the "original aesthetic sin" was the loss of universal principle in the welter of the material world, from which grew the further, active sins of individualism and a depletion of spiritual sense.[33] The artist's calling in this context, Mondrian continued, was to recover by the transformation of his mind the "underlying principles behind appearances, the permanent structure that encompassed change," and so to show forth the true cosmos "of balance and order."[34] In Kuyperian terms, it was to recover creational norms, the original divine purpose for cosmic development. But this recovery was not available by going backwards, Mondrian warned, exactly as Kuyper repeatedly admonished his followers against "repristination." "Always further" was Mondrian's mantra, and functionally Kuyper's constant advocacy.[35] The two, in fact, shared the same Hegelian notion of the mind's role in historical development. Mondrian said of the artist what Kuyper prescribed for the Christian intellectual: he (and "he" it was for both of them) must be — is — the voice of his time, expressing the vision of eternity in the forms of the age.[36] Finally, the two anticipated the same ironic conclusion at the end of the process: the institutional matrix to which they devoted their lives would wither away. For

---

32. Henkels, *Mondrian*, 173, 180. For a brief statement in English of Kuyper's concept of human development under divine ordinances, see "The Ordinances of God," in James Skillen and Rockne McCarthy, eds., *Political Order and the Plural Structure of Society* (Atlanta: Scholars Press, 1991), 242-57.

33. Cited in Cheetham, *Rhetoric of Purity*, 42.

34. Milner, *Mondrian*, 57, 60.

35. Jaffé, *Piet Mondrian*, 9. A classic locus of Kuyper's warnings of "repristination" is *Lectures on Calvinism*, 171.

36. Henkels, *Mondrian*, 180.

Mondrian, art — as for Kuyper, the church — would disappear in the New Jerusalem, their prophetic function having been fulfilled in the full redemption of humanity.[37]

Two more analogies may be briefly noted. One is that for Mondrian as much as for Kuyper, the artist had a moral vocation — to set forth the uncluttered ideals of ultimate purpose, inspiring the viewer to live in that light, along those lines, toward that promise. Painting thus burst beyond its particular boundaries to work the transformation that would harmonize all spheres. Mondrian saw his as the painterly side of an emerging revolution in architecture, music, and theater, but also in social life that would propel unending progress in and toward a dynamic order of harmony. Mondrian, says one observer in words to warm the Kuyperian heart, aspired to the complete integration of art and life.[38] But secondly, Mondrian, like Kuyper, drew back significantly from forthright immersion in the democracy that each viewed to be the society of the future. Kuyper's commentary deemed only certain types of art to be safe for the untutored masses; Mondrian executed exactly the type of art that those masses (perhaps to Kuyper's relief) could not appreciate. Kuyper played the censor, Mondrian the elitist; Kuyper did not trust, and Mondrian did not kneel, to the lures of the democratic age.

It is hard to stop being a Calvinist if one is born into it, irrespective of one's later journeys outside that circle. Hans Jaffé noted as much about Mondrian's art: it was iconoclastic, emptied of sensuality, obedient to law, religious in devotion, sectarian in zeal, ethical and democratic in purpose. Jaffé attributes to Mondrian a distinctively Dutch characteristic from that language's first word in art criticism: *schoon,* meaning at once beautiful and pure.[39] This essay means to move this analysis from the categories of Dutch and Calvinist to Dutch Neo-Calvinist. In terms and in a structure of argument that closely paralleled those of the worldview in which he was raised, Mondrian as the quintessential Modernist aimed, just as Kuyper taught, to penetrate through the forms of nature to exhibit the "objective" and universal meaning behind it — its ultimate spiritual truth.

---

37. This aspect of Kuyper's ecclesiology is summed up in his *Encyclopaedie der Heilige Godgeleerdheid* (Amsterdam: J. A. Wormser, 1894), vol. 3, 215-18. In the next life, he says there, the church as an institution will "fall away and nothing but the organism [of godly people] will remain" (215). For Mondrian, see Henkels, *Mondrian,* 180: "Art and life would be identical in the paradise on earth that man would make for himself."

38. Jaffé, *Piet Mondrian,* 57; Henkels, *Mondrian,* 165, 180.

39. Jaffé, *Piet Mondrian,* 41-42; on *schoon,* 46.

The Music God Likes and the Calvinist Tradition

John Barber

The advancement of enlightened awareness promulgated by the "Age of Reason" produced the decentralization of God in wide-ranging areas of human intellectual thought and life, including the arts. The drastic reshaping of the cultural disciplines known for centuries as the seven liberal arts into the modern system began with the Abbe Batteux. In his treatise *Les beaux arts reduits a un meme principe* (1746), he successfully separates the fine arts, which have pleasure as their end, from the mechanical arts, which are intended for usefulness. The focal point of his argument is that the goal of all the arts ought to be the "imitation of beautiful nature."

Following closely the trend set by Batteux, the *Encyclopédie* formalized the radical humanizing of the arts. Diderot and d'Alembert exploited Lord Bacon's scheme of subsuming all knowledge under the three human faculties of memory, reason, and the imagination. Subsequently, in his famous *Discours preliminaire*, d'Alembert concludes with a main division of knowledge into philosophy, history, and the fine arts, corresponding to Bacon's reason, memory, and imagination, respectively. The effect was to yank artistic ingenuity in the arts from its starting place in the Creator and reestablish it upon the new autonomous foundation of human imagination.

In our day, the enlightened trend continues to find fertile expression among secularists. Surprisingly, however, its influence can also be found among thoughtful Christians engaged in the visual and performing arts. This influence is most notably detected in the visceral reaction among a growing number of Christian academics to the proposition that there is a type of art that, in comparison with other forms of art, has the capacity to glorify God in a unique way. The positive and categorical attitude that has become all too commonplace is that it is enough for a Christian artist to seek great art in the values of beautiful colors, proportions, and shapes only. But as for a specific type of art that stirs God, and even prompts God's approval, the Christian community of artists very often perceives God as indifferent. The unspoken thought is that it is sufficient that God has given us the gift of creativity. It is therefore ours to use at our discretion. But do not those who take this position continue to rear the child birthed by Batteux and heard crying in the nineteenth century, *"l'art pour l'art"* ("art for art's sake")?

Although the Christian community continues to witness an evisceration of gospel values from the arts generally envisioned, the specific form of art considered in this essay is music. The formative inquiry is this: Does God have musical tastes, such that there is a form and function of music that glorifies God — indeed, that God desires above all others? Or is such a claim dogmatic? The answer proposed looks back in time before the European Enlightenment, when the moral dimension of life before God was most prominent in Christian thought. This vaulting back designates the development of a single voice in Christian theology, but one so well advanced on the relationship of God to music that it may very well prompt an invigoration of the centrality of the glory of God in our craft.

In the conception of the relationship of music to God, the Calvinist tradition offers important distinctions and pointers that move us toward the idea that God has musical preferences. This is as good a place as any to define more precisely the word "likes" in the title of this essay. One can like something for its appealing nature: it is cute, pleasing, or engaging. Following the Calvinist ideal, however, the word "likes" is taken here in a more restricted sense: that it is pleasing and acceptable to the Lord, that it glorifies the Lord. Given this understanding, then, the music God likes is shaped by two controlling factors: the moral dimension of music, which includes both text and tune, and the spiritual state of the musician. Of first concern is the moral dimension of music.

I

John Calvin's iconoclastic and restrictive view of images, his equally restraining enforcement against the use of musical instruments in congregational worship, and his use of exclusive metrical psalms, sung unaccompanied and in unison in public worship, have been well documented by the literature on the subject. Influences weighing on Calvin's decisions to limit congregational singing to the psalms have received wide attention by scholars as well. Nonetheless, a few important points drawing from the historical and intellectual trends of Calvin's day can augment the connection between Calvin's positions on exclusive psalmody and his belief in the moral dimension of music.

Calvin's support for canonical psalmody is based first and foremost in a guiding principle of the Reformation: *sola scriptura*. The Reformer of Geneva envisioned that if the Word of God is the sole basis for faith and practice, then congregational singing should not merely be *based* on the words of Scripture, such as Luther had thought, but should incorporate the very words of Scripture. After all, God has given us his own songbook in the middle of the Old Testament. Why look further?[1] Calvin's deep belief in the sacred and moral nature of the Book of Psalms, and that singing God's own words back to him is the preeminent way to glorify God in song, helped him remain steadfastly devoted to their supreme usage in congregational worship, despite other musical innovations taking place during the early years of the Reformation.[2]

Yet a point that deserves wider attention regarding Calvin's position on canonical psalmody focuses on the transposition of values shared between Calvin and Renaissance culture. Any assessment of music in Calvin's thought must consider not only Calvin the Protestant Reformer, but also Calvin the Christian humanist.[3] The beginnings of Calvin's humanist sym-

---

1. Calvin's love for and commitment to the Book of Psalms is noted in the preface to the Principal Genevan Psalter, written from Geneva, June 10, 1543. See the facsimile edition of: "*Les Pseaumes mis en rime francoise par Clément Marot et Théodore de Béze. Mis en musique a quatre parties par Claude Goudimel. Par les héritiers de Francois Jacqui*" (1565). Published under the auspices of La Société des Concerts de la Cathédrale de Lausanne and edited, in French, by Pierre Pidoux and, in German, by Konrad Ameln (Kassel: Baerenreiter-Verlag, 1935).

2. On this point see Charles Garside Jr., *The Origins of Calvin's Theology of Music: 1536-1543*, Transactions of the American Philosophical Society, Volume 69, Part 4 (Philadelphia: The American Philosophical Society, 1979), p. 26. Also helpful is Louis F. Benson, *The Presbyterian Reformed Review* 8 (1897): 422.

3. E.g., "Between 1527 and 1534 . . . Calvin inhabited the Erasmian world of thought and breathed its spiritual atmosphere; he remained in major ways always a humanist of the late Renaissance," William J. Bouwsma, *John Calvin: A Sixteenth-Century Portrait* (Oxford: Oxford University Press, 1988), 13. I do not join Bouwsma in as far as he makes Calvin out to be too close to Erasmus in humanist affinities. The best study of Calvin and the French humanists remains Josef Bohatec, *Budé und Calvin: Studien zur Gedankenwelt des französischen Frühhumanismus* (Graz, 1950).

pathies trace to his legal education at the hands of humanist scholars who had abandoned the glosses of medieval copyists for the *fontes* of ancient Roman law theory. Becoming deeply familiar with the pioneers of biblical philology, such as Valla, Erasmus, and Lefevre, Calvin carried his early training into his work as a Reformer. Scholars have seen in Calvin's writings "humanist linguistic and textual techniques for the interpretation of Scripture" as well as a characteristically humanist sense of "the importance attached to the study of the Fathers" and "the acceptance of a kind of Christian philosophy."[4]

The humanist pedigree is evident in Calvin's perception of music. This connection is first seen in comparison with Erasmus. The conjecture that Erasmus broke away from the early medieval tradition that envisioned the psalms as a medium for praise and prayer to find in them a repository of prophetic indicators of Jesus Christ[5] is an incomplete generalization of his position on the Book of Psalms. Erasmus also held to an equally important early monastic position, which viewed the psalms as the Word of God and as a medium for praise and spiritual growth.

In the preface to his edition of the Greek New Testament, he states,

> I wish that even the weakest woman should read the Gospels — should read the Epistle of Paul; and I wish that they were translated into all languages, so that they might be read and understood not only by Scots and Irishmen, but also by Turks and Saracens. I long that the husbandman should sing portions of them to himself as he follows the plough, that the weaver should hum them to the tune of his shuttle and that the traveler should beguile with their stories the tedium of his journey.[6]

Features of Erasmus's wishes are certainly time-bound. Nonetheless, his comments on the import of the commoner singing the Scriptures for moral edification append directly to Calvin's desire to publish a version of the Book of Psalms for public praise and as an instrument for spiritual growth. The image painted by Roland Bainton of Erasmus as "a blend of Stoicism

---

4. Alister E. McGrath, *A Life of John Calvin* (Oxford: Oxford Univ. Press, 1990), 57; Alexandre Ganoczy, *The Young Calvin* (Philadelphia: Westminster, 1987), 181.

5. Howard N. Wallace is an example of this. See Wallace, *Words to God, Word from God: The Psalms in the Prayer and Preaching of the Church* (Burlington, Vt.: Ashgate Publishing), 10.

6. Quoted in Frederick Seebohm, *The Era of the Protestant Revolution* (Kessinger Publishing, 2006), 92.

and the Sermon on the Mount. . . . Syncreticism, allegorization, moralization, the reduction of dogma, the spiritualizing of everything external,"[7] in contradistinction to Calvin, the man of *sola scriptura*, does not do full justice to how much the two men had in common.

Other parallel developments relevant to music linked Calvin with his times. Bourgeoning musical changes were happening during the period of the European Renaissance largely due to the influence of humanism and its renewed interest in the Classical view of the dignity of humanity. The new program in music followed developments in other arts and sciences somewhat closely, especially the blending of religious and secular subject matter heard in the works of composers such as Dufay and Ockeghem. Calvin's disapproval of the use of secular subject matter in music and musical embellishment has been well established, but what has not been stressed enough by the standard literature is that before Calvin set out to codify Scripture into a clear and regular system of song singing, Renaissance humanism was already showing great interest in the psalms, and for a related reason.

Once Calvin was in exile in Strasbourg for three years he was able to start work on the French Psalter, which he and Beza finished in 1562 in Geneva.[8] However, after taking the original songs to his congregation in Strasbourg, Calvin felt that his work was of insufficient quality, so he enlisted the help of French court poet Clément Marot, who had earlier versified most of the psalms in French during the first part of the sixteenth century for princes and their courtiers. Marot's settings were central to the Renaissance ideal of the "finished man" who viewed music as a means of moral instruction and courtly sophistication. The process was simple. A man or woman of refinement communicated his or her favorite psalm to Marot, and he wrote the poems. Since a common practice was then to have the song sung in the court or in the center city, Calvin must have been aware of the utilization of the psalms as a means of moral refinement, even entertainment — in a secular setting, no less — and of Marot's involvement. In fact, this could be a reason Calvin chose Marot.

Due to this transposition of values it is difficult to qualify Calvin's exploitation of the psalms as a means to nurture expressly Christian virtues as an inspired and original product of the central tenets of his theology. Al-

---

7. Roland Bainton, "Man, God, and the Church in the Age of the Renaissance," in *The Renaissance: Six Essays* (New York: Harper and Row Publishers, 1962), 93.

8. Published in 1539 as *Aulcuns pseaulmes et cantiques mys en chant*, it contains metrical versifications written by Calvin himself.

though Calvin's codification of the Psalter draws currency from humanist, cultural developments, he still achieves a sacred end: the use of the moral dimension of music as an important catalyst for corporate worship — pleasing to God and uplifting to the flock.

Nowhere is Calvin's commitment to the humanist moral ideal for music more aptly expressed than in his appeal to the ancient Greek doctrine of ethos. According to this doctrine, to the extent one listened to good music, one became a good person; to the extent one listened to bad music, one became a bad person. This simple idea was rooted in the ancients, principally Plato and Aristotle, who thought that music shared a close association with mathematics. Because mathematics was understood to express the workings of the universe, music was believed to articulate a primary reality.[9] Greek philosophers were therefore keenly aware of the moral qualities of music and approached both musical style and musical instruments with a degree of caution.[10] On this basis Plato's *Republic* limits instrumentalists to the use of the lyre and cithara.[11] In Greek thought, music therefore employs a spiritual dimension and functions as both form and forum for moral training.[12]

In the preface to the Principal Genevan Psalter, Calvin appeals to the Greek doctrine of ethos to reveal his great appreciation for the power of music to inflame or to inspire the heart as justification for the paramount need to sing the psalms:

> But still there is more: there is scarcely in the world anything which is more able to turn or bend this way and that the morals of men, as Plato

---

9. Augustine took up this theory in his highly influential treatise *De Musica*.

10. The doctrine of ethos deals with the moral qualities of music and seems to be related to the idea of a cosmic dimension in music discovered by Pythagoras. The doctrine of ethos, however, goes beyond the Pythagorean conception that music merely shares in the greater cosmic order, and holds that it may also affect the universe in some way.

11. See Smith's essay "The Contest of Apollo and Marsyas: Ideas about Music in the Middle Ages," in *By Things Seen*, ed. David L. Jeffrey (Ottawa, Canada: University of Ottawa Press, 1979), 81.

12. According to Dr. Grout, "The Greek doctrine of ethos, then, was founded on the conviction that music affects character and that different kinds of music affect it in different ways. In the distinction made among the many different kinds of music, we can discern a general division into two classes. . . . The first class was associated with the worship of Apollo; its instrument was the lyre, and its related poetic forms, the ode and the epic. The second class was associated with the worship of Dionysus; its instrument was the aulos, and its related poetic forms, the dithyramb and the drama" (Donald Jay Grout, *A History of Western Music*, 3d ed. [New York: W. W. Norton and Company, 1980], 9).

prudently considered it. And in fact, we find by experience that it has a sacred and almost incredible power to move hearts in one way or another. Therefore we ought to be even more diligent in regulating it in such a way that it shall be useful to us and in no way pernicious. . . . It is true that every bad word (as St. Paul has said) perverts good manner, but when the melody is with it, it pierces the heart much more strongly, and enters into it; in a like manner as through a funnel, the wine is poured into the vessel; so also the venom and the corruption is distilled to the depths of the heart by the melody.[13]

Here Calvin makes clear the power of music to inflame the human heart with spiritual zeal or pernicious sensations. In reaction he wanted singing to be without accompaniment. In the original tunes by Louis Bourgeois the music is thus monophonic.[14]

II

How do the thoughts expressed thus far connect to today's church musician? In modern times the doctrine of *sola scriptura* continues to inform the fundamental structures of approaches to, and attitudes about, music for congregational use. Still, a lack of consensus on exactly *how* Scripture ought to enlighten the role of music in our devotional life together is seen optimally in the uneased tension often called "worship wars." To generalize: the "battle lines" are drawn between those who advocate for traditional music and those who prefer a contemporary or edgier style of music in worship. The latter form is typically heard among Pentecostals and charismatics, but it is not without its impact on many older, mainline churches. Representatives of contemporary music point to the pages of the Old Testament to show the precedent of dancing and vociferous praise to enthusiastic praise bands, while the conventional group appeals more to the New Testament to support what it perceives as the proper interpretation of "the regulative principle of

---

13. For Calvin's views on Jubal and the musical arts, in which he makes similar remarks, see his *Commentary on Genesis*, n.d., http://www.iclnet.org/pub/resources/text/m.sion/cvgn1-11.htm (accessed December 3, 2010).

14. Although Bourgeois did also provide four-part harmonizations, they were reserved for use *at home*. I will have more to say on the psalms for home use later in this paper. Many of the four-part settings are syllabic and chordal, a style which has survived in many Protestant church services to the present day.

worship." Fundamentally the question both sides are asking is, "What music best glorifies God: traditional or contemporary?"[15] In other words, "Which one does God like?"[16] While it may seem counter-intuitive, Calvin offers the contemporary church musician a degree of latitude. How so?

III

It is significant that Calvin's penchant for canonical psalmody was motivated not only by his ardent notion that the music God enjoys most is that which God himself inspired holy men of old to compose. As mentioned earlier, Calvin's choice of music was every bit as much actuated by Christian and Classical humanism — in short, the cultural trends of his day. This point is really not surprising. From the earliest times church music has been influenced strongly by an exchange of ideas between church and culture. Even more generally, the precise relationship the church has shared with its contiguous culture has always been one of mutual dialogue: the church informing culture, and culture informing the church.

The Huguenot Renaissance composer Claude Le Jeune[17] offers a particularly apt conjunction of the dialogue between Calvinist composer and cultural trends. In 1537, Calvin sought to codify the practice of exclusive psalmody throughout Geneva. Psalms were to be sung in the metrical style and in unison. Before long, however, Le Jeune exchanged the tunes and composed settings of the psalms in contrapuntal style, what have been equated to free motets.[18] He produced 347 psalm settings, the most famous of which during

---

15. As there is likely no need to define further the nature of these two forms of worship, it is important to note that there is a third soldier on the battlefield. This is the modern Puritan who interprets even the traditionalist's use of hymns, organs, and pianos as a departure from the guiding principle of *sola scriptura* or what is today called "the regulative principle" of worship.

16. This brief dissection does not consider "blended" services or those that still ascribe to Calvin's practices.

17. Le Jeune was the most famous composer of secular music in France in the late sixteenth century. In case it be said that the composer was dissonant to Calvin's sweeping religious priorities, he was discovered to have authored an anti-Catholic tract in 1589, which forced him to flee Paris during the siege that year. Upon his death in Paris he was buried in the Protestant cemetery of La Trinité.

18. See Anne Harrington Heider, "Preface," in *Claude Le Jeune, Les Cent Cinquante Pseaumes de David,* Recent Researches in the Music of the Renaissance, vol. 98 (Madison, Wis.: A-R. Editions, 1995), 10. The Renaissance period was a time when the motet blossomed

his lifetime was his *Dodécacorde,* a series of twelve psalm settings published in La Rochelle in 1598.[19] What is important is the fact that each of the psalms is set in one of the twelve modes first established by Renaissance theorist Gioseffo Zarlino. Richard Freedman notes the importance of this move:

> The *Dodécacorde* contains music of great subtlety, especially in the ways that it combines melodies from the Genevan Psalter with polyphony that vividly reflects the imagery and emotional aspects of those sacred hymns. As such the *Dodécacorde* can be understood as a culmination of a long process of elaboration of the monophonic Psalter. The *Dodécacorde* is also notable for the ways in which it reflects upon and accumulates a long tradition of musical thought, in particular the modal theories of Gioseffo Zarlino in the 1573 revision of the *Istitutioni harmoniche*.... Le Jeune took special care in his cycle not merely to select psalm tunes that would illustrate this twelve-tone system, he actually revised the official Genevan melodies to make them correspond more neatly to Zarlino's theoretical ideal. This is a wholly remarkable and ... unprecedented approach to this repertory of sacred tunes.... Le Jeune's use of this modal system as a framework for the presentation of his spiritual polyphony also has direct analogies with an extensive Protestant tradition of inscribing new meaning in familiar forms.[20]

As Freedman elucidates, Le Jeune's purpose in revising the melodies of the Genevan Psalter in accord with Zarlino's system was to bring out "the imagery and emotional aspects of those sacred hymns." Like Calvin, Le Jeune wanted the sacred psalms to stir not merely the head, but more importantly the heart of the hearer. That Calvin would have disapproved of the use of polyphony is unmistakable. But does not Le Jeune follow the more important path of his predecessor with his desire for the psalms to in-

---

for both worship and entertainment. Secular motets were typically set to a Latin text in praise of a monarch, commemorating some public triumph, or as in the case of Dufay's motet *Nuper rosarum flores* (1436) written to commemorate the completion of Brunelleschi's massive dome atop the Cathedral of Florence.

19. Features of the music indicate his intent, which clearly exceeds Calvin's knowledge. His rendering of Psalm 52 uses sixteen voices while his collection of all 150 psalms, published posthumously, was set for four and five voices.

20. Richard Freedman, "Le Dodécacorde de Le Jeune comme site pour des significations spirituelles," *Revue de musicologie* 89:2 (2003): 297. For the importance of the twelve tones in Renaissance music, see Harold S. Powers, "Tonal Types and Modal Categories in Renaissance Polyphony," *Journal of the American Musicological Society* 34:3 (Autumn 1981): 428-70.

flame and inspire the heart with spiritual zeal? And, like Calvin, did not Le Jeune listen to the cultural trends of his day when giving shape to his new psalm settings?

After her half-sister Elizabeth succeeded Catholic Mary Tudor in 1558, the Calvinist tradition of psalmody was reinstated in England. New metrical Psalters were produced during the period — most notably the New Version of the Psalms of David by Nahum Tate and Nicholas Brady first published in England in 1696. Tate was poet laureate of England, as well as being a playwright and an adapter of others' plays. Brady was an Anglican clergyman, poet, and author. The work of these poets opened the way for scriptural hymnody in English worship of the late 1600s. Also significant during this period was the devotional poetry of Herbert, Crashaw, Vaughan, Herrick, and John Donne.

But of particular interest is the work in 1697 by George Herbert: *Select Hymns Taken Out of Mr. Herbert's Temple,* with a preface stating that they were for the use of "Private Christians . . . in their Closets or Families." Herbert's stress on interior worship was critical in the divide of the day between ceremonialists and Puritans over music. Both sides looked to Herbert as a spiritual son. According to Guibbory, "For [Henry] Vaughan in the early 1650s, Herbert's *Temple* took the place of the disestablished church, providing the forms and inspiration for worship," while at the same time Puritan "Richard Baxter praised Herbert's 'heart-work' . . . and dissenters embraced Herbert as 'Our Divine Poet.'"[21] Opposing forces to legitimize two differing forms of worship, both claiming the Reformed legacy, claimed Herbert. Noteworthy is the fact that the debate centered on a writer of hymns and paid little attention to the role of exclusive Psalmody.

Although Calvin would have been uncomforted by the high role of hymnody in the seventeenth-century English church, it is again his steadfastness to the moral and spiritual nature of music that carries through from Tate and Brady to Herbert, and from there splintering into ceremonialist and Puritan camps. This is yet another example of how the *spirit* of Calvin's desires for music continued even though the *letter* was in decline.[22] But had

---

21. Acssah Guibbory, *Ceremony and Community from Milton to Herbert: Literature, Religion, and Culture Conflict in Seventeenth-Century England* (Cambridge: Cambridge University Press, 1998), 44.

22. By the 1690s, the use of exclusive psalmody was waning, though the Church of England and a few of the Calvinist congregations held fast to the Psalter. But the rise of evangelical Protestants, all still claiming the Calvinist heritage, had created a fertile ground for Isaac Watts's first collection of hymns in 1707: the *Hymns and Spiritual Songs.*

not Calvin himself opened the door to these innovations? The 1543 edition of the Genevan Psalter also contained musical versions of the Song of Simeon, the Lord's Prayer, the Ten Commandments, and the Apostles' Creed.[23]

IV

Yet another way Calvin proffers the contemporary church musician of today a degree of latitude is seen in his celebration of the Reformation in a new liturgical design, in which original song-settings were crucial. In the main Calvin was not doing anything new. Throughout Scripture God's mighty acts are celebrated in song: Moses' Song of Deliverance, Deborah and Barak's Song of Victory, Hannah's Song, David's Song of Victory, Mary's Song of Praise — all fall on the heels of God's declaration to save his people, to do a new thing in the earth, or to recall his deeds of loving-kindness. Are we to argue that Calvin's exploitation of the psalms of Scripture limits us in congregational singing to those same psalms? Or can we find in Calvin's replication of the scriptural pattern an encouragement to speak afresh musically in today's world in response to God's saving acts? In the Calvinist tradition, it is this latter course that represents the standard.

For example, in the year 1756, while attending an evangelistic meeting held in a barn at Codymain, Augustus Montague Toplady was converted. He became a strong Calvinist and the author of many popular hymns, but none as memorable as "Rock of Ages," first published in 1776. Although legend has it that Toplady wrote the words to the hymn commemorating his escape from a violent storm into a cave for shelter, the words "Nothing in my hand I bring, Simply to thy Cross I cling; Naked, come to thee for dress; Helpless, look to thee for grace; Foul, I to the fountain fly; Wash me, Saviour, or I die" must also recall that night in the barn at the village of Codymain.

The Wesley brothers and George Whitefield began preaching in England and eventually crossed over to the American Colonies during the first half of the eighteenth century to help spawn America's Great Awakening. As almost on cue, the revival produced yet another, fresh outpouring of new hymns. Calvinistic Methodist John Cennick, writer of hymns like "Jesus My All to Heaven Is Gone," and the Anglican preacher John Newton, of "Amaz-

---

23. I owe some of the thoughts in this paragraph to Duck Schuler, "History of the Genevan Psalter," Part 3, *Credenda Agenda* 15:1, http://www.credenda.org/issues/15-1musica.php (accessed January 12, 2011).

ing Grace" and "Glorious Things of Thee Are Spoken," are the two most important individuals in the creation of Great Awakening–era hymns.

The Second Great Awakening in America brought about a revitalization of hymn-singing and the introduction of new hymns once again. Though it is typical to emphasize the impact the Wesleyan tradition had on the creation of new hymns during this period, one of the most influential hymnbooks of the Second Great Awakening was Calvinist evangelist Asahel Nettelton's *Village Hymns*.

Protestant churches of today are at conflict over styles of music. Shall we preserve the traditional hymns that have stood the test of time? Or should we engage our sensitivities in styles and sounds that reflect the times in which we live? It must be remembered that Calvin intended for the Reformation to be a continuing movement. We are *always* reforming. There thus remains a need for sustained commitment to spiritual revitalization within our churches and to embodied Christian living in the world. Is it not, then, oxymoronic that so many Christians who are hard at work to revive and reform church and society are committed only to the songs of yesterday's reformations and revivals? True commitment to a program of ongoing reform entails a readiness to express joy at the outcome in the form of a new collection of psalm-settings, spiritual songs, and hymns. Christians must be prepared to follow Calvin's main concern for the glory of God through the moral and spiritual integrity of music, but also to listen to the voice of culture, while not abandoning themselves to the whims of culture. Christians must also be willing to maintain their rich heritage in church music. It is a delicate balance, to be sure, but one the churches must embrace.

V

The next main point to be considered here is that, in Calvin's thought, the music God likes is conditioned by the spiritual state of the musician. This idea opens up the wider consideration of secular music — although the term "secular" is used reservedly — for according to neo-Calvinist cultural thought the supposed *sacred-secular* distinction is casuistic. Nevertheless, the term is used here for the sake of argument.

Appreciation for Calvin's view on the moral nature of music is increased by a deepened awareness of the spiritual relationship of the musician to God. This parallel issue relates two theological tenets of Calvin's thought:

the spiritual antithesis between God and non-Christian[24] and the doctrine of common grace.

The phrase "spiritual antithesis" is not to be confused with Barth's idea that despite the hypostatic union of the two natures of Christ the metaphysical polarity between God and the world is preserved. Calvin's view on the antithesis is in contradiction to the Roman Catholic belief that fallen man has lost only the *donum superadditum* (supernatural gift of God's grace) while in large part retaining his natural endowments. Quite the opposite: Calvin believed that total depravity not only renders sinners unable to do anything profitable unto salvation, but also makes it impossible for even their natural gifts to produce anything truly good in God's eyes. It is with this idea in mind that he states,

> Now the soul is not reborn if merely a part of it is reformed, but only when it is wholly renewed. The antithesis set forth in both passages [John 3:6 and Romans 8:6-7] confirms this. The Spirit is so contrasted with flesh that no intermediate thing is left. Accordingly, whatever is not spiritual in man is by this reckoning called "carnal." We have nothing of the Spirit, however, except through regeneration.[25]

That nothing of the Spirit is in us except through regeneration led Calvin to insist that only Christian presuppositions should inform the elements of public worship, including music. Here, however, Calvin provides a way of thinking that appears to present a curious ambiguity. On the one hand, he is willing to make use of Plato's doctrine of ethos as a basis for restricting the use of instruments in corporate worship, while on the other hand, he believed that Plato's philosophic insights were as a whole totally eclipsed by the gospel. Calvin appears to have resolved this seeming ambiguity through selective utilization of Plato as support for his more prominent position on the moral dimension of music.

VI

Calvin's position on the antithesis leads rather naturally to the question of music more generally envisioned. Does Calvin completely disregard the mu-

---

24. For more on this, see John M. Frame, *Cornelius Van Til: An Analysis of His Thought* (Phillipsburg: Protestant & Reformed, 1995), 187-213.
25. *Institutes* II.iii.1.

sic of non-Christians? No — in fact, he recognized God's presence in all things, but with an important caveat. Herman Bavinck's description of Calvin's position on the *semen religionis* (seed of religion) is explanatory.

> Calvin, taking as his starting point "the seed of religion," saw incontrovertible signs and testimonies of God's majesty in "every particle of the universe"; in the starry heavens, in the human body, in the soul, in the preservation of all things (etc.) but, having said this, he immediately reminds us that this "seed of religion," though ineradicably implanted in all humans, can be choked and cannot bear good fruit. Humans, having lost the capacity to see God, need the eye of faith. In other Reformed theologians we see natural theology occupying the same place.[26]

Bavinck's distillation of Calvin centers on the fact that although the non-Christian is born in the *imago Dei,* and for that reason bears testimony to God's majesty, such can only be conferred upon the unbeliever in a general sense. In the contracted sense of a life that *gives majesty* to God the non-Christian "cannot bear good fruit." Musicians are not exempt. Calvin's distinction that the non-Christian *testifies* to God's majesty while only the Christian *gives* majesty to God suggests that music happens within a moral context shared by both musician and God. Music is simply a creative extension of a musician's spiritual values and worldview, which help to define her relationship to God. Every note of the composer, even the tone one produces as a musician, must therefore be done with the quality of aesthetic deference to the Lord of all creativity for it to bear good fruit.

In the Stone Lectures delivered at Princeton in 1898, Abraham Kuyper gave voice to the antithesis of consciousness that exists between Christians and non-Christians: "We, of course, have to acknowledge two kinds of human consciousness: that of the regenerate and the unregenerate; and these two cannot be identical."[27] Though Kuyper's remarks are set in the context of science, they are no less profitable for an appreciation of the antithesis of consciousness between Christian and non-Christian musicians.

---

26. Herman Bavinck, *Reformed Dogmatics,* vol. 2: *God and Creation* (Grand Rapids: Baker Academic, 2004), 78. Here Bavinck is referencing John Calvin, *Institutes* I.iv.1; I.v.1-10, 11-15.

27. Abraham Kuyper, *Calvinism: Six Stone-Lectures,* "Calvinism and Religion," Kuyper Foundation, Online Books and Essays, July 17, 2003, http://www.kuyper.org/main/publish/books_essays/printer_17.shtml 137 (accessed March 3rd, 2011). Op. cit. Peter Heslam, *Creating a Christian Worldview: Abraham Kuyper's Lectures on Calvinism* (Grand Rapids: Eerdmans, 1998), 183.

But if this is the case, are we to infer that only Christians are capable of composing and/or performing great music? Ludwig van Beethoven was enamored with the philosophy of Immanuel Kant and is not thought of as a Christian. Yet he is considered one of the greatest composers of all time. Does God not think that Beethoven bore good fruit? Unquestionably Beethoven and other exceptional unbelievers like him demonstrated technical genius and aesthetic vision in their compositions, and accordingly their life production was great. But in the Calvinist tradition, "great" is interpreted in a particularized way.

Dutch Calvinist Klaas Schilder clarifies this particularization when he opposes it to the spiritual deficit in unbelieving artists. He observes, "Our conclusion then is that culture is never more than a mere attempt and that, since it is restricted to remnants only, it is a matter of tragedy. God has indeed left something behind in fallen man. But these are only 'small remnants' of his original gifts . . . they can never produce any work that is sound."[28] The upshot of Schilder's position is that, except people receive back those elements of the *imago Dei* lost to sin, *how* the expressions of culture are produced is by "small remnants" of that image, and *what* is produced is not spiritually whole.

Bavinck explains the situation this way. "God is present in his creatures in different ways. . . . There is a difference between his physical and his ethical immanence. To suggest an analogy: people, too, may be physically very close to each other, yet miles apart in spirit and outlook."[29] So it is the ethical presence of God in his redeemed creatures that brings their music before him in an enhanced way.

Neo-Calvinist Cornelius Van Til offers great insight into the nature of this enhancement. He argued that there is no such thing as a "brute fact" — a part of reality that somehow escapes divine interpretation. Consequently, there is no such thing as "brute music." The composing and playing of all forms of music, as they articulate some moral position, summon holy judgment. Minus a redemptive relationship between musician and Creator, even if the music may reflect the interests of beauty in a broad sense, on the whole the Calvinist view of the antithesis cautions us to determine the value such music has before God not only in terms of beautiful tones, harmonies, and textures, but also according to the ethical *values* that flow from the musician's heart as defined by her redemptive relationship to God.

---

28. Klaas Schilder, *Christ and Culture* (Winnepeg, Manitoba: Premier Printing, 1977), 59.
29. Bavinck, *Reformed Dogmatics*, vol. 2, 169.

VII

This current point having to do with the spiritual state of the musician is inextricably woven together with the deep-centered issue of motivation. Why do I play, compose, and sing before the public? To impress the music critics? To draw attention to myself? Or do I do it as an offering to God? These concerns bleed over to yet another, related issue: the moral statement all music makes. What was Richard Wagner really saying in much of his music about race relations? What was his motivation? Despite the July 2001 performance of the overture to *Tristan und Isolde* at the Israel Festival in Jerusalem, Wagner's music has been unofficially banned in public in Israel ever since *Kristallnacht* in 1938. As much as one may love the rich, soaring textures of the tone poems of Richard Strauss, is the worldview of his famed *Thus Spake Zarathustra*, in which he brings to mind the philosophical novel of Nietzsche by the same name, one Christians can support? Further, one may ask, does God, sovereign over the creation and Giver of the Law at Sinai, receive pleasure from the chance music of John Cage? If so, then God's delight in music would seem to be something other than a matter of moral degree, but a matter of relative focus. However one might answer these sorts of questions they are difficult to be sure and remain ones with which we ought to wrestle. The Calvinist stance that no offering of music is immune from holy judgment may well provide an important starting-point in addressing these concerns.

Reformed scholar David Prowlison looks to the Calvinistic worldview for such a starting point. In speaking to the idols of culture he addresses not only our cultural impetus, but sets even this concern within the heightened context of our most fundamental loyalties.

> The deep questions of motivation are not "What is motivating me?" The final questions are, "Who is the master of this pattern of thought, feeling or behavior?" In the biblical view, we are religious, inevitably bound to one god or another. People do not have needs. We have masters, lords, gods, be they oneself, other people, valued objects, Satan. The metaphor of an idolatrous heart and society captures the fact that human motivation bears an automatic relationship to God: Who, other than the true God, is my god?[30]

30. David Prowlison, "Idols of the Heart and 'Vanity Fair,'" n.d., Restoring Christ to Counseling and Counseling to The Church, http://www.ccef.org/idols-heart-and-vanity-fair (accessed February 15, 2011).

In light of the antithesis, how then does Calvin account for human achievement among non-Christians? He does so through the concept of God's universal or common grace to man. Though Calvin cannot be credited with having first coined the phrase "common grace" — in fact, he never used the term — he is seminal in the formation of the idea. In explaining the honesty, courage, and other virtues exemplified by the Roman commander Camillus, Calvin reasons,

> The most certain and easy solution of this question, however, is, that those virtues are not the common properties of nature, but the peculiar graces of God, which he dispenses in great variety, and in a certain degree to men that are otherwise profane.[31]

Calvin's remarks, though centered on the heroic nature of those destined for command, are no less applicable to the gifted nature of those destined for music. In fact, Calvin's thought on what Kuyper later termed "common grace" had more to do with explaining all the positive cultural contributions of fallen men, while Kuyper looked to common grace more as a justification for Christian participation with non-Christians in a variety of cultural endeavors.

VIII

This is a suitable point at which to note a finer distinction still between Calvin and Kuyper on common grace. Noted previously is Kuyper's clarity on the antithesis in the area of science especially. Nonetheless, Kuyper's views on common grace do not seem to take into account adequately the import of the antithesis as found in Calvin. It could even be argued that Kuyper's position on common grace is oddly out of place with his own view on the antithesis.

Intrinsic to the Kuyperian notion of common grace is the belief that unregenerate people are properly competent to execute their cultural responsibilities without need of regeneration. Now Kuyper would *not* say that fallen people realize their cultural tasks to the glory of God. Nonetheless, it was Kuyper and Bavinck, the latter of whom I have quoted in support of the antithesis, who used Revelation 21:24-26, which says, "The nations will walk by its light . . . and the kings will bring the glory and honor of the nations into

---

31. *Institutes* II.iii.4.

it," to say that God is so pleased with the excellencies of unregenerate culture that God will gladly receive such products into heaven. Not only does this position raise insoluble philosophical problems in juxtaposition to the antithesis, but also it is not exegetically sound. Verse 27, which presents a continuance of the idea started in verse 24, states unmistakably that the nations and the kings that bring the glory of their cultures through the gates of the city are those who know the Lamb of God in salvation. It says, "[A]nd nothing unclean, and no one who practices abomination and lying, shall ever come into it, but *only* those whose names are written in the Lamb's book of life" (italics added).

Calvin, in contrast, takes the antithesis to its logical conclusion. Nothing but that which proceeds from the Spirit of regeneration will enter heaven. In the same section of the *Institutes* most recently quoted, Calvin, though admitting that the unregenerate evidence "the peculiar graces of God," nevertheless cautions us against all spiritual presumption.

> But because however excellent anyone has been, his own ambition always pushes him on — a blemish with which all virtues are so sullied that before God they lose all favor — anything in profane men that appears praiseworthy must be considered worthless. Besides, where there is no zeal to glorify God, the chief part of uprightness is absent; a zeal of which all those whom he has not regenerated by his Spirit are devoid.[32]

In support of Calvin's position are the words of Jesus: "And whoever in the name of a disciple gives to one of these little ones even a cup of cold water to drink, truly I say to you, he shall not lose his reward" (Matthew 10:42). If we cannot so much as give a cup of cold water to a thirsty child and be rewarded by heaven lest we be his disciple, why do we think we can compose a symphony and have God receive it unto his glory lest we be his disciple?

In its long history, Calvinism has been a lightning rod. Perhaps no less controversial are the thoughts expressed in this essay, which lead inevitably to the view that an off-pitch melody warbled by a poor Dutch farmer to the glory of God is more pleasing to God's ear than is a top performance of *Nussun Dorma* sung by an unbeliever. Yet one thing in particular Calvin ought to be broadly applauded for is his insistence on the need for unrestricted zeal for the glory of God in all areas of human endeavor. As the first question of the Shorter Catechism asks, "What is the chief end of man?" the

---

32. *Institutes* II.iii.4.

answer that "Man's chief end is to glorify God, and to enjoy him forever" means that no area of cultural work, including music, is exempt from this fundamental claim. If such a position is to be viewed as "dogmatic," then let it be so. But dogma viewed simply as a system of belief is an inescapable and regular part of life.

Calvin's restrictions on music may seem antiquated to many. But, as demonstrated, even Calvin himself was not exempt from certain cultural influences. Should one also invest something from the culture into the patterns of regular worship, or choose to pursue music on the world stage, one ought to bear in mind two things: first, the moral nature of music; and second, the spiritual state of the musician's life before God. In all, the aspiration of every musician should be to sing, play, and compose to the glory of God. According to Calvin, this is the music God likes.

The Vampire Squid:
Abraham Kuyper on Public Entertainment

Clifford B. Anderson

"People think they come together in the Theatre, and it is there that they are isolated."

Jean-Jacques Rousseau, *Letter to D'Alembert* (1759)

In the waning months of 1880, Abraham Kuyper entered into a polemical exchange about the place of public entertainment in Christian life. The proximate cause of this controversy was a troupe of English bell-ringers. The "Royal Poland Street Temperance Handbell Ringers," conducted by Duncan Miller, embarked on a tour of the Netherlands in November 1880 and performed, at the invitation of a prominent Dutch pastor, a benefit concert for a Christian orphanage.[1] Why did Kuyper object to this performance? Was he just a curmudgeon? The controversy over the bell ringers might have passed forgotten were it not for the questions it raised about the role and place of entertainment in the Christian life.

I

As the name suggests, the Royal Poland Street Temperance Handbell Ringers were a group of Christian musicians active in the temperance movement. A

---

1. Abraham Kuyper and Frederick Lodewijk Rutgers, *Publiek Vermaak: Asterisken en Artikelen Over het Ook Destijds aan de Orde Zijnde Vraagstuk* (Amsterdam: Standaard, 1924), 5.

history of the temperance movement relates the group's origins in a chapter aptly titled "Music and Song as Aids to Temperance."[2]

> In the early part of the year 1866 Mr. C. J. Havart, secretary to the Poland Street (London) Young Men's Teetotal Society, felt moved to make an effort to raise the character of temperance entertainments, and conceived of the idea that campanology might be made subservient to the ends of teetotalism. Having had some connection with Mr. Duncan S. Miller, who from boyhood had made hand-bell ringing a hobby, and having a love for the art himself, Mr. Havart sought his friend's assistance, and a band was formed in connection with the society. They commenced with a peal of ten bells, and after some reorganization of the members they increased the number of bells to seventeen. On Saturday, March 24, 1866, the Poland Street Hand-bell Ringers made their first public appearance. . . . Encouraged by their success they continued their efforts, became more and more proficient, and increased the number of bells to something over seventy. In April, 1870, they made their first appearance (by command) before her majesty the queen and the members of the royal family at Osborne House, Isle of Wight. Since that time they have made several appearances before members of the royal family, and are therefore justly termed the "Royal Poland Street Handbell Ringers."[3]

By the 1870s, the Poland Street Handbell Ringers had struck an alliance with the famous Baptist preacher Charles Spurgeon (1834-1892). Miller conducted bell-ringing concerts at the Metropolitan Tabernacle in London, entertaining children in Spurgeon's Sunday School.[4] They toured extensively and, in 1882, also traveled to Canada and the United States.[5]

Several contemporaneous reports about the concerts survive. Perhaps the fullest is by Charles Maurice Davies, a historian and journalist who coincidentally penned a history of the Netherlands in 1841.[6] Davies devoted a chapter of *Unorthodox London*, a book of sketches of offbeat religious events in London, to his experience attending a concert of the Royal Poland Street

---

2. Peter Turner Winskill, *The Temperance Movement and Its Workers: A Record of Social, Moral, Religious, and Political Progress*, vol. 2 (London: Blackie, 1891), Chapter 25.

3. Winskill, *The Temperance Movement and Its Workers*, 2:138f.

4. Christopher Crayon, "The Royal Hand-Bell Ringers," *The Chautauqaun: A Monthly Magazine Devoted to the Promotion of True Culture* 2:6 (March 1882): 370.

5. Winskill, *The Temperance Movement and Its Workers*, 2:139.

6. Charles Davies, *History of Holland, from the Beginning of the Tenth to the End of the Eighteenth Century* (London: J. W. Parker, 1841).

Handbell Ringers in 1873.[7] He recounts his receipt of two tickets to a "Campanological Concert," which he decided to attend along with a girl (presumably a relative) of twelve years old. "It was, strangely enough, to a Baptist Tabernacle the tickets invited me; and when I entered I found the space below the pulpit occupied with a long table on which were placed multitudinous bells of all sizes, up from the muffin-bell of domestic life to the size of a small pail."[8] The event combined bell ringing, playacting, and admonition against the dangers of drinking. Davies captures the light-hearted tone of the performance in his description of its opening scene.

> Their conductor, Mr. Miller, on entering with his four confreres, immediately proceeded to request the expulsion of all babies, then the five indulged in a sort of burlesque opening in verse. . . . All sorts of entertainments are suggested, just as in the opening of a pantomime; and, of course, everybody knows that campanology will eventually carry off the palm.[9]

The players excelled at their bell ringing according to Davies, offsetting the comical staging with beautiful renditions of religious and secular compositions. Toward the end of the concert, Duncan Miller delivered "a sermon on tract distribution," which Davies thought "a mistake."[10] In this juxtaposition of musical entertainment and morality, it was music that cast a lasting spell. Davies records that the pastor of the Baptist Tabernacle — whom he does not name — exclaimed at the concert's finale that he could "*lay* in bed all day and dream of the music he had been hearing that evening."[11]

Another source strengthens the supposition that the unnamed pastor was Spurgeon. A reporter attended a concert at the Metropolitan Tabernacle in 1882, commenting on the relaxed and mirthful exchanges between Duncan Miller and Charles Spurgeon.

> Mr. Miller has a knack of amusing children, and he has determined to devote his energies in that direction. The time has come, as he told us on Friday, when it is the duty of Christian men to find wholesome moral entertainment, not music-hall slang, for their young people, and that he

---

7. Charles Davies, *Unorthodox London or, Phases of Religious Life in the Metropolis* (London: Tinsley Bros., 1873), 351-55.
8. Davies, *Unorthodox London*, 352.
9. Davies, *Unorthodox London*, 352.
10. Davies, *Unorthodox London*, 354.
11. Davies, *Unorthodox London*, 355.

succeeded, at any rate, I may say, there are a thousand of the Tabernacle Sunday-school children ready to declare, to say nothing of their pastor, who never looked better than he did the other night sitting at the far end among the boys, with a face all smiles and fun. Indeed, it would be difficult to say who did enjoy themselves most, Mr. Spurgeon or the children, or Mr. Miller and his men.[12]

According to the account, Spurgeon went so far as to announce that he would award a "patent" to Miller for performances before his Sunday school.[13] Who would not be enthusiastic at the "sight of the children" who "all looked so happy, so clean, so comfortable, so respectable . . . ?"[14] Who would object to such innocuous and happy entertainment, gently decked with Christian morals and admonitions to temperance? Who would call for a boycott on such performances? Who but Abraham Kuyper?

II

The Royal Poland Street Handbell Ringers gave a charitable performance in Amsterdam on November 6, 1880. The performance was arranged by Carel Steven Adama van Scheltema (1815-97), a Protestant pastor active in the temperance movement,[15] to benefit a Christian orphanage administered by Johannes van 't Lindenhout (1836-1918), a Christian evangelist and social worker.[16] The concert was advertised in the papers, stressing the troupe's artistry with their 124 bells, calling attention to their 3,300 public performances in England, and noting that they had performed nine times for the British royal family.[17] The concert was successful, drawing several hundred people and selling out the hall. A reviewer in *Het Nieuws van de Dag* praised the concert in words similar to those attributed to Spurgeon: "one would like most to follow along with closed eyes and in the sweetest dreams."[18] The

12. Crayon, "The Royal Hand-Bell Ringers," 370f.
13. Crayon, "The Royal Hand-Bell Ringers," 371.
14. Crayon, "The Royal Hand-Bell Ringers," 371.
15. J. A. Zeilstra, "Adam van Scheltema, Carel Steven," in *Biografisch Lexicon voor de Geschiedenis van het Nederlandse Protestantisme*, vol. 3 (Kampen: Kok, 1988), 15f.
16. F. L. van 't Hooft, "Lindenhout, Johannes van T.," in *Biografisch Lexicon voor de Geschiedenis van het Nederlandse Protestantisme*, vol. 1 (Kampen: Kok, 1978), 124f.
17. See, for example, advertisement, *Het Nieuws van de Dag*, November 5, 1880.
18. "Gemengd Nieuws," *Het Nieuws van de Dag*, November 9, 1880.

reviewer commented briefly, "songs were also sung — joyful ditties during which all kinds of humorous gestures were made."[19] The reviewer also remarked, "Whoever intended to have what is typically referred to as an 'edifying' evening would have gone seriously wrong."[20]

As it happened, among the audience that evening was Frederick Lodewijk Rutgers (1836-1917), a former Amsterdam pastor who had become a professor of church law and history at the newly organized *Vrije Universiteit*.[21] In a letter to the editor of *De Standaard* composed after the outbreak of the controversy, Rutgers recounted his experience of the concert. He evidently enjoyed the campanology and did not object to the singing that took place. But he raised questions about the character of the performance as a whole. His first concern was about false advertising. He had been led to believe that this was to have been a Christian concert, but the event itself was entirely "neutral" in its perspective.[22] Admittedly, the newspaper advertisements made no reference to Christianity, but they did note that the performance was a benefit concert for an orphanage run by a leading Christian social worker. More significantly, the comical tone disturbed him. He disliked the farcical faces and gestures made by the singers. "It was not spiritual, nor comical, nor pleasant, nor anything of the kind; it was just 'drollery,'" he wrote with disdain about the first song.[23] He disliked the excessive laughter accompanying a song about the desire of a giant man for a tiny woman. And he objected to the closing act, during which the singers put on colorful nightcaps and poked their heads through the curtains as they sang to suggest that they had already retired for the evening. While he did not question the goodness of the cause, Rutgers asked how the performance could properly be termed "Christian."

Kuyper published a "three star" editorial on November 15, 1880, about the Royal Poland Street Handbell Ringers.[24] "Their whole show, however admirable from an artistic perspective, was a regrettable mistake," he wrote, ruing that these "jokers" had been introduced with "an anointed word."[25] He

---

19. "Gemengd Nieuws," *Het Nieuws van de Dag*, November 9, 1880.
20. "Gemengd Nieuws," *Het Nieuws van de Dag*, November 9, 1880.
21. Doede Nauta, "Rutgers, Frederick Lodewijk," in *Biografisch Lexicon voor de Geschiedenis van het Nederlandse Protestantisme*, vol. 1 (Kampen: Kok, 1978), 303f.
22. Kuyper and Rutgers, *Publiek Vermaak*, 18f.
23. Kuyper and Rutgers, *Publiek Vermaak*, 20.
24. Kuyper and Rutgers, *Publiek Vermaak*, 5. The so-called "three star" editorials were short commentaries printed in *De Standaard* under three asterisks.
25. Kuyper and Rutgers, *Publiek Vermaak*, 5.

backhandedly criticized Van 't Lindenhout and Adama van Scheltema by excusing them from criticism on the grounds that they must have received bad advice from their English contacts.

What is not apparent from the editorial is that Adama van Scheltema had already clashed with Kuyper during his period as a pastor in Utrecht.[26] Scheltema was a forerunner in the temperance movement in the Netherlands. In 1844, he committed to abstaining from Dutch gin *(jenever)* and other hard alcohol. Contact with the Total Abstinence Society in England convinced him in 1861 that Christians should swear off all forms of alcohol. He was out in front of the teetotal movement in the Netherlands, which had gained ground more quickly in England. He was orthodox in doctrine, but concerned to draw on the church's influence to reform the morals of his period.

Scheltema responded to the editorial in *De Standaard* with a letter to the editor.[27] He refused the "excuse" offered him by Kuyper, stating that he had been acquainted with Duncan Miller since 1871 and thus knew well the content of his bell-ringing performances. Furthermore, he called attention to the close connection between Duncan and Spurgeon, which should dispel any concern that Miller's performances were unchristian. He noted that Miller and his troupe were teetotalers, whose moral standpoint was much superior to moderate drinkers and smokers among the ranks of the Reformed.[28] The appeal to Spurgeon elicited the wry comment from Kuyper that though Spurgeon was "as a popular preacher a talent without equal," he was "anything but a trustworthy theologian."[29] Or, as he put it with a little Dutch pride, "What commands our interest is exclusively the question whether Dutch Christians should go about exchanging their customs, which they have accepted since the Reformation, for the — in our opinion — *lower ranking* practices of Christian circles in England."[30] The question, in other words, touched on a matter of principle. Was it permissible for Christians to attend public entertainment that not only lacked a sacred basis but was entirely secular, so long as it served a virtuous cause?

The "three star" editorials and letters to the editor continued into December. Kuyper's remarks about England and his characterization of the performance as "profane" evoked the expected responses. An anonymous

---

26. Biographical details are drawn from Zeilstra, "Adam van Scheltema, Carel Steven," 15f.
27. The letter is reprinted in Kuyper and Rutgers, *Publiek Vermaak*, 6f.
28. Kuyper and Rutgers, *Publiek Vermaak*, 6f.
29. Kuyper and Rutgers, *Publiek Vermaak*, 7.
30. Kuyper and Rutgers, *Publiek Vermaak*, 8.

"Christian" sent a letter to the *Algemeen Handelsblad*, for example, full of indignation that a concert that had provided "a pleasure-full, joyful evening" and raised 4,000 pounds for the orphanage should be dismissed as profane.[31] Who was Kuyper to judge whether such public entertainment was unchristian?

The most significant outcome of this nearly forgotten polemical exchange was a series of fifteen articles on "Public Entertainment," which Kuyper published in *De Standaard* from December 15, 1880, to February 21, 1881.[32] The series is significant, not only because Kuyper dealt with the place of entertainment in the Christian life, but also because it represents an early articulation of his understanding of the sphere of the arts, which he would subsequently develop in his rectoral address "Het Calvinisme en de Kunst"[33] in 1888 and the chapter on "Calvinism and Art" in his *Lectures on Calvinism* of 1898.[34]

III

What is the distinction between art and entertainment? Today, we typically conjoin the two — as in the "Arts and Entertainment" section of the *Philadelphia Inquirer* or the A&E Network. Is art just a form of entertainment? Is entertainment a kind of art? Anyone who knows Kuyper's manner of thinking will see where we are headed. Kuyper excelled at making distinctions, sharpening blurred boundaries, and distinguishing collapsed spheres. It comes as no surprise, then, that he opened his series by articulating the distinction between art and entertainment.

As with all his writings about art, Kuyper anticipated the criticism of Calvinism as the enemy of artistic expression.[35] The purpose of the arts according to Kuyper is to give expression to the unity undergirding the plurality of appearance. Kuyper saw this theme running from the Greeks to the Medieval Church to the Renaissance to contemporary naturalism, adjusting for differing understandings of the nature of that underlying unity. By contrast, he argued, Calvinists abandoned the conviction of the unity of the

---

31. Letter to the editor, *Algemeen Handelsblad*, November 28, 1880.
32. J. C. Rullmann, *Kuyper-Bibliographie* (The Hague: Bootsma, 1923), vol. 2.
33. Abraham Kuyper, *Het Calvinisme en de Kunst: Rede bij de Overdracht van het Rectoraat der Vrije Universiteit op 20 October 1888* (Amsterdam: J. A. Wormser, 1888).
34. Abraham Kuyper, *Lectures on Calvinism* (Grand Rapids: Eerdmans, 1931).
35. See Kuyper and Rutgers, *Publiek Vermaak*, 26ff.

world. The doctrine of election divides the world, creating a division too profound for artists to heal. The world of body and matter resisted too strongly re-formation by the Christian artist, Kuyper suggested. The Reformers had therefore retreated inwards to fulfill the human desire for art, giving expression to the Spirit in poetry and song. Only poetry is properly a Protestant art because it is so thoroughly inward, though Calvinism had expressed itself to an adequate degree in music and painting. But that is as far as he would go in 1880. "A Protestant sculpture, architecture, drama, or, what else more there might be, is simply *unthinkable*."[36]

Kuyper's vision of the arts is underdeveloped in the 1880 series on public entertainment. In 1888, he developed a theocentric conception of the arts by drawing on the concept of God's glory.[37] Still, his encomium of the poetry of Jacob Cats (1577-1660) in his 1888 lecture forms a line of continuity with his perspective of 1880. The emphasis in 1880, however, was on the danger of the arts to the religious life. We must remain vigilant, Kuyper contended, in every encounter with the arts, because idolatry is always at hand in artistic creations.[38] In his perception of a life-struggle between Christianity and the arts, Kuyper showed his modernity; as Gordon Graham relates in *The Re-Enchantment of the World: Art versus Religion*, Friedrich Nietzsche (1844-1900), his contemporary, had predicted that the human impulse for religion would turn to the arts as Christianity became discredited.[39]

What, then, of entertainment? Is entertainment also an existential threat to Christian faith? Not at all, according to Kuyper. Entertainment is innocuous. Far from avoiding entertainment, Kuyper considered that Christians needed to seek it out. He expressed his reasoning with a metaphor: "The bow, our ancients were in the habit of saying, cannot always be tense."[40] This quotation derives from an anecdote about John the Evangelist recorded in John Cassian's *The Conferences*.[41] (Interestingly, Miguel de Cervantes drew on the same story to defend the theatre. In Chapter XXI of *Don Quixote*, the

36. Kuyper and Rutgers, *Publiek Vermaak*, 29.
37. Abraham Kuyper, "Calvinism and Art," in *Christian Thought: Lectures and Papers on Philosophy, Christian Evidence, Biblical Elucidation*, trans. J. Hendrik DeVries, vol. 9 (New York: Wilbur B. Ketcham, 1892), 264ff.
38. See Kuyper and Rutgers, *Publiek Vermaak*, 36.
39. Gordon Graham, *The Re-Enchantment of the World: Art Versus Religion* (Oxford: Oxford University Press, 2007), 28f.
40. Kuyper and Rutgers, *Publiek Vermaak*, 30.
41. John Cassian, *John Cassian: The Conferences,* trans. Boniface Ramsey (Mahwah, N.J.: The Newman Press, 1997), 842.

Canon of Toledo remarks apropos of the work of novelists and playwrights, "the bow can't always be bent, nor can our frail human nature subsist without some honest recreation.")[42] To Kuyper, God had ordained periods of human rest in order to avoid exhaustion and strain. The ordained forms of rest are nightly sleep, observation of the weekly Sabbath, and regular recreation. Recreation is crucial because the sinful disorder of the world fosters imbalances not only between body and soul, but also between parts of the body. A letter carrier develops strong legs but weak arms in the course of his work, whereas a cobbler develops powerful arms but frail legs. Recreation restores bodily balance. The same applies in at a higher degree to those whose work requires mental strain but little physical exertion.[43]

Why Kuyper was alive to the dangers of one-sided mental exertion will be immediately understood. He himself had suffered from nervous exhaustion at two crucial points in his early career — after the completion of his Groningen prize thesis in 1861 and after his participation in the holiness conference at Brighton in 1875. In his mature years, he institutionalized periods of rest, travelling each summer to a spa in Dresden, Germany, to unwind from his prodigious labors.[44] Kuyper complained that children did not receive the same consideration. He criticized the "miserable school system that keeps still tender brains in constant tension and delivers to us clever miracle children as candidates for an early 'little old men' existence."[45]

How do we sort out good entertainment from bad? Kuyper drew on the twin commandment to love God and neighbor (cf. Matt 22:37-39) as the touchstone for all Christian existence. He argued that this twin commandment provides several criteria. With respect to the love of God, does the entertainment actually produce the intended effect — namely, relaxation — and thus allow us to return refreshed to our vocations? Or does the entertainment lead to forgetfulness of God or, worse, to activities contrary to divine law? With respect to the love of neighbor, the questions are similar: does the entertainment enable us to return with renewed vigor to serving

---

42. Miguel de Cervantes Saavedra, *Don Quixote*, trans. John Rutherford (London: Penguin Books, 2000), 337; Thompson notes the resemblance between Cervantes and Cassian without, however, suggesting that Cervantes read Cassian. See Colin Thompson, "Eutrapelia and Exemplarity in the Novelas Ejemplares," in *A Companion to Cervantes's Novelas Ejemplares*, ed. Stephen F. Boyd (Woodbridge: Tamesis Books, 2005), 263f.

43. Kuyper and Rutgers, *Publiek Vermaak*, 30f.

44. Jan de Bruijn, *Abraham Kuyper: Een Beeldbiografie* (Amsterdam: Prometheus-Bert Bakker, 2008), 353.

45. Kuyper and Rutgers, *Publiek Vermaak*, 31.

our neighbors? Or do such activities render us hostile toward fellow human beings? Finally, does our entertainment involve us in "solidarity of guilt" with our neighbor?[46]

To summarize, Kuyper distinguished art and entertainment on theological grounds. The arts constitute a sovereign sphere of existence, with a distinct calling to witness to the glorious beauty of God's creation. The arts are also a dangerous sphere because the artist may be tempted to assay the impermissible, namely, the restoration of the unity of the world from its fractured, fallen state. Entertainment, by contrast, is not a sphere as such. Relaxation has no intrinsic purpose, but only a utilitarian function. Sleeping at night, resting on the Sabbath, and taking part in fun and games all serve in different ways to restore our strength. They are ordained not so much for their own sake, but for the sake of our vocations.

IV

Kuyper adjudicated several forms of entertainment in his series on "Public Entertainment," but his focus was the theatre. He concentrated on the theatre because he evidently considered the bell-ringers' performance a form of musical theatre (i.e., public entertainment) rather than a concert (a form of art). "Concerts," he argued, "are only pleasurable for a very small circle. More aristocratic."[47] If the bell-ringers were putting on musical theatre, that begged the question of whether the theatre is a permissible form of entertainment. Kuyper, though, recognized that he was swimming against the tide by defending the Calvinist position. The controversy over the bell-ringers showed that many Christians were no longer convinced that there was any harm in attending theatrical productions. He thus called on another authority, Gustave Tophel, a pastor in Geneva who had recently published a book titled *The Limits of Christian Liberty: Three Discourses Followed by an Appendix with Regard to the Question of the Theatre*.[48] Kuyper encouraged its translation into Dutch and provided a preface.[49] In his preface, he referred

---

46. Kuyper and Rutgers, *Publiek Vermaak*, 33.
47. Kuyper and Rutgers, *Publiek Vermaak*, 39.
48. Gustave Tophel, *The Limits of Christian Liberty: Three Discourses, Followed by an Appendix with Regard to the Question of the Theatre,* trans. George E. Shipman (Chicago: Foundlings' Home Print, 1882).
49. Abraham Kuyper, "Voorwoord," in *Behoort een Christen in de Komedie? Drie Pleidooien,* by Gustave Tophel (Amsterdam: Kruyt, 1881).

to the threat, subsequently averted, that "our good Bell-ringers would push open the comedy door for our Christian folk."⁵⁰

Tophel's work comprises three sermons, only the third of which deals directly with the theatre. He wrote during a period in which actors and most actresses were commonly regarded as Lotharios and prostitutes. Drawing on existing prejudices, Tophel questioned whether Christians could legitimately attend the theatre without participating, at least indirectly, in their sinful and pitiable state. He tried to persuade his readers not to patronize the theatre by appealing to Paul's exhortation in 1 Corinthians 8 that Christians should not eat food dedicated to idols if doing so would injure the faith of weaker companions. In this case, could Christians afford to attend the theatre if doing so might tempt weaker Christians to fall prey to its temptations?

> How would you feel, you who hesitate to condemn the theatre, if, not your own daughter, not even a distant relation, but a simple protégée, a young girl of your acquaintance, should manifest a desire to enter the theatre? That child, why you would rather see it die than to suffer such a fall! Well, if such is the fear with which the theatre inspires you for those who are dear to you can you, without a palpable inconsistency, use it for your own amusement? Will you make sport for yourself with that which ruins souls, and, whether believers or not, shall we not say with Vinet again, "If the theatre devotes its agents to immorality, and sometimes, even to infamy, by the task imposed upon them, how can we allow ourselves to encourage it?"⁵¹

Kuyper relied on Tophel's line of argument, not repeating him word for word, but giving expression to similar prejudices against actors and actresses. These arguments depend on an underlying premise that we no longer share, namely, that the profession of acting is at best unseemly and at worst immoral. This is an old prejudice, which reaches back to the ancients and was given Christian expression by Tertullian.⁵² Its connection to orthodox Christian doctrine is, in fact, tenuous — as Kuyper more or less admits in his preface. "And, what I especially may not pass over in silence," he wrote, "[Tophel's sermons] address the Christian from a standpoint that really is neither puritanical, nor Calvinistic, but might instead be qualified as inclining toward the Groningen school."⁵³

50. Kuyper, "Voorwoord," v.
51. Tophel, *The Limits of Christian Liberty*, 59f.
52. On Tertullian, see Kuyper and Rutgers, *Publiek Vermaak*, 23.
53. See Kuyper, "Voorwoord," v.

V

Kuyper's arguments against the comedy in particular, the theatre more broadly, and public entertainment in general sometimes have the air of a musty old chest, full of all kinds of half-forgotten memorabilia, which on inspection might have been better left shut. Kuyper repeats numerous prejudices of his era, which rankle in our egalitarian and enlightened age. His remarks about the ethical turpitude of the theatre, moral perils of the actor's profession, and the disjunction between high arts and public entertainment would prove unacceptable to most Christians today.

Yet the distinguishing characteristic of Abraham Kuyper's arguments against public entertainment could easily be missed in our rush to shut the lid on this old-fashioned Calvinist. What makes Kuyper intriguing is his ability to retrieve classical Calvinist teachings and provide them with modern underpinnings. What is forward-thinking is his anticipation of our culture of mass entertainment. For Kuyper, the problem was not entertainment per se, but the conjunction of "public" and "entertainment." To put it differently, Kuyper opposed the professionalization of entertainment, arguing that it eroded the sphere of the family by turning its members into individual consumers of entertainment.[54]

Kuyper made these claims in article twelve of his series. These represent his final set of arguments against the theatre before he moved in articles thirteen and fourteen to the related topics of concerts and "spiritual games" [i.e., liturgical drama] and then concluded the series. Kuyper was against comedy because, along with everything else, it "banishes the sense of household and tempts toward expenditures, which are not appropriate for our citizenry."[55] This strikes a distinctively Kuyperian note. In his understanding, society is composed of families, not individuals. He feared the atomization of society, whereby all social judgments would be evaluated against individual preferences. The sovereignty of the spheres was meant to impede the process of atomization or, better put, the development of a mass culture. The theatre represented a threat to the family because it removed entertainment from its sphere into the realm of the public, of anonymous individuality.

---

54. In his criticisms of the professionalization of entertainment, Kuyper's arguments parallel Rousseau's criticisms of the effect of the professional theater on public festivals. See Jean-Jacques Rousseau, *Letter to D'alembert and Writings for the Theater*, trans. Allan Bloom, Charles Butterworth, and Christopher Kelly (Hanover: University Press of New England, 2004), 343ff.

55. Kuyper and Rutgers, *Publiek Vermaak*, 63.

Kuyper predicted that families would spend less and less time enjoying one another's company and more and more effort planning their next outings. The household would become a "boring" place with only the old folks and young babies left behind.[56] Meanwhile, he calculated the enormous sums necessary to bring families on outings, money most families could not afford. The upshot is that families would lose the ability to entertain themselves and depend on professionals for entertainment, draining their spiritual and financial existence. He warned against such an outcome with strong words: "And while what is good and noble dwindles, the world of pleasure, with comedy at its center, swells and squeezes, has thrown itself as a deadly vampire against the breast of our society, and clasps it with its polyp arms, and shall not rest until all of the noble life spirit in it has been asphyxiated."[57] Public entertainment, in other words, is a vampire squid.

VI

Today we live in a mass-entertainment society. Entertainment is supplied to us continuously and ubiquitously. We have become consumers of amusements on a scale hardly imaginable in the late nineteenth century. Today, staying home is about professional entertainment as much as going out is. There is no point belaboring or rehearsing this point. Many others have already made the effort and we may all draw our own conclusions about how the professionalization of entertainment has affected families, churches, and small towns.

Here I note only the irony that Abraham Kuyper himself has been accused of precipitating the development toward the mass society, even as he aligned himself against it. Jeroen Koch, author of the rather unsympathetic *Abraham Kuyper: Een Biografie,* casts Kuyper as an "artist and actor [*toneelspeler*]" — a master of political theatre.[58] "In form and content, church, theatre, and politics were fused together in the Anti-Revolutionary leader."[59] Koch has a point. Kuyper, for example, infused his parliamentary speeches with dramatic, prophetic flair that inspired his followers while alienating his fellow members of parliament. These political theatrics contributed to the

---

56. Kuyper and Rutgers, *Publiek Vermaak,* 63f.
57. Kuyper and Rutgers, *Publiek Vermaak,* 65f.
58. Jeroen Koch, *Abraham Kuyper: Een Biografie* (Amsterdam: Boom, 2006), 290.
59. Koch, *Abraham Kuyper,* 290.

passing of the classic "liberal" parliament of rational and open debates and to the coming of party democracy, in which parliamentarians address their colleagues, but always direct their speeches to a mass audience. Politics as public entertainment? We know something about this today, too, and Kuyper, as the founder of the first modern political party in the Netherlands, also contributed to that form of theatre. Ironically, then, Kuyper may have fed the vampire squid with his political theatrics even as he struck at its tentacles in musical theatre.[60]

---

60. On the afterlife of this controversy, which flared up again among the *Gereformeerden* after the First World War, see Tjark Ebbens, "Beroering door de Opvoering: Studententoneel aan de Vrije Universiteit, 1920-1926," *Documentatieblad voor de Nederlandse kerkgeschiedenis na 1800* (2003): 23-42. This second episode of the controversy over the legitimacy of the theatre as a form of public entertainment explains why Kuyper's newspaper articles on the subject from the 1880s were collected and published in pamphlet form in 1924.

To Transcend and to Transform: The Neo-Calvinist Relationship of Church and Cultural Transformation

James Eglinton

1. Introduction

In surveying Reformed theological trends at the outset of the twenty-first century, it becomes apparent that talk of "transforming the culture" has become common parlance in various circles within the Reformed community. Furthermore, many of those in such circles have self-identified as neo-Calvinist or Kuyperian. Indeed, the concept of cultural transformation has become closely associated with the Kuyperian theological identity.[1] Those who locate "transforming the culture" at the center of the neo-Calvinist mandate, however, have not been without critics. Indeed, there now appears to be something of an anti-Kuyperian backlash forming. These critiques come from a variety of sources, the Reformed philosophical theologian Paul Helm[2] and the exponents of the Two Kingdoms school at Westminster Seminary California[3] being noted examples.

---

1. Among recent publications, see, for example, Richard Mouw, *Abraham Kuyper: A Short and Personal Introduction* (Grand Rapids: Eerdmans, 2011), ix-x, 28-37, 105-10.

2. For Helm's critique of the reading of Calvin in relation to culture found in the works of Abraham Kuyper and Herman Bavinck, see Paul Helm, *Calvin at the Centre* (Oxford: Oxford University Press, 2010), 323. For an example of Helm's popular-level critique of later Kuyperian trends, see Paul Helm, "On Getting Involved in Politics" (http://paulhelmsdeep.blogspot.com/2010/10/on-getting-involved-in-politics_15.html, accessed 19 May 2011): "'Culture' is another rather queasy word, don't you agree? Think of the Kuyperians everlastingly talking about 'transforming culture.'"

3. See, for example, David VanDrunen, *Natural Law and the Two Kingdoms: A Study in the Development of Reformed Social Thought* (Grand Rapids: Eerdmans, 2010).

A common critique of the Kuyperian "cultural transformation" trend is that it is based on an inadequate grasp of the church's uniqueness in relation to human culture, and consequently it has often amounted to little more than a Christianized gentrification without sufficient basis in a confessional churchly tradition. A group of hipster seminary grads wish to "transform the culture" in an up-and-coming urban area. They arrive, iPads in satchels, as bespectacled and tattooed *reformissional* fashionistas ready to implement their plan for cultural renewal. A coffee house is opened and a community arts program begun. The twitteratti in their number begin to tweet, and a high-end website is regularly updated. That, the pop-critique goes, is the sum total of their gospel mission. And it is all done in the name of Kuyperianism or neo-Calvinism. Insofar as there is little direct engagement with the *ecclesia* itself to accompany this aspiration of "cultural transformation," as will be seen, it does seem that such an attempt at transformation amounts to little more than a baptized form of urban gentrification.

While I deliberately deal in stereotypes here, what I describe is essentially what one finds in critiques (albeit perhaps weighted at the popular, rather than scholarly, side of the debate) of neo-Calvinism in its theology of cultural transformation. Immediately apparent as one wades into this debate is the range of closely related, important questions it prompts: can a neo-Calvinist cultural project exist in isolation from the living, confessional ecclesiastical context in which it began? Can one be neo-Calvinist in relation to culture, but not in relation to the church? Can independent, non-confessional congregational contexts be the locus of a neo-Calvinist cultural movement? Conversely, can one be a neo-Calvinist in relation to the church, but not in relation to the culture? (Closely related is the issue of whether the practice of neo-Calvinist politics is possible without connection to the church.)

Bearing in mind that the neo-Calvinism of Bavinck and Kuyper, in its cultural aspect, appeared in tandem with a carefully defined ecclesiology (one that gave a central place to confessional subscription, and, as will be seen, viewed the *ecclesia* via the distinctions of invisibility/visibility and organism/institution), this essay will focus not on whether the aforementioned anti-Kuyperian observations are correct. Rather, it will center on an important area of said critique — that much Kuyperian cultural transformation is vacuous and unconvincing when it appears detached from the church, and fails to question rigorously the church's uniqueness in the world — and will ask whether such an approach to cultural transformation, if it indeed exists, can credibly be called "neo-Calvinist."

There is, it appears, a widespread suspicion towards the cultural transformation aspect of Kuyperian theology. In responding to this, I will argue that the neo-Calvinist concept of cultural transformation should be understood in relation to several theological loci that must be carefully maintained in a deliberate order of priority: the neo-Calvinist cultural project can only be understood in relation to the church. This is say, without a highly nuanced set of ecclesiological commitments, neo-Calvinist cultural renewal becomes increasingly difficult to sustain. In short, I will argue that there is considerably more to neo-Calvinism than a bare theology of "we must transform the culture."

2. Neo-Calvinism in Context

Before speaking about the neo-Calvinist understanding of the role of the church in relation to culture, it is important to first sketch the broad trends in mainstream Dutch ecclesiology, which shaped the context within which a distinctively neo-Calvinist ecclesiology and theology of church and gospel in relation to culture developed in the mid-to-late nineteenth century.

a. Groningen

In Groningen, theology and the rising spirit of nineteenth-century European nationalism combined through the influence of the Utrecht professor Philip Willem van Heusde. Appointed professor of Greek and History at Utrecht in 1804, van Heusde was amongst the first Dutch advocates of Schleiermacher, Lessing, Herder, and the German *Vermittlungstheologie* (and as such he represents the Dutch appropriation of nineteenth-century Germany Protestant efforts to wed the traditional Reformed confessions with modern science, philosophy, and historical scholarship). He portrayed history as a process of education towards a morally ideal "humanity."[4] In the backdrop to the rise of neo-Calvinism, van Heusde is a significant figure, primarily for his influence on the founders of the Groningen school, and secondarily for his effect on his nephew J. H. Scholten, the founder of the opposing Leiden school (within which Bavinck and Kuyper were educated, and against which they reacted).

Between 1829 and 1830, a group of van Heusde's acolytes, known as the

---

4. K. H. Roessingh, *De moderne theologie in Nederland; hare voorbereiding en eerste periode* (dissertation, Groningen, 1914), 35.

"Heusdiaans," were appointed to teach in Groningen. Replicating the nationalist concerns of van Heusde, the Groningen school attempted to expel all "foreign" influences and create a pure Dutch theology and church.[5] These appointments included the fabulist Louis Gerlach Pareau, Johan Frederik van Oordt, and Willem Muurling. A fourth *Heusdiaan*, Petrus Hofstede de Groot, was appointed head of the Groningen Seminary. Hofstede de Groot was educated at Groningen rather than Utrecht and as such was not directly taught by van Heusde. However, while a student, he was given a manuscript copy of van Heusde's *Lectures on the History of Philosophy*, a book which marked him deeply. Van Heusde's reading of Plato was of particular importance to the *Heusdiaans*.[6] The driving sentiment conveyed to these men was that practical matters (in terms of Christian living and personal experience of Christ) are more important than doctrinal specifics: *"Niet de leer, maar het leven. . . . Niet de leer, maar de Heer!"*[7]

In charting the Groninger school's rise to prominence, one notes the sense in which it promoted a stated unwillingness to look outside the Netherlands for a basic theological identity. By positioning themselves against the perceived Heidelberg- and Geneva-centrism of rural Calvinism, it was asserted, they maintained an indigenous Dutch appropriation of Christianity. The Groninger school insisted that it was distinctly Dutch and needed not look abroad for theological direction. Mackay cites "a sympathetic critic of the time":

> It is not to the credit of our national Church that it should go for its spiritual milk and meat to Scotsmen and Englishmen, the French and the Swiss. Foreign books and teachers give foreign twists to our piety. Even in the kingdom of God nationality cannot be disregarded without impunity. And although there is no distinction before God between Jew and Gentile, let every one remain as he is called: he who is called as a Dutchman, a Dutchman let him remain.[8]

---

5. James Hutton Mackay, *Religious Thought in Holland during the Nineteenth Century* (London: Hodder and Stoughton, 1911), 57.

6. Mackay, *Religious Thought in Holland*, 50.

7. English: "Not doctrine, but life. . . . Not doctrine but the Lord!"

8. Mackay, *Religious Thought in Holland*, 57. Frustratingly, in following the convention of his time, Mackay does not reference this quotation. The sentiment was common to the Heusdiaans and came from van Heusde's own insistence on interpreting an individual's behavior and actions as the effect of his nationality. Cf. Jasper Vree, *De Groninger godgeleerden. De oorsprongen en de eerste periode van hun optreden (1820-1843)* (Kampen: J. H. Kok, 1984), index s.v.

In 1842, Hofstede de Groot published an historical overview of Dutch theology.[9] This work asserted that the Brethren of Common Life, a fourteenth-century sect established in the Netherlands by Geert Groote (1340-84), represented a pure, Dutch theology. This indigenous faith, Hofstede de Groot claimed, was replaced by the imposing alien force of Calvinism. The Polish Reformer Jan Łaski, as a non-Dutch theologian lauded by the Groningers, was deemed acceptable by association as he was a close friend of the Dutchman Erasmus and worked in the Dutch churches in Emden and London.[10]

In this sense, the Groninger theologians coincided with the period of Restoration under King Willem I (1813-1840), wherein Dutch culture generally began seeking a keener self-identification in a new Europe.[11] Within this context, the Groningen school seems to display a curious set of double standards with regard to foreign ideas. Despite its aversion to much Reformed theology (on the grounds of its non-Dutch origins), its intellectual catalyst (via van Heusde) was undoubtedly German; Lessing, Herder, and Schleiermacher were van Heusde's major influences.[12] This influence was passed on to the Heusdiaans, who, like Herder and van Heusde, espoused a fervent nationalism.[13]

The Groninger school represented a move to bind the Dutch Reformed Church *(Nederlandsche Hervormde Kerk)* strictly to Dutch culture and society by making all Dutch persons members in an established national church.[14] That an ecclesiological agenda was central to the Groningen school is evident in the new subtitle given to their publication *Waarheid in*

---

9. For an overview of Hofstede de Groot's works, see J. B. F. Heerspink, *Dr. P. Hofstede de Groot's leven en werken* (Groningen: Noordhof, 1898).

10. Jan Łaski or John à Lasco (1499-1560) was a leading Polish reformer. The sole extant work by Łaski is a catechism prepared under his direction. He became of interest in Germany and the Netherlands in the 1840s, largely through the rise of Dutch nationalism as led by Hofstede de Groot. See Polnischer Baron, *Humanist und europäischer Reformator Hrsg. v. Christoph Strohm* (Tübingen: Mohr Siebeck, 2005).

11. Hendrikus Berkhof, *Two Hundred Years of Theology* (Grand Rapids: Eerdmans, 1989), 97.

12. Roessingh, *De moderne theologie in Nederland*, 35; D. H. Kromminga, *The Christian Reformed Tradition, from the Reformation to the Present* (Grand Rapids: Eerdmans, 1943), 113.

13. Kathleen Powers Erickson, *At Eternity's Gate: The Spiritual Vision of Vincent Van Gogh* (Grand Rapids: Eerdmans, 1998), 17-18.

14. For more information on the Groningen school, see James Eglinton, "Trinity and Organism: Towards a New Reading of Herman Bavinck's Organic Motif" (Ph.D. dissertation, University of Edinburgh), 11-16.

liefde in 1857: "Dedicated in particular to building up the Evangelical Catholic church of the future."[15]

Their goal was that membership in the *volkskerk* and in the Dutch state were intended to function as two sides of the same coin. The bar for membership in this *volkskerk* was very low: it prioritized Dutch nationality over Christian belief. In relation to their ideal, "Membership in the *volkskerk* and membership in society were virtually indistinguishable, illustrated by the fact that until 1811 baptismal records were the only registration of newborn children in the Netherlands."[16]

The Groningers were critical of both traditional Reformed and Lutheran ecclesiologies. Hofstede de Groot charged the Heidelberg Catechism (the confessional standard of the Dutch Reformed Church) with blurring the true meaning of the *ecclesia:* "To understand the doctrine of the true Church, the word Church must first be explained. With the victory of the particularism of Calvinism at the Synod of Dort, insight into the meaning of the Church began to disappear. Luther did not see that separate Christians, each one for himself, can never realize the end of God in the appearance of Jesus Christ; that this can only be realized in the Communion of Saints, a doctrine which Luther did not understand."[17]

In its ecclesiology, as Hofstede de Groot's *Theologica Naturalis* suggests, the Groninger school was heavily influenced by Jansenism. They laid a strong emphasis on spiritual community. Interestingly, the Groninger theologians chose to abandon the Reformed relationship between Old and New Covenants. Instead, they emphasized the New Covenant's attachment to the history of the church.

> Much confusion has arisen in philosophy from not placing sufficiently in the foreground the fact that man is a social being, and can only become man in society. Man, as a solitary being upon a lonely island, is a creature of the imagination, not an actuality. Real men are born of parents, who care for them. They come into a small circle, gradually becoming wider, of brothers and sisters, relations, neighbors, fellow-men, and, unless he lived in this constantly widening human society, the child would not become a

---

15. *Waarheid in liefde, een godgeleerd tijdschrift, voor beschaafde christenen* (1845ff.: J. Zoon, 1837-1872). Between 1857-61, its subtitle was: *Nieuwe reeks, bijzonder gewijd aan de opbouwing der evangelisch-catholieke kerk der toekomst.*

16. John Halsey Wood, "Church, Sacrament and Society: Abraham Kuyper's Early Baptismal Theology, 1859-1874," *Journal of Reformed Theology* 2 (2008): 278.

17. Hofstede de Groot, cited in Mackay, *Religious Thought in Holland*, 62-63.

man. In his mother's womb he lives the life of a plant, newly born that of an animal, and an animal he would remain were he not taken up into human society and there gradually formed into a man. The consciousness of the spiritual world, of which the child must become a member, would remain dormant in him if it were not awakened by seeing and hearing other men in whom this consciousness has become awake. It would sleep like the spark in the flint, which has not been struck by iron; like the flame in the oil, which has not been set alight by another flame. In man, viewed apart from society, we can look only for a capacity for the spiritual life. To find the beginning of the spiritual life we must thus go outside the individual, and seek for it in the spiritual society in which he lives.[18]

Just as the Groningen Christology sets the tone of its ecclesiology, this concept of church has a formative effect on its soteriology. Pareau's *Compendium Theologiæ Christianæ Moralis* demonstrates this relationship. It interprets Christ's mission as being to establish a community committed to the spiritual and intellectual formation of people. The church is to strive for the development of Christ's divine-humanity in its human members.

b. Leiden

In Leiden, the home of nineteenth-century modernist Dutch theology, ecclesiology moved in the opposite direction. There, one finds the likes of Johannes Scholten and Lodewijk Rauwenhoff casting serious doubt on whether the church has any relevance to modern culture at all. Scholten, the nephew of van Heusde, lived with his uncle while studying in Utrecht. Following his graduation, he spent two years working as the pastor of a rural congregation. His time as student and clergyman entailed firsthand experience of the various dominant schools of thought: the anti-Reformed bent of the *Heusdiaans*, the older mainline pre-Groninger theology of the Utrecht theological faculty, and then the type of Calvinism deeply ingrained in rural Dutch life. After his period in the pastorate, Scholten moved to teach theology at the University of Franeker. His time there marks a rejection of the *Heusdiaan* school of thought; indeed, his opening professorial address at Franeker accused the Groningen school of espousing heretical Christology.[19]

---

18. Hofstede de Groot, *Theologica Naturalis*, cited in Mackay, *Religious Thought in Holland*, 63-64.

19. Johannes Scholten, *Oratio de vitando in Jesu Christi historia interpretanda docetismo*,

Following his stay in Franeker, Scholten moved to Leiden, where he was to teach alongside Lodewijk Rauwenhoff and Abraham Kuenen. Scholten's mature theology,[20] as taught at Leiden, is marked by two central aspects. First, under the influence of Alexander Schweizer's *Die Glaubenslehre der evangelisch-reformierten Kirche*,[21] Scholten came to view the Reformed faith as centered on the formal principle of divine self-revelation and the material principle of unqualified divine sovereignty. At this point in his theological development, Scholten maintained that Reformed theology found its fulfillment in idealism.[22] Secondly, a high-profile debate with Cornelis Opzoomer led Scholten to abandon idealism in favor of empiricism.[23] His doctrine of God became distant and monistic. His worldview became rigidly mechanical in character, with every event in the time-space continuum being determined by a vast, unbreakable process of cause and effect. In short, his core commitment to absolute divine sovereignty became adherence to cosmic predeterminism with an original, divine cause.

In this context, an omnicausal deity provided Scholten with a convincing reason for assenting to the prevailing determinism of contemporary natural science. Theism, he believed, was a suitable foundation for a mechanical worldview. A critical reading of Scholten might suggest that his particular principle of determinism provided the hermeneutic with which he then formed a doctrine of God, rather than allowing God's self-revelation to shape the relationship of God's will to cosmic history.[24] Such a claim finds momentum in Scholten's own theological development. Particularly as he moved towards empiricism, his determinism adopted a rigid, antisupernaturalist pose. In tandem with this, his doctrine of God became less Trinitarian.[25] Such an outcome fits neatly with Scholten's earlier assertion

---

nobili, ad rem Christianam promovendam hodiernae theologiae munere (in *Annales Academi, 1839-40*, Hagae-Comitis, 1842), 265.

20. Scholten published accounts of his own theological development: *Herdenking mijner vijfentwintigjarige ambtsbediening* (Leiden, 1865); and *Afscheidsrede bij het neerleggen van het hoogleeraarsambt aan de Universiteit te Leiden* (Leiden, 1881).

21. Alexander Schweizer, *Die Glaubenslehre der evangelisch-reformierten Kirche, Dargestellt und aus den Quellen belegt*, 2 vols. (Zürich: Orell, Füssli und Com, 1844-47).

22. Berkhof, *Two Hundred Years of Theology*, 98.

23. Berkhof, *Two Hundred Years of Theology*, 98-103.

24. Scholten's statement that his doctrine of God is reached by "reflection grounded upon observation [of the cosmos]" (*"bespiegeling gegrond op waarneming,"* De leer der Hervormde Kerk (Leiden: P. Engels, 1848-50) 4:lxi) also hints at this verdict.

25. This fact was not lost on Bavinck, who critiqued Scholten for this very point: Herman Bavinck, *Reformed Dogmatics: God and Creation*, ed. John Bolt, tr. John Vriend

that the specifics of God's being (in particular his tri-unity) are less important than the material principle of predestination.[26]

It is hardly surprising that within such a system, ecclesiology would take a low place. Indeed, Scholten and Rauwenhoff believed the church had nothing to contribute that the secular state could not provide. The church, it was argued, could offer no miracle, virgin birth, or resurrection. Rather it could provide only poverty relief and some kind of social community. Even so, they argued that the state was also well placed to order society and care for the poor.

While the Groningers sought to make the church ever present (albeit passively and somewhat anonymously) in Dutch culture, the Leiden school called for disestablishing the church on the grounds of its irrelevance to culture.[27] Reflecting the optimistic, evolutionary spirit of the nineteenth century, the Leiden school maintained that humanity was predetermined to develop into moral perfection through the leading of the state. Within this scheme, the church was largely superfluous. Rauwenhoff once quipped that, "What actually lay in the beautiful dream of the Kingdom of God on earth can be fulfilled in and through the state."[28] Although Scholten did not call for the abandonment of "church" altogether (as the church could still be useful, though not essential, as a social forum), this low view of the church nonetheless set the scene within which various Leiden-influenced ministers abandoned both church and ministry in the mid-nineteenth century.[29]

c. The Leiden-Groningen Ecclesiological-Cultural Rivalry and the Rise of Neo-Calvinism

Viewed in this context, the rivalry between the Leiden and Groningen schools (particularly in relation to ecclesiology) played an important role in the de-

---

(Grand Rapids: Baker Academic, 2004), 43. See also Herman Bavinck, *Philosophy of Revelation* (London: Longmans, Green and Co., 1909), 46.

26. Scholten, *De leer der Hervormde Kerk*, 18-20.

27. See Eglinton, "Trinity and Organism," 18-23.

28. Cited by John Halsey Wood, "Church, Sacrament, and Society," 279; L. W. E. Rauwenhoff, cited in Cornelis Augustijn, "Kerk en Godsdienst 1870-1890," *De Doleantie van 1886 en haar Geschiedenis*, ed. Wim Bakker (Kampen: Kok, 1984), 58-62.

29. In this context, one finds the likes of Conrad Busken Huet, Allard Pierson, and C. B. Huet making high-profile exits from the church. Allard Pierson, *Brief aan mijn laatste gemeente* (Arnhem, 1865); Hederscheê, *Modern-godsdienstige richting in Nederland* (Amsterdam: Van Holkema & Warendorf, 1904), 136.

velopment of neo-Calvinism. In the aftermath of the French Revolution, ecclesiology became a much debated topic across nineteenth-century Europe.

In the Netherlands, various nineteenth-century events highlight the significance of ecclesiology at that time. The Secession of 1834 *(Afscheiding)* was closely followed by Roman Catholic emancipation. The revision of the Dutch constitution, under the liberal leadership of Johan Thorbecke, created a secular welfare state — thus moving directly into the church's diaconal role.

The Groningen school seized upon the opportunity to further ecclesiological debate in this context. In 1856, it organized an academic competition on ecclesiology, posing the question: "Had the church been an aim or a means for Jesus, or both?"[30] This concern for the church was also seen in the Groninger publication *Waarheid in liefde.*[31]

In 1859, the Groningen theological faculty staged another essay competition. The topic on this occasion was the ecclesiology of John Calvin and Jan Łaski. It has been speculated that the Groningers chose a Calvin-related topic in order to combat the influence of the professedly "pro-Calvin" Scholten in Leiden.[32] Hofstede de Groot's writings on Scholten from this period would certainly add weight to such a suggestion.[33] The fervently nationalistic Heusdiaans, of course, were keen to include Łaski in the study due to his proximity to the Dutchman Erasmus and his role in the Dutch churches in Emden and London. Indeed, Hofstede de Groot had been raised in Emden, in the shadow of Łaski's influence.[34] Furthermore, the anniversary of Łaski's death was soon to occur. By this point, the Groningers had publicly rejected almost all of Calvin's theology[35] and no doubt hoped that exposure to the quasi-Dutch Łaski would demonstrate a better approach to the church. The competition specified a comparison of the ecclesiologies of both Calvin and Łaski with specific reference to their respective personal life

---

30. This competition was won by E. R. Borgesius (Groningen) and J. Knappert (Leiden).

31. *Waarheid in liefde, een godgeleerd tijdschrift, voor beschaafde christenen* (1845ff.: J. Zoon, 1837-1872).

32. Jasper Vree and Johan Zwaan, *Abraham Kuyper's Commentatio (1860), The Young Kuyper about Calvin, a Lasco, and the Church, I: Introduction, Annotations, Bibliography and Indices* (Leiden: Brill, 2005), 17.

33. Petrus Hofstede de Groot, *Beantwoording van J. H. Scholten, hoogleeraar te Leiden* (Groningen: A. L. Scholtens, 1859), 137. At this time, Hofstede de Groot held a *privatissimum* in Groningen on Scholten's handling of the Reformed tradition.

34. Heerspink, *Dr P. Hofstede de Groot's leven en werken*, 3-11.

35. Vree, "P. Hofstede de Groot en de armenverzorging door vrouwen. Een hoofdstuk uit de geschiedenis van de Groninger inwendige zending," 218.

contexts. Such an emphasis on the nationality of a particular theologian was typical of the Groningen approach.[36]

There is also another layer of complexity in the rivalry between Leiden and Groningen on this point. As has already been stated, the Leiden theologians typified the optimistic, evolutionary spirit of the nineteenth century: within their scheme, the church was redundant. The Groningen theologians took a similar position in terms of the prevailing culture of optimism: Christ would lead by example as humanity strode on towards moral perfection. However, their intense nationalism meant that the *volkskerk* remained a key element in their model of Dutch culture. Thus, Christ would lead through the church.

As such, the Groningers staged this competition hoping not only to prove that *their* Łaski was more worthwhile than *Scholten's* Calvin, but also to enforce that the Dutch *volkskerk* was a better option than the Leiden school's theories on church and state.

The competition caught the attention of a young Leiden student, Abraham Kuyper, who entered and eventually won the competition. This essay will not delve into the history of Kuyper's prize-winning work, which has been extensively described elsewhere.[37] Suffice it to say that Kuyper's innovative handling of the Calvinist tradition (particularly in relation to the church) was central to the birth of what is now labeled "neo-Calvinism."

3. Neo-Calvinism on Church in Relation to Culture: The Visible Church

In the face of Groningen and Leiden, it is fascinating to observe that as neo-Calvinism firmed up its ecclesiological identity, it proposed a third way in terms of church in relation to culture. The historical context of this development is important in understanding why the original neo-Calvinists were so concerned with the relevance and application of Christianity to culture: they wrote *contra* the Leiden school's belief that cultural betterment would occur passively and had no crucial need of Christianity, and *contra* the Groningen

---

36. Vree and Zwaan, *Abraham Kuyper's Commentatio (1860), The Young Kuyper about Calvin, a Lasco, and the Church, I: Introduction, Annotations, Bibliography and Indices*, 18.

37. Abraham Kuyper, *Disquisitio historico-theologica, exhibens Johannis Calvini et Johannis à Lasco de Ecclesia Sententiarum inter se compositionem* (Den Haag en Amsterdam, 1862).

re-creation of Christianity as an ever-present but docile factor in nationalist culture.

As has been established, then, the Groningen-Leiden rivalry should be seen as the backdrop to various emphases in the development of neo-Calvinist ecclesiology. In the first place, the ecclesiologies of neo-Calvinist dogmaticians Abraham Kuyper and Herman Bavinck responded to their contextual debate on ecclesiology by following the Reformed tradition back to John Calvin.[38] As such, one finds at the core of their concept of "church" a reliance on the classical Calvinist distinction between the church as visible and invisible.[39] The factor of *invisibility* is used to account for the mystery and sovereignty of divine election, the true catholicity of the church as transcending geographical and temporal boundaries, and the purity of the church as containing only those who truly believe. In that sense, the concept of the "invisible church" is received by the neo-Calvinists from Calvin and kept in substantially the same form.

The factor of *visibility*, on the other hand, accounts for the church's presence in the world. It contains a mix of true and false believers and, as it (to a certain extent) makes the invisible church visible within human culture, *it forms the basis within which one must examine a neo-Calvinist theology of gospel in relation to culture.* The definition of the visible church that one finds in the ecclesiologies of Bavinck and Kuyper will (or at least should) give definition to a neo-Calvinist theology of Christianity in relation to culture.

In short, the *visible* church was understood by both Bavinck and Kuyper to be two things simultaneously: an institution and an organism.[40]

a. The Visible Church as Organism

The ascription of a living element within the visible church is important to Bavinck's ecclesiology. The church, created by the living Holy Spirit, is a new community of faith and worship. Its spiritual essence is characterized by a

---

38. Cf. John Calvin, *Institutes* IV.xvi.19.
39. Eglinton, "Trinity and Organism," 201-24.
40. Bavinck, *Reformed Dogmatics: Holy Spirit, Church and New Creation*, ed. John Bolt, trans. John Vriend (Grand Rapids: Baker Academic, 2008), 288; Abraham Kuyper, "Common Grace," in *Abraham Kuyper: A Centennial Reader*, ed. James D. Bratt (Grand Rapids: Eerdmans, 1998), 187-201; John Halsey Wood, "Going Dutch in the Modern Age: Abraham Kuyper's Struggle for a Free Church in the Nineteenth Century Netherlands" (Ph.D. dissertation, St. Louis University, 2010), 103-15, 141-51.

necessary vitality. In this context, Bavinck draws on the heavily organic illustrations used in Scripture to refer to the church: it is a body, a vine, and a field.[41]

Trying to simultaneously maintain Reformed doctrines of election and ecclesiology, Bavinck views Scripture's organic pictures of the church as referring to the visible, rather than invisible, *ecclesia*. The significance of this point should not be glossed over: the organic motif is employed here to convey the idea that through the Holy Spirit's creative power, there exists on earth a church teeming with spiritual life. (Hendrikus Berkhof's account of Bavinck's ecclesiology suggests that the organic visible church idea is mentioned by Bavinck only "in the passing."[42] However, this seems to understate the significance of the motif within Bavinck's theology of church. Furthermore, Berkhof's highly minimalist portrayal of the "church as organism" within Bavinck's thought seems odd when one considers the regularity with which Bavinck applies the organic motif to the church.)[43]

This fledgling neo-Calvinist ecclesiology applied the organic motif to the church to account for the visible church's marked unity in diversity. This point was brought into Kuyper's ecclesiology by a trip to Brighton in 1875, where he found himself serving communion to French and Prussian officers who had previously been at war.[44] According to Bavinck, however, the overwhelming focus of this organic visible church idea is that *within the church-as-organism, unity precedes diversity*.[45] "In the first place, therefore, the ingathering of the elect must not be conceived individualistically and atomistically.... The church is an organism, not an aggregate; the whole, in its case, precedes the parts."[46]

This grounding of diversity upon pre-existing unity is, according to

---

41. Herman Bavinck, *Reformed Dogmatics: Holy Spirit, Church and New Creation*, 254.

42. Hendrikus Berkhof, *Christian Faith: An Introduction to the Study of the Faith* (Grand Rapids: Eerdmans, 1986), 399: "Bavinck (GD IV, par. 53), however, refers in passing to the concept of 'the church as organism' enunciated by Kuyper (over against 'the church as institution')."

43. Cf. Herman Bavinck, *Reformed Dogmatics: Sin and Salvation in Christ*, ed. John Bolt, trans. John Vriend (Grand Rapids: Baker Academic, 2006), 524; *Reformed Dogmatics: Holy Spirit, Church and New Creation*, 280-81, 285, 301, 303-5, 330-32, 340, 375, 448.

44. See James Bratt, "Raging Tumults of the Soul: The Private Life of Abraham Kuyper," *Reformed Journal* 37 (Oct.-Nov. 1987): 11. Cf. Herman Bavinck, *Christelijke Wereldbeschouwing* (Kampen: Kok, 1904), 50.

45. Bavinck, *Christelijke Wereldbeschouwing*, 51; "[. . .] leert zij, dat het geheel aan de delen, de eenheid aan de veelheid voorafgaat."

46. Bavinck, *Reformed Dogmatics: Sin and Salvation in Christ*, 524.

Bavinck, the basis for the *ecclesia*'s catholicity.[47] The same thought is applied to the *catholicity* of the church over time and space. The "church militant" is but a small portion of the invisible church: "[It] must be noted that the universal church is antecedent to the particular or local church. The church of Christ is an organism in which the whole is prior to the parts."[48] The same question of priority lies at the core of his section on "The Church as Organism and Institution."[49]

b. The Visible Church as Institution

In drawing on Scripture's richly pictorial ecclesiology, Bavinck is quick to note that the organisms in question possess a distinctly ordered existence. A body requires a head; every kingdom needs a monarch; a vineyard has a gardener; a flock must have a shepherd. Similarly the visible church is not just an organism, but is also an institution. Bavinck defines this on two levels: first, it is institutional in terms of its elder- and deacon-led government, and second, it is so in its possession of the means of grace. Thus Bavinck's contention is that this institutional element is strictly necessary: "Government is indispensable for the church as a gathering of believers."[50]

It should be acknowledged that Bavinck makes a great effort to keep the pairings of visible-invisible and organism-institution separate: "As stated earlier, this distinction [between organism and institution] is very different from that between the invisible and visible church."[51] By one, then, he does not mean the other. Rather, the organism-institution is the definition of the *visible* church. Those who regard the organic church as the invisible church, he says, ignore the fact that the as-yet-uncalled elect are not presently members of the church militant. In this viewpoint, "the church becomes totally invisible, remains an idea, and has no corresponding reality."[52] Those who

---

47. Bavinck, *Reformed Dogmatics: Holy Spirit, Church and New Creation*, 280-81.
48. Bavinck, *Reformed Dogmatics: Holy Spirit, Church and New Creation*, 301.
49. Bavinck, *Reformed Dogmatics: Holy Spirit, Church and New Creation*, 329-32.
50. Bavinck, *Reformed Dogmatics: Holy Spirit, Church and New Creation*, 329.
51. Bavinck, *Reformed Dogmatics: Holy Spirit, Church and New Creation*, 304. This point is stressed again on p. 330.
52. Bavinck, *Reformed Dogmatics: Holy Spirit, Church and New Creation*, 304. It has been argued elsewhere that due to the Westminster Confession's lack of definition concerning the visible church, this criticism applies somewhat directly to much of Westminster Calvinism in Scotland: James Eglinton, "Some Benefits of Going Organic: Herman Bavinck's Theology of the Visible Church," *Theology in Scotland* 17:1 (Spring 2010): 23-36.

twin the visible church solely with the institutional church, from Roman Catholicism to the Anabaptists, receive a parallel critique.[53]

Worth stating in passing is that Bavinck posits a strict concatenation between the visible church's organic and institutional facets. Neither takes precedence: the presence of one always necessitates the other. "The church, accordingly, was never without a government; and it did not provide its own but received it from God. Over and over the institution and the organism were called into being by God at the same time and in conjunction with each other."[54] One cannot have a living church without the institutional factors established by Christ, and vice versa. The church must be both visible and invisible, and in its visibility it must be both organism and institution.[55]

This understanding of the visible church (which is the ground of the church's interaction with its host culture) as both an organism and an institution, I will argue, led Bavinck and Kuyper to forge a third way, within which they moved away from both Groningen and Leiden. Kuyper supported the Leiden idea of disestablishing the church, and as such he came to strongly disagree with the Groningen concept of an established *volkskerk* within which all Dutch citizens were automatically members.[56] However, he also strongly disagreed with the Leiden idea that the church has nothing distinctive to offer. For Kuyper, the church is not the state; the two are separate and distinctive. The church has the gospel, and the secular state does not. Stated broadly, the Kuyperian movement, in its original context, sought to disestablish the church while establishing the basis upon which it continues to influence (and exert its relevance towards) its host culture.

4. How to Assert the Church's Uniqueness while Remaining Active in the Culture

(a) Kuyper: Institutional Church as Safe Haven (Transcendence), Organic Church as Outreach (Transformation)

Kuyper attempted to explain the sense in which the concept of the visible church, as organism and institute, preserves the church's distinctive identity

---

53. Bavinck, *Reformed Dogmatics: Holy Spirit, Church and New Creation*, 304.
54. Bavinck, *Reformed Dogmatics: Holy Spirit, Church and New Creation*, 330; cf. p. 340.
55. Bavinck, *Reformed Dogmatics: Holy Spirit, Church and New Creation*, 305.
56. For a thorough discussion of the development of Kuyper's beliefs on the separation of church and state, see Wood, "Going Dutch in the Modern Age," 117ff.

and message, while also guarding the participation of its members in secular culture. In this context, John Halsey Wood points out that the element of disestablishment is a significant innovation in what is otherwise a classically Calvinistic ecclesiology. It was "a deviation that imprinted his ecclesiology with a distinctively modern tint."[57] The basic pattern by which such a modified, modern Calvinistic ecclesiology worked is as follows: the church as institution serves as a safe haven for believers in the world, whereas the visible church organically spreads throughout the wider culture. In this context Kuyper argues for the existence of "four terrains."[58]

First, there is terrain abounding in common grace but untouched by special grace.[59] This terrain, he writes, is typical of non-Christian cultures which nonetheless display commendable sophistication. (China was Kuyper's chosen example: "Common grace operates there in no small measure but special grace has not yet influenced that gigantic empire to the extent of changing Chinese life.")

Secondly, there is the terrain of the institutional church, which comes about solely by special grace. Here, Kuyper has in mind "those instituted churches" that make no effort to sanctify their host cultures. He refers to them as "churches that . . . limit themselves to fulfilling their own task."[60] In this context, one may think of churches that heavily stress the transcendence of the gospel or means of grace, but which deny any responsibility to transform or affect their surrounding environments.

Thirdly, there is the terrain of common grace illuminated by special grace. Kuyper regarded this terrain as typical in much of late-nineteenth-century European and North American culture, where the common grace-laden host cultures benefited from Christianity, without the majority of those within the culture embracing special grace. There, "a wide variety of customs, usages, mores and laws are current that clearly manifest the influence of divine revelation and are followed by a broad class of people who want nothing to do with faith or conversion."[61]

Fourthly, there is the terrain of special grace which has been enriched by common grace. "Finally you find the fourth terrain wherever the church as organism manifests itself, i.e., where the personal confessors of Jesus in their own circle allow the life of common grace to be controlled by the principles

---

57. Wood, "Going Dutch in the Modern Age," 117ff.
58. Kuyper, "Common Grace," 199.
59. Kuyper, "Common Grace," 199.
60. Kuyper, "Common Grace," 199.
61. Kuyper, "Common Grace," 199.

of divine revelation."⁶² In this context, Kuyper explained that Christian art, schools, and scholarship are Christian in a very different sense than that of the Christian nation or state. The adjective applied to a nation, he believed, carries only a nominal meaning, whereas the organic church's role in society, whereby Christians understand and participate in common grace activities through the lens of special grace, is markedly different. For Kuyper, a Christian school is *Christian* in a way that a Christian nation can never be.

Unlike Bavinck, who uses the organic motif primarily to emphasize that the church's unity precedes its diversity, Kuyper's outstanding emphasis is that the motif explains how and why church members conduct themselves outside of the church institute: in other words, *how Christians act within the wider host culture.*

(b) Bavinck: Gospel as Pearl of Great Price (Transcendence), Gospel as Leaven (Transformation)

Such a thought has a direct equivalent in Bavinck's writings. This equivalent, however, is expressed in Christ's own language, rather than the language of the organic. It is found in the New Testament imagery of the pearl and the leaven. In his penultimate Stone Lecture (1909), Bavinck outlined the relationship of the church (by way of its individual members, and in its congregational unity) to its host culture. Here, Bavinck stated that the gospel is two things. It is first a "pearl of great price" (cf. Matt. 13:46).

> But this is certain, — if the gospel is true, then it carries with it its own standard for the valuation of all culture. Jesus has shown this distinctly in the attitude which he adopted towards all earthly things and natural relations. He was no ascetic. . . . And he was as little an epicurean. . . . Neither shallow optimism nor weak pessimism finds in him an ally. . . . He accepted the social and political conditions as they were, made no endeavor to reform them, and confined himself exclusively to setting the value which they possessed for the kingdom of heaven. And in that connection he said, that nothing a man possesses in this world — food or drink, covering or clothing, marriage or family, vocation or position, riches or honor — can be compared with that *pearl of great price* which he alone can present.⁶³

---

62. Kuyper, "Common Grace," 200.
63. Herman Bavinck, *Philosophy of Revelation* (London: Longmans, Green and Co., 1909), p. 257 (emphasis added).

In this context, Bavinck, on the basis of common grace, praised the worth of human culture. However, on the basis of special grace, he admitted that human culture is not that pearl of great price to which the Christian must ascribe ultimate value. To borrow Kuyper's language, the gospel gives Christians an institutional solidarity in a world characterized by common, rather than special, grace. However, the wider context of Bavinck's theology concerning common and saving grace means that he cannot lapse into pietism and withdraw that pearl from the world. To act consistently with his theology of common and saving grace,[64] he invokes another piece of New Testament imagery: the kingdom of heaven is like a "leaven" (cf. Matt. 13:33). "Christ did not portray for his disciples a beautiful future in this world, but prepared them for oppression and persecution. But, nevertheless, the kingdom of heaven, while a pearl of great price, *is also a leaven* which *permeates the whole of the meal.*"[65]

Thus, while the gospel (as the *transcendent* pearl of great price) provides an institutional haven for Christians in the world, it also (as the *transforming* leaven) provides the impetus and rationale for their involvement therein. Although Bavinck relies on New Testament imagery, rather than the organic motif (*à la* Kuyper), to explain this dynamic tension, the picture is strikingly similar in both theologians.

In order to produce a Christian nation, one can construct a neo-Calvinist argument along these lines: one needs not a *volkskerk,* but rather a visible church which, as an *institution,* is separate from the state (indeed, as the pearl of great price, it is worth more than nationalism) and which, as an *organism,* is the leaven that uses special grace to enrich the nation's pre-existing common grace. In his application of this principle, Bavinck also attacks the thinking of the Groningen and Leiden schools for their submission to the general spirit of passive optimism prevalent in nineteenth-century Europe: "The kingdom of God, although analogous to a mustard seed and a leaven and a seed that sprouts and grows aside from any knowledge and involvement of human beings (Matt. 13:31, 33; Mark 4:27), nevertheless does not reach its completion by way of gradual development or an ethical process."[66]

---

64. Bavinck's idea is that common grace preserves the (corrupted) goodness of the creation until its restoration in special grace. See Bavinck, "Common Grace," trans. Raymond Van Leeuwen, *Calvin Theological Journal* 24:1 (April 1989): 51.

65. Bavinck, *Philosophy of Revelation,* 268 (emphasis added). He also references the "gospel as a leaven" idea in *Reformed Dogmatics: Holy Spirit, Church and New Creation,* 395-96, where the same idea is expressed.

66. Bavinck, *Reformed Dogmatics: Holy Spirit, Church and New Creation,* 684.

5. Precedence: Which Comes First — Transformation or Transcendence?

John Bolt makes two helpful points on Bavinck's pearl and leaven ideal, both of which demonstrate that while Bavinck does not use the organic motif here (as does Kuyper), the principle operates from the same paradigm. First, Bolt draws the reader's attention to the issue of concatenation: the church must hold the gospel as *both* a pearl *and* a leaven. Secondly, he highlights the issue of priority: "furthermore, [the gospel] is a treasure or pearl first and foremost; the leavening role is *secondary*."[67]

This point, it has been suggested, leads to a divergence between Kuyper and Bavinck. Presumably basing it upon Kuyper's wish to combat the *volkskerk* emphasis on the church as a national institution (and consequently, in his desire to emphasize the organic element), Gerben Heitink has argued that Kuyper played the organism against the institution: "Kuyper saw the church as an organism, that is, as the community of Christians who are present everywhere in society through the Christian organizations. This he viewed as essential: the church as an institution is of secondary importance and must serve the organism."[68]

However, this presentation of Kuyper as a low-church theologian requires deeper scrutiny. It risks misunderstanding the nature of his response to the Groningen school. Rather than respond to their *volkskerk* ideal *by* antithesis, Kuyper responded *with* an antithesis. This is to say, he did not react against their model by rejecting the institutional (or leaving it in a secondary place) and embracing the organic church. Instead, he drew an antithesis between his model of the visible church (as organism and institution) and the *volkskerk*.[69] When critiquing the *volkskerk* ideal, he writes, "This, then, is the system of the *national church [volkskerk]*. Directly opposed to it is the system of the *church as organism*."[70] Kuyper's general tendency was to place the two aspects of the visible church in a mutually supportive, concatenous dynamic.[71]

---

67. John Bolt, "A Pearl and a Leaven," in *John Calvin and Evangelical Theology: Legacy and Prospect*, ed. Sung Wook Chung (Milton Keynes: Paternoster, 2009), 263.

68. Gerben Heitink, *Practical Theology: History, Theory, Action Domains* (Kok: Kampen, 1993), p. 72.

69. Kuyper, "Common Grace," 193.

70. Kuyper, "Common Grace," 194.

71. Kuyper, "Geworteld en Gegrond (1870)," *Predicatiën, in de jaren 1867 tot 1873, tijdens zijn Predikantschap in het Nederlandsch Hervormde Kerkgenootschap, gehouden in Beesd, te Utrecht en te Amsterdam* (Kampen: J. H. Kok, 1913), 325-51.

Kuyper recognized that both the organism and the institute were necessary aspects of the church, and that they had a reciprocal relationship: the organism naturally issuing in an external form or institution and the institution nourishing the organism.[72]

There are perhaps various reasons that little has been previously written to demonstrate the coherence of Bavinck and Kuyper on the role of the church in relation to culture. Evidently, Kuyper has been portrayed in some quarters as a figure who opposes Bavinck on the priority of the organism-institution relationship. This is perhaps an unfair portrayal of Kuyper. It may also be that because Kuyper wrote so much on this application of the *church-as-organism* concept, more has been written on this as a Kuyperian, rather than Bavinckian, ideal.[73] Although their ecclesiologies use the same terminology in different ways (Kuyper's use of the "pearl of great price" is very different to that of Bavinck),[74] one does well to remember the typically neo-Calvinistic distinction between essence and form. Between Bavinck and Kuyper, the form differs, but the essential agreement between Kuyper's emphasis on organism-institute and Bavinck's pearl-leaven concepts demonstrates that Bavinck should in no way be excluded from this discussion. Both are concerned to express the relationship of church and culture via the categories of *transcendence* and *transformation*.

Although Bavinck prefers to express this aspect of ecclesiology with the language of the pearl and the leaven rather than the organic motif, the concepts behind the illustrations are cogent within the wider neo-Calvinist worldview. As such, this model of Christianity as culture-producing and culture-renewing depends on a balance of various neo-Calvinist principles, all of which originate in the unity and diversity of the Godhead.

---

72. Wood, "Church, Sacrament, and Society," 287-88.

73. Herman Ridderbos, "Het is taak van de 'kerk als organisme' om een appel te doen op de samenleving," in *De Kerk: Trefpunt van sociale en politieke aktie?* ed. K. Runia (Kampen: Uitgeversmaatschappij J. H. Kok, 1987), 23-28; Jasper Vree, "Organisme en instituut: De ontwikkeling van Kuypers spreken over kerk-zijn (1867-1901)," in *Abraham Kuyper: vast en veranderlijk, De ontwikkeling van zijn denken,* ed. Cornelis Augustijn and Jasper Vree (Zoetermeer: Uitgeverij Meinema, 1998), 86-108.

74. Abraham Kuyper, "Calvinism: Source and Stronghold of Our Constitutional Liberties," in *Abraham Kuyper: A Centennial Reader,* 303.

6. Conclusion

If the stereotypes portrayed by the anti-Kuyperian backlash are in some way accurate (i.e., if those who "transform the culture" evince little more than a set of aesthetic concerns within a broader social context of urban gentrification) and those who talk of transformation never stress the more important element of transcendence, it seems that Kuyper and Bavinck would respond univocally in saying that it is nigh on impossible for neo-Calvinist cultural transformation to take place in such a setting. The issue of precedence is highly important to both Bavinck and Kuyper: unless one has an external, higher, transcendent standard by which to assess a host culture, on what basis may one ever talk of its transformation? The neo-Calvinist position is nothing less than this: the gospel can only transform that which it first transcends.

The stereotype of "Kuyperians everlastingly talking about 'transforming culture'"[75] should drive Kuyperians to ask whether their speech makes plain that the gospel's transcendence of culture takes priority over cultural transformation. If such reflective practice leads one to observe an incorrect prioritization of transformation over transcendence, this order must be changed if one is to be anything other than tenuously "Kuyperian." Kuyperians must endlessly talk of transcending the culture, which will itself serve as the catalyst for cultural change.

Closely related to this point is the issue of a confessionally based church context as the original locus of neo-Calvinist cultural renewal. The significance of ecclesiology centered on confessional subscription within the original Kuyperian cultural movement cannot be understated. (In 1888, for example, when the Kuyperian project moved to counter its nemesis modernist approach to church and culture, it did so by insisting that its *Broederking* members subscribe unreservedly to the Belgic Confession, the Heidelberg Catechism, and the Canons of Dort.)[76] Central to the notion of the visible-institutional church, in the Kuyperian sense, is the issue of confessional subscription. In a typical moment of boldness, Kuyper went as far as to claim that confessional subscription (or the lack thereof) is the difference between "a *church* and a *group of friends*."[77]

---

75. Helm, "On Getting Involved in Politics."
76. Cf. Wood, "Going Dutch in the Modern Age," 142.
77. Abraham Kuyper, "Conservatism and Orthodoxy: True and False Preservation," in *Abraham Kuyper: A Centennial Reader*, 75.

At the start of this essay, the question as to whether a non-confessional-church setting can be the locus of a neo-Calvinist cultural movement was raised. To begin towards an answer by working backwards from transformation to transcendence, one notes that for Bavinck and Kuyper, the gospel can only transform that which it first transcends. In addition, the Kuyperian contention seems to have been that the visible church-as-institution serves to safeguard the gospel's transcendent aspect. The culture can only be changed by a transcendent evangel, which, in turn, depends on the visible (institutional) church as safe haven, as bearer of the means of grace and as kept in a continuity of truth by its confessional commitment.

As such, it seems that considerable questions linger over the issue of whether, for example, a Kuyperian cultural movement is viable within the context of contemporary non-confessional evangelical Christianity. A related question must also be asked: is it even possible to maintain some kind of a neo-Calvinist political project in the present-day Netherlands without reference to the church?

The general thrust of much anti-Kuyperian sentiment, then, seems to be that Kuyperians deny the importance of the church. These debates must cause those who self-identify as Kuyperian to ask whether this is true, and consequently, to ask whether anything other than an ecclesiocentric vision is possible in a Kuyperian approach to culture.